LET GOD BE GOD

ALSO BY RAY C. STEDMAN:

Adventuring through the Bible
Authentic Christianity
Body Life
The Fight of Faith
For Such a Time as This
Friend of God
God's Blueprint for Success
God's Final Word
God's Loving Word
God's Unfinished Book
Hope in a Chaotic World
Is This All There Is to Life?
Let God Be God
Letters to a Troubled Church
On the Way to the Future
Our Riches in Christ
The Power of His Presence
Psalms: Folk Songs of Faith
Reason to Rejoice
Spiritual Warfare
Talking with My Father
The Way to Wholeness
What on Earth Is Happening?

ABOUT RAY C. STEDMAN

Portrait of Integrity: The Life of Ray C. Stedman by Mark Mitchell

LET GOD BE GOD

life-changing truths from the book of job

RAY C. STEDMAN

WITH JAMES D. DENNEY

Discovery House®
from Our Daily Bread Ministries

Let God Be God: Life-Changing Truths from the Book of Job
©2007 by Elaine Stedman
All rights reserved.

Discovery House Publishers is affiliated with Our Daily Bread Ministries,
Grand Rapids, Michigan.

Requests for permission to quote from this book should be directed to
Permissions Department, Discovery House, P.O. Box 3566, Grand Rapids,
MI 49501, or contact us by email at
permissionsdept@dhp.org.

Library of Congress Cataloging-in-Publication Data
Stedman, Ray C.
    Let God be God : life-changing truths from the book of Job /
    by Ray C. Stedman ; edited by James D. Denney.
        p. cm.
    ISBN 978-1-57293-180-0
    1. Bible. O.T. Job—Criticism, interpretation, etc. I. Denney, James
    D. II. Title.
    BS1415.52.S74 2007
    223'.106—dc22   2006038002

Edited by James D. Denney

Interior design by Sherri L. Hoffman

Printed in United States of America
Eleventh printing in 2018

CONTENTS

PUBLISHER'S PREFACE

Ray Stedman (1917–1992) served as pastor of the Peninsula Bible Church from 1950 to 1990, where he was known and loved as a man of outstanding Bible knowledge, Christian integrity, warmth, and humility. Born in Temvik, North Dakota, Ray grew up on the rugged landscape of Montana. When he was a small child, his mother became ill, and his father, a railroad man, abandoned the family. From the age of six, Ray grew up on his aunt's Montana farm. He came to know the Lord at a Methodist revival meeting at age ten.

As a young man he moved around and tried different jobs, working in Chicago, Denver, Hawaii, and elsewhere. He enlisted in the navy during World War II, where he often led Bible studies for civilians and navy personnel, and even preached on local radio in Hawaii. At the close of the war, Ray was married in Honolulu (he and his wife Elaine had first met in Great Falls, Montana). They returned to the mainland in 1946, and Ray graduated from Dallas Theological Seminary in 1950. After two summers interning under Dr. J. Vernon McGee, Ray traveled for several months with Dr. H. A. Ironside, pastor of Moody Church in Chicago.

In 1950, Ray was called by the two-year-old Peninsula Bible Fellowship in Palo Alto, California, to serve as its first pastor. Peninsula Bible Fellowship became Peninsula Bible Church, and Ray served a forty-year tenure, retiring on April 30, 1990. During those years, Ray Stedman authored a number of life-changing Christian books, including the classic work on the meaning and mission of the church, *Body Life*. He went into the presence of his Lord on October 7, 1992.

This book, *Let God Be God*, has been edited from a sermon series that Ray Stedman preached on the book of Job. In lively, everyday language, he offers solid biblical comfort and counsel on such deeply personal and agonizing questions as:

- Why does God allow affliction in my life?
- Why doesn't He answer my prayers?
- Why does God allow the wicked to prosper while the godly suffer?
- What's the best thing I can do or say to help people who are suffering?
- How should I respond to people who falsely accuse me of sin? What's wrong with defending myself?
- Is it God's will that I suffer? Does He take delight in my pain?
- If evil seems to reign on earth, is God truly in control?
- Why is life so unfair?
- Is it a sin to question God when I suffer?
- How does my suffering play a part in God's eternal plans and purposes?
- What does my suffering have to do with spiritual warfare?
- What does it truly mean to share in the sufferings of Christ?

In this book, Ray Stedman also squarely addresses some of the perplexing mysteries of the book of Job. Here are just a few of the tough questions Stedman tackles in these pages:

- If Job was "blameless" as God said, why did He rebuke Job at the end of the book?
- Why did Job have to repent in dust and ashes?
- Why did God rebuke Job's three "miserable comforters" but not the bold young man named Elihu?
- And what about Job's ten children who were killed at the beginning of the book—didn't their lives mean anything to God?
- Is it true that we find the earliest announcement of the Christian gospel in Job, the oldest book in the Bible?
- What were the strange creatures God spoke of, behemoth and leviathan? What is the strange connection between those two beasts and the book of Revelation?
- What is Satan's "unholy trinity"?
- Did Job actually make statements that reflect our current understanding of astronomy?
- What did God mean when He told Job about "storehouses" of snow and hail that He had reserved for times of war?
- What is the significance behind the names of Job's daughters?

Even if you've studied the book of Job many times before, you'll discover new and profound insights in Ray Stedman's teaching. You'll learn surprising truths about the nature of suffering, the character of God, and the reality of your own humanity in this book. Though the book of Job is probably the oldest book in the Bible, its truths are still as fresh and relevant today as they were four thousand years ago.

Can a book about suffering sparkle with warmth, humor, and encouragement? Yes, it can—and Ray Stedman's *Let God Be God* is that book. So turn the page and prepare to be instructed, inspired, and comforted by the life-changing truths of one of the oldest and greatest stories in human history—the story of Job.

—DISCOVERY HOUSE

THE TOUGHEST QUESTION

An Overview of Job

Johnny Gunther was an active, fun-loving, straight-A student at Deerfield Academy in Massachusetts. He excelled in math, science, and chess. In early 1946, his life was overshadowed by the discovery of a large, malignant tumor in his brain. Over the next fourteen months, Johnny endured two operations, painful spinal taps, daily X-ray treatments, experimental injections of mustard gas, and a severe dietary regimen. (Many of the treatments Johnny was subjected to in the 1940s are now known to have no therapeutic value.)

During his treatments, Johnny amazed his doctors with his courage, optimism, and ability to survive a particularly aggressive tumor. For a while, in early February 1947, he grew stronger as the tumor appeared to shrink. But in April, as Johnny was taking his College Board exams, he suffered bouts of short-term amnesia. Doctors discovered that the tumor had taken a particularly aggressive and deadly form called *glioma multiforme*.

Though Johnny's illness had hurt his attendance at school, he'd built up so much extra credit that he was able to graduate with his class on June 4. When Johnny returned to Deerfield Academy for his final weeks of school, his classmates couldn't hide their shock at his thin and wasted appearance. He wore a turban to cover his bald, surgery-scarred scalp. Though his life was ebbing, he aced his final exam in chemistry. On June 4, he received a standing ovation as he walked across the platform to receive his diploma.

On June 12, Johnny Gunther was admitted to the hospital, where he experienced worsening bouts of amnesia, headaches, vomiting, and tremors. The doctors told his parents that he was dying of a cerebral hemorrhage. Just a few days after entering the hospital, Johnny received the news that his application to Columbia University had been accepted. Early on June 30, 1947, Johnny went into a coma from which he never woke up. He was pronounced dead that night at 11:02.

Johnny's father, journalist John Gunther, recounted this story in a book that has become a modern classic, *Death Be Not Proud*. One of the most poignant ironies of Johnny Gunther's story is the fact that his cancer attacked him at the very site of his personality, his intellect, and his human potential.

We hear a tragic story like that of Johnny Gunther's, and we have to wonder: Why? Why was the life of this promising young man cut short? Why did he have to endure so much suffering? Why is life so unfair?

This is the toughest question of our existence: Why do we suffer? The reason this question is so hard is that it touches the deepest part of our being. It affects our faith and colors our view of the world.

We know that God is loving and all-powerful. We know He has the power to heal us and take away our suffering, and we know He loves us. Still, we suffer, and we wonder why God doesn't take us out of our suffering. We wonder why He leaves us in our pain. Doesn't He care? Has He forgotten us? Has He turned His back on us?

These are the questions that throb at the heart of the book of Job.

AN EPIC DRAMA, A RECORD OF HISTORY

Job is the first of five poetical books in the Old Testament. (It is followed by Psalms, Proverbs, Ecclesiastes, and the Song of Solomon.) These five books of ancient Hebrew poetry are often called the Wisdom Books, because they have condensed the deep wisdom of God into one powerful and concise section of God's Word. In these five books, the great riddles of life are asked and answered.

I also like to think of these five books as the Music Books, because they contain the rich, soul-swelling music of Scripture. These books reflect the sorrow and the joy of our lives and our relationship with God. In these books, you'll find every emotion of the human experience.

The feelings expressed in the book of Job are primarily those of affliction, distress, grief, misery, and doubt. Here is the cry of man's wounded spirit, the deep groaning of a man who desperately struggles to trust in God, even though everything in his life is crumbling. Human beings were made to know God and trust in Him. So when our suffering reaches such a white-hot intensity that life seems senseless and chaotic, then our only hope is to cling to God in faith.

Open the book of Job whenever you find yourself going through pain and trials, whenever you cry out, "Why, Lord?" In those pages, you'll find a man who has experienced agony and loss beyond our ability to comprehend. Job questions God, seeks answers from God, and even becomes angry with God—yet he remains faithful. In the end, we see that Job emerges from his time of trial with his faith-relationship with God intact.

The book of Job is probably the oldest book in the Bible, and its author is unknown. Some scholars think Moses may have written it, while others date it as late as the time of Solomon. One thing is certain: This book was given by the Holy Spirit to encourage, comfort, and instruct us.

Job is a profound work, a story of great beauty and emotional intensity, majestically and artistically crafted. As poetry, Job is an epic drama, much like such Greek epic poems as *The Iliad* and *The Odyssey* of Homer. Some Bible scholars believe that the story of Job may have been presented as a dramatic stage play in which actors recited the parts of the different characters in the book. This idea is suggested by the unique structure of the book. Though most of the book is composed of dramatic poetry, it begins with a prose prologue and ends with an epilogue in prose. The prologue and epilogue may have served as program notes that were read to the audience at the beginning and end of the dramatic presentation.

Though the book of Job is a work of poetry, it was also written as a record of historical events. Job was a man who actually lived. The vast majority of scholars of the Jewish Torah have always considered Job to have been a living historical figure, as have most evangelical Christian scholars. Ezekiel 14 names Job (alongside Noah and Daniel) as a historical human being of surpassing righteousness and faithfulness to God (see verses 14 and 20). Job is also referred to in the New Testament epistle of James: "You have heard of Job's perseverance and have seen what the Lord finally brought about" (5:11).

According to the opening lines of the book, Job lived in the land of Uz, the location of which is now unknown. He was one of the most prominent and prosperous citizens of the land. References to a man named Job have been found on ancient tablets that are thought to be around four thousand years old. Job probably lived in roughly the same historical era as Abraham—around 2,000 BC.

THE BATTLEGROUND

In the opening scenes of Job, we are given some program notes that explain the background of Job's drama—background that even Job himself doesn't know. Here we catch our first glimpse of an answer to the eternal question,

"Why do we suffer?" This scene, in which Satan issues a defiant challenge to God, tells us that senseless human suffering often arises out of Satan's rebellion against the government of God.

As the book opens, we see God conferring with His angelic creation. Among these angels is Satan, who arrogantly strides in. He has just returned from traveling around the earth, and he says, in effect, "Human beings only love You out of self-interest because You bless them. Take those blessings away, and they will curse You to Your face."

So God replies, "Very well. Let's test your theory, and let's let a righteous man named Job be the proving ground."

This scenario that is laid out at the beginning of the book of Job reminds me of the way combat was waged in the Pacific during World War II. On December 7, 1941, a sneak attack at Pearl Harbor in Hawaii brought the United States into World War II. At the beginning of the war between Japan and the United States, it looked as though this conflict would be staged in the middle of the Pacific, around the Hawaiian Islands. But very early in the war, events took a sudden turn, and, without warning, the whole theater of battle shifted abruptly to the South Pacific, an area several thousand miles from Hawaii. For the first time, Americans began to hear of places with names like Guam, Guadalcanal, Wake Island, Mindanao, and Bataan. In those obscure, out-of-the-way corners of the world, the greatest powers on earth were locked in mortal combat.

This is much like what happened in the life of Job. Here was a man who was simply living his life, completely unaware that he had suddenly become the center of God's attention—and Satan's as well. Like tiny Guam or remote Wake Island, there was nothing special about Job. Yet his life was about to become a strategic battleground in the cosmic struggle between God and Satan. The soul of Job was about to become Ground Zero, and Satan was preparing to launch his first major assault.

AN OVERVIEW OF JOB

Job 1 shows us how, one after another, all the props are pulled out of Job's life. First, foreign raiders take all of Job's oxen. Then his donkey herds are decimated. Next, his flocks of sheep are wiped out in a storm, followed by his great herd of camels. Finally comes the most devastating news of all: all of Job's children—seven sons and three daughters—are killed by a tornado.

Though reeling from his losses, Job responds in faith: "Naked I came from my mother's womb, and naked I will depart. The LORD gave and the LORD has taken away; may the name of the LORD be praised" (Job 1:21).

Job's faith deals Satan a stinging setback, so Satan asks God to change the rules of the game. He says, "Let me attack Job more directly. Let me strike Job's own body." God agrees, and the result is that Job is stricken with boils, producing almost unendurable pain. Watching Job's sufferings, his wife gives up on God. In Job 2:9, she turns on him and says, "Are you still holding on to your integrity? Curse God and die!"

Despite his losses and suffering, Job remains faithful to God. "You are talking like a foolish woman," he replies. "Shall we accept good from God, and not trouble?" And then the writer of the book of Job adds, "In all this, Job did not sin in what he said" (2:10).

Then comes the final test: In Job 2:11, this suffering saint is visited by three would-be "comforters," who provide no comfort at all! These three friends are Eliphaz the Temanite, Bildad the Shuhite, and Zophar the Naamathite. The book shifts its focus from Job's sufferings to his controversy with these three friends. Their conversation occupies the major part of the book.

Initially, these three friends seem to respond with genuine empathy. They hardly recognize Job because he is so disfigured by his sufferings. Upon seeing him, they weep, tear their clothes, and cover themselves with ashes. For seven days and nights they sit with him, not saying a word. Had they simply maintained their silent presence, Job would have felt supported and cared for. Unfortunately, they break their silence. As they speak, they magnify Job's suffering.

From their limited human perspective, Eliphaz, Bildad, and Zophar attempt to answer the question that haunts us all: Why must we suffer? All three of these friends come to the same mistaken conclusion. With dogmatic certainty, they agree that Job's suffering is a punishment for hidden sin in his life. So they argue with him, accuse him, and try to break down his defenses. Some comfort!

It's true that God sometimes uses painful circumstances to get our attention when we have wandered away from Him. And it's also true that when we violate God's laws (for example, by overeating, smoking habitually, abusing drugs, or engaging in promiscuous sex), our bodies pay a price in poor health and even early death. But it is also true (as the title of a best-selling book states) that "bad things happen to good people."

Job's three "comforters" stubbornly insist that sin is the only explanation for Job's circumstances. They accuse him. They argue with him. They use different approaches: sarcasm, cajoling, and recrimination. These are just variations on a recurring theme, however: "Job, admit it—all of these sufferings are God's punishment of your hidden sin!" Their premise—which is false—is that if God is just and loving, the righteous will always be blessed, and the wicked will always suffer. That sounds logical, unless *you* are the one who is suffering.

Job replies that he can't confess sin he never committed, and he can think of nothing he has done to offend God. Moreover, their argument that the wicked always suffer is simply untrue. In fact, the wicked seem to prosper and flourish while the righteous often suffer.

THE ANSWER OF THE LORD

In Job 38, this suffering saint finally hears from an authoritative source: The Lord Himself answers Job. Out of the fury of the whirlwind, God comes to him and says,

> Who is this that darkens my counsel
>   with words without knowledge?
> Brace yourself like a man;
>   I will question you,
>   and you shall answer me (vv. 2–3).

In other words, "Do you want to debate with Me, Job? First, let Me see your qualifications. I have a list of questions. If you can handle these questions, then perhaps you ready to debate Me."

Then, in chapters 38 through 40, we find one of the most remarkable passages in all of Scripture. God takes Job on a tour of nature and asks him question after question:

> Where were you when I laid the earth's foundation? (38:4).

> Have the gates of death been shown to you?
>   Have you seen the gates of the shadow of death? (38:17).

> Can you bind the beautiful Pleiades?
>   Can you loose the cords of Orion?
> Can you bring forth the constellations in their seasons

or lead out the Bear with its cubs?
Do you know the laws of the heavens? (38:31–33).

Do you give the horse his strength
or clothe his neck with a flowing mane? (39:19).

Can you pull in the leviathan with a fishhook
or tie down his tongue with a rope? (41:1).

Here, almighty God, maker of heaven and earth, creates a poetic word picture of the complex and intricately designed universe He has fashioned. Only a superhuman intellect could comprehend the full range of creation in its variety, scope, and power. Job—a finite and fallible human being—can only respond by falling on his face before God, confessing:

My ears had heard of you
but now my eyes have seen you.
Therefore I despise myself
and repent in dust and ashes (42:5–6).

Ultimately, we must accept the fact that God does not exist for man, but man exists for God. We are God's instruments, and we exist to carry out His plans and purposes, which transcend our limited understanding.

As the book draws to a close, God rebukes Job's friends and directs Job to pray for his three misguided "comforters." In the end, God restores everything Job has lost and doubles it. He had seven thousand sheep before; God gives him fourteen thousand. He had five hundred oxen and five hundred donkeys; God gives him a thousand of each. He had three thousand camels; God gives him six thousand. God even replaces Job's sons and daughters.

You might say, "But no new child can replace a lost child in a parent's heart! Nothing could remove that grief." And you are right. Notice that Job had seven sons and three daughters before disaster struck, but God did not give him fourteen sons and six daughters afterwards. God did not double the number of Job's offspring as He had doubled the size of his herds. Why? Because his first ten children were not lost to him forever. They were in glory with God, and he would one day be reunited with them.

Job expresses this confidence and assurance when he says, "I know that my Redeemer lives, and that in the end he will stand upon the earth. And after my skin has been destroyed, yet in my flesh I will see God" (Job 19:25–26). He had no doubt that he would survive death and corruption, and so would his children. Nothing, not even ten new children, can replace even one child who leaves this world too soon. But Job knew his Redeemer, and he knew that he and his children would all be together again in the presence of the Lord.

The account closes with the words, "And so he died, old and full of years" (Job 42:17). But notice this: Job dies without an answer to his question. God never explains to Job why he has suffered so intensely.

You and I, as readers of the book of Job, do gain a glimpse into the answer: Everything we endure takes place against a backdrop of Satan's rebellious challenge to God's righteous government of creation. Though this answer is given to us, it is never explicitly divulged to Job while he lives.

If the book of Job were filmed as a movie, you would see the film open with three main characters on the screen—God, Satan, and Job. In the middle of the film, several more characters would enter the picture: Job's three "comforters," followed by Elihu. By the end of the film, most of these characters would have departed. Even Satan, the instigator of these events, fades completely out of the picture. From the beginning to the end, the camera slowly zooms in until there are only two figures framed on the screen: God and Job.

The book of Job is the story of a dynamic relationship between two friends. It's sometimes a stormy relationship marked by pain and anger as well as delight and joy, but the bond is unbreakable. God never lets go of Job, and Job never lets go of God. Though Satan believed he could destroy this relationship by afflicting Job, the relationship between God and Job emerges even stronger because of Job's trial of suffering.

The deepest note of this book is sounded when Job says, in the very depths of his pain and desolation, "But he knows the way that I take; when he has tested me, I will come forth as gold" (Job 23:10). Our sufferings often seem meaningless, yet there is a lesson for us all in Job's life and the lives of all those who endure persecution, martyrdom, injury, cancer, multiple sclerosis, poverty, and countless other types of trials. The lesson is that testing purifies us and reveals the gold of proven, refined character within us.

British journalist Malcolm Muggeridge became a Christian after living most of his life as an atheist. In his book *A Twentieth Century Testimony* (Thomas Nelson, 1978), Muggeridge observed:

> Contrary to what might be expected, I look back on experiences that
> at the time seemed especially desolating and painful with particular

satisfaction. Indeed, I can say with complete truthfulness that every-thing I have learned in my seventy-five years in this world, everything that has truly enhanced and enlightened my existence, has been through affliction and not through happiness, whether pursued or attained. In other words, if it ever were to be possible to eliminate affliction from our earthly existence by means of some drug or other medical mumbo jumbo . . . the result would not be to make life delec-table, but to make it too banal and trivial to be endurable (p. 72).

In the New Testament, the apostle Paul expresses a parallel thought: "And we know that in all things God works for the good of those who love him, who have been called according to his purpose" (Romans 8:28). That is also the triumphant song of Job, a song of faith in a God who redeems even our deepest pain and suffering.

An Outline of the Book of Job

Prologue: The losses and sufferings of Job (Job 1:1–2:13)

1. The abundance of Job (1:1–5)
2. The attacks of Satan; Job loses everything (1:6–2:10)
3. Job's friends arrive and silently mourn with him (2:11–13)

Drama: Job and his three "comforters" (Job 3–37)

1. The first debate (3:1–14:22)
   A. Job's first speech (3:1–26)
   B. Eliphaz: The innocent do not suffer (4:1–5:27)
   C. Job's anguished reply and plea for empathy (6:1–7:21)
   D. Bildad: Job must have sinned (8:1–22)
   E. Job questions God's seeming affliction of him (9:1–10:22)
   F. Zophar's accusations (11:1–20)
   G. Job rebukes his accusers; God will vindicate him
      (12:1–14:22)

2. The second debate (15:1–21:34)
   A. Eliphaz's second accusation (15:1–35)
   B. Job responds: "You are miserable comforters!" (16:1–17:16)
   C. Bildad's second accusation (18:1–21)
   D. Job responds to Bildad (19:1–29)
   E. Zophar's second accusation (20:1–29)
   F. Job's response to Zophar (21:1–34)

3. The third debate (22:1–26:14)
   A. Eliphaz's third accusation (22:1–30)
   B. Job responds to Eliphaz (23:1–24:25)
      1. He will come forth as gold (23:1–17)
      2. The wicked do not seem to suffer (24:1–25)
   C. Bildad's third accusation (25:16)
   D. Job responds to Bildad (26:1–14)

4. Job's ultimate defense (27:1–31:40)
   A. Job's first monologue (27:1–28:28)
      1. He defends his innocence (27:1–23)
      2. Where can wisdom be found? (28:1–28)
   B. Job's second monologue (29:1–31:40)
      1. Job reminisces over past joys (29:1–25)

     2. Job laments his pain and humiliation (30:1–31)
     3. Job again defends his innocence (31:1–34)
     4. Job prays to meet God face to face (31:35–40)
     5. Interruption and monologue of young Elihu
       (32:1–37:24)

Moment of Truth: **God's dialogue with Job (Job 38:1–42:6)**

  1. God speaks to Job from the whirlwind (38:1–40:5)
    A. God's first confrontation, questioning of Job (38)
       1. The realm of Creation (38:1–38)
       2. The animal kingdom (38:39–39:30)
    B. Job's response (40:1–5)
    C. God's second confrontation of Job (40:6–41:34)
       1. Can Job save himself? (40:6–14)
       2. The power of the behemoth (40:15–24)
       3. The power of the leviathan (41:1–34)
    D. Job's second response (42:1–6)
       1. Job confesses his finiteness and ignorance (42:1–3)
       2. Job repents (42:4–6)

Epilogue: **The deliverance and restoration of Job (Job 42:7–17)**

THE TEST

The First Council of Nicea, convened by Emperor Constantine in AD 325, was the first worldwide conference of the Christian church. At this council, many of the great doctrinal matters of the Christian faith (such as the deity of Christ) were settled for all time. There the Nicene Creed, a creed of orthodox faith still recited in churches to this day, was adopted.

Of the 318 delegates to the First Nicene Council, only twelve were whole in body. All of the rest had been maimed or crippled as a result of being tortured for their faith. Some had lost an eye or a hand. Others had suffered broken or dislocated limbs. Some had been scarred by branding irons. In the early days of the Christian church, no one thought it was strange or unfair to suffer for Christ. Suffering was considered a normal part of the Christian life. It was expected.

Most of us, as American Christians, have grown up feeling that we are entitled to a life of ease, comfort, and prosperity. When suffering comes into our lives, we cry out in protest against the unfairness of it all. But when we read the writings of some of the great Christian saints of the past, we often find a more mature and accepting view of suffering. For example, Oswald Chambers, the great nineteenth-century Christian writer from Scotland, observed, "Suffering is the heritage of the bad, of the penitent, and of the Son of God. Each one ends in the cross. The bad thief is crucified, the penitent thief is crucified, and the Son of God is crucified. By these signs we know the widespread heritage of suffering."

In Job 1, we see that this same heritage is shared by a man of the ancient Middle East, a righteous and godly man named Job.

A BLAMELESS AND UPRIGHT MAN

We are introduced to Job in these verses:

In the land of Uz there lived a man whose name was Job. This man was blameless and upright; he feared God and shunned evil. He had seven sons and three daughters, and he owned seven thousand sheep, three thousand camels, five hundred yoke of oxen and five hundred donkeys, and had a large number of servants. He was the greatest man among all the people of the East.

His sons used to take turns holding feasts in their homes, and they would invite their three sisters to eat and drink with them. When a period of feasting had run its course, Job would send and have them purified. Early in the morning he would sacrifice a burnt offering for each of them, thinking, "Perhaps my children have sinned and cursed God in their hearts." This was Job's regular custom (Job 1:1–5).

These first three opening verses reveal some significant facts about Job. First, we learn that he was an upright and godly man. He is called "blameless," and make no mistake, this does not mean that Job was sinless. The Hebrew word that is translated "blameless" is *tam*, which means complete, lacking nothing, balanced and integrated in his character. Like all human beings but Jesus Himself, Job was born in sin, and he sinned during his lifetime. Yet he is described as "blameless" (complete) because he dealt with his sin in the way that God required. When Job sinned, he was sorry for his sin, he confessed it to God, and he repented and turned away from his sin.

These verses also tell us that Job "feared God and shunned evil." Job was complete and upright because he had an awe and respect for God plus a fear of offending the righteousness of God. He was complete and upright because he loved God, and he turned away from evil. We also learn that Job was a family man, the father of ten children: "He had seven sons and three daughters."

Next, verse 3 tells us that Job was a prosperous man, much like a rich rancher, owning thousands of sheep and camels, hundreds of yoke of oxen and donkeys, and employing a large number of servants. Job wasn't merely rich. He was *famous* for his wealth—the "greatest man" in Middle Eastern society.

We sometimes make the mistake of thinking that the Bible condemns prosperity and prosperous people. It's true, of course, that God's Word warns that riches are a snare for the unwary. Ezekiel 28:5 warns, "By your great skill in trading you have increased your wealth, and because of your wealth your heart has grown proud." Similarly, the apostle Paul writes: "People who want to get rich fall into temptation and a trap and into many foolish and harmful desires that plunge men into ruin and destruction. For the love of money is a root of all kinds of evil. Some people, eager for money, have wandered from the faith and pierced themselves with many griefs" (1 Timothy 6:9–10).

Notice in this passage that it is not money itself that is the root of all kinds of evil; it is "the *love* of money." Job was prosperous; he had money. But Job didn't love money. He loved God, and God had made him rich. Job possessed wealth, but wealth didn't possess Job.

Finally, these opening verses tell us what kind of father Job was. He was a man who genuinely and tenderly loved his children. We learn that Job's sons had an interesting custom. They would hold a feast or party in their homes, and they would invite their three sisters to eat and drink with them. After the feast was over, Job would send for them and call them together to worship God. He would give sacrificial offerings for each of them because of a special concern he felt for them. His concern was this: "Perhaps my children have sinned and cursed God in their hearts."

Now doesn't that seem a little strange? Why was Job afraid that his children might have "cursed God in their hearts"? Hadn't he raised them well? Hadn't he taught them to love God, just as he did? Of course he had. But Job had a special reason for concern.

The Amplified Version brings out a fact in these verses that we don't readily see in the New International Version: "His sons used to go and feast in the house of each on his day (birthday) in turn, and they invited their three sisters to eat and drink with them" (Job 1:4).

The Amplified Version tells us that these feasts or parties were held on the birthday of each of these seven sons. So there were seven of these feasts every year. Whenever his sons had a birthday party, Job responded by holding a special time of prayer, worship, and sacrifice to God. Why? Because Job understood that when people need spiritual help the most is *when things are going well*.

Times of stress and trial tend to drive us into the arms of God, but people have a tendency to fall away from God during times of prosperity and celebration. Job demonstrated a keen insight into human psychology and spirituality. He understood that the pressure to deny and forsake God is at its worst when things are going well.

Job did not sacrifice a *sin offering* on behalf of his children (as described in Leviticus 4), because a sin offering had no value if the sinner himself did not actively repent of his sin. Instead, Job gave a *burnt offering* on behalf of his children (as described in Leviticus 1).

In the Scriptures, a burnt offering is always a symbol of total dedication to God, an awareness of God's rightful ownership of us. A burnt offering is the sacrifice of a male animal, the healthiest and most perfect animal of the herd or flock, completely without blemish. The perfection of the burnt offering symbolizes the perfect sacrifice of the Lord Jesus. Centuries after the death of Job, Jesus the Messiah would stand before Pontius Pilate, who would declare, "I find no fault in Him at all" (John 18:38 NKJV). The physical perfection of the burnt offering symbolized the moral and spiritual perfection of Jesus, the great sacrifice for our sin.

When Job sacrificed a burnt offering for the sake of his children, he expressed the burden of his heart for them. Job desired that all of his children might belong wholly to God. So Job committed his children to God by means of this burnt offering. The sacrifice of the burnt offering completes this picture of Job as not merely a godly man but a good and loving father to his children.

FROM THE PHYSICAL TO THE INVISIBLE

In verse 6 the scene shifts to that world of invisible reality that the New Testament calls "the heavenly realms." It is the place Paul spoke of when he wrote, "Praise be to the God and Father of our Lord Jesus Christ, who has blessed us in the heavenly realms with every spiritual blessing in Christ" (Ephesians 1:3). This realm is not up above the clouds or off in outer space. It's here — it's all around us — but it's invisible to us. We are separated from this realm by an invisible barrier. We can't see what's going on in that unseen realm, but we know it is the place where God and His angels are engaged in a great struggle against Satan and his demons.

Here, in Job 1:6, the curtain lifts, and we catch a glimpse of the drama taking place behind the scenes of history. I am reminded of the scene in 2 Kings 6, where the heathen king of Aram sends a strong force of men and chariots to capture the prophet Elisha in the city of Dothan. When Elisha's servant awakens in the morning and sees Aram's army all around, he panics and says to Elisha, "Oh, master, what shall we do?" And Elisha replies, "Don't be afraid. Those who are with us are greater than those who are with the army of Aram." Then Elisha prays, "O Lord, open my servant's eyes so he may see!"

In that instant the Lord lifts the curtain that hides the heavenly realm from the servant's eyes. The servant looks and sees the horses and chariots of fire all around Elisha's house, providing a zone of security and protection against the armies of Aram.

This is a description of the invisible realm that surrounds you and me at all times. It surrounded Job. We humans cannot see that realm unless God lifts the curtain and reveals it to us. That is what He does in Job 1:6–12. God raises the curtain on this drama in the heavenly realms and allows us to see what Job himself could not see:

> One day the angels came to present themselves before the LORD, and Satan also came with them. The LORD said to Satan, "Where have you come from?"
>
> Satan answered the LORD, "From roaming through the earth and going back and forth in it."
>
> Then the LORD said to Satan, "Have you considered my servant Job? There is no one on earth like him; he is blameless and upright, a man who fears God and shuns evil."
>
> "Does Job fear God for nothing?" Satan replied. "Have you not put a hedge around him and his household and everything he has? You have blessed the work of his hands, so that his flocks and herds are spread throughout the land. But stretch out your hand and strike everything he has, and he will surely curse you to your face."
>
> The LORD said to Satan, "Very well, then, everything he has is in your hands, but on the man himself do not lay a finger."
>
> Then Satan went out from the presence of the LORD.

An impressive scene! It reminds us of John's vision in Revelation 4, where he sees thousands of angels gathered in the great audience chamber of heaven, in the presence of God Himself.

In verse 6, the word translated *angels* is literally *the sons of God* in the original Hebrew. No one knows how many angels there are, but their number seems countless. The text suggests that they were required to periodically come before God and report their activities to Him.

Where did the activities of the angels take them? Well, consider the universe God has made. According to the American Astronomical Society, our own sun is one star out of an estimated four hundred billion stars in the Milky Way galaxy, which is just one galaxy out of an estimated 240 billion galaxies in the known universe. How many planets there might be in such a vast universe is anyone's guess, but God could have assigned an angel to every planet in the universe. If we push back the limits of our imagination, we begin to see that God is interested in far more than this little planet of ours. He and His angels have an entire universe to oversee.

That is the scene we glimpse in these opening verses of Job. The ministering angels of the Lord have gathered from all over the universe to report to God on their activities, and in the midst of them was Satan.

The name *Satan* means "the adversary," and it's an apt name. That's how Satan first appears in the book of Job. We see him there in the midst of all the angels of heaven, and there is no question that he comes as an adversary—an enemy of God and an enemy of humanity. Clearly, this is Satan after his fall. The books of Ezekiel and Isaiah describe the fall of Satan (see Ezekiel 28:11–18 and Isaiah 14). There we are told that he was once the greatest of angels, but he became arrogant and proud. In opposition to God, who created him, Satan led a rebellion.

Now he has returned to the courts of God, where he once had a place of honor as the greatest of angels. I find it fascinating that Satan, though fallen and an enemy of God, still has access to Him. God's adversary has not been excluded from His presence. Some people think that Satan has been bound in hell or that he has been consigned to some sort of underground furnace, but this is not true. Satan, in this scene, has been granted access to heaven.

A STRANGE WAR

Job 1 gives us the first hint of why the book of Job was written. This book has much to say to us about the reasons for our suffering in this world, and especially why innocent people suffer.

And there is yet a deeper level of truth behind the book of Job. In this scene, we see that the book of Job was written, in part, to reveal to us the relationship between God and Satan. Our Lord does not want us to be confused or uninformed about the power of this vicious enemy called Satan. The adversary is deadly and powerful; he hates God, and he hates us. But Satan is not the equivalent of God. He is under the authority of God.

Some people seem to think that there are two gods in the universe, a good God and an evil god named Satan, and they struggle against each other on even terms. That is not so. Satan is not God's equal. The book of Job shows us right from the start that God is in control of all things. All the forces of the universe are His to command. All of time and space are under His authority. Nothing ever takes God by surprise. There is nothing beyond the reach of God's will, not even Satan.

God is the almighty, maker of heaven and earth. When we pray to God, we do not command Him. He is not our heavenly bellboy, waiting to serve us when we issue a command. No, God is the great sovereign of the universe. Every living thing in the universe must acknowledge that He is Lord of all. Even rebellious Satan must confess that God is in control; there is nothing Satan can do in heaven or on earth except with God's permission.

I've heard some people suggest that the book of Job is the record of a great battle between God and Satan and that Job is caught in the middle of the battlefield. Though I see how people might get such an impression, I have to wonder: Isn't this a strange war, in which one side must get permission from the other before it attacks?

When Julius Caesar invaded Gaul and Britain, did he first ask, "May I?" Did Napoleon ask permission of Czar Alexander before he invaded Russia in 1812? Did Hitler ask Poland's permission before the Blitzkrieg in 1939? Yet that is exactly the situation we encounter in the book of Job. Satan comes to God and asks permission to invade Job's life.

What we are witnessing here is not a battle in the conventional sense. It is not warfare—and certainly not war between two equal forces. God clearly has authority over Satan. If this is not warfare, what is it? It's a test. We need to see that Satan is testing God and His creation through Job. Though Satan brings this test about, God permits it. He has authority over Satan.

Have you ever noticed who challenges whom in this account? Those who are vaguely aware of the story of Job tend to think that Satan challenges God. In reality, it is the other way around: God challenges Satan. When Satan comes to the courts of heaven, God says, "Satan, where have you come from?"

Satan replies, "I've been roaming through the earth and going back and forth in it." What does Satan mean? Under questioning from God, Satan admits what he's been up to. He's been roaming all over the earth, trying to stir up trouble among human beings. He has been tempting and trying and tormenting the human race.

So God says to Satan, "Have you considered my servant Job? There is no one on earth like him; he is blameless and upright, a man who fears God and shuns evil." In other words, God tells Satan, "Have you been trying to attack my servant Job? He is a righteous, complete, balanced man. He turns from evil the moment he sees it."

Satan replies, "Does Job fear God for nothing? Have you not put a hedge around him and his household and everything he has? . . . But stretch out your hand and strike everything he has, and he will surely curse you to your face." Satan is saying, "I can't get to Job. Sure, I've tried. I've been thinking and plotting and trying to figure out a way to bring him down, but You have him protected so I can't get to him. God, You're not playing fair! Of course Job loves you. Look at all the blessings you've showered on him. But take all of those blessings away, and he'll curse you to your face!"

At that, God says, in effect, "Let's see if you're right. Attack all of his blessings and possessions, and let's see if he truly loves Me or if he only loves the wealth I've allowed him to possess."

THE SATANIC ACTIVITY AND THE SATANIC PHILOSOPHY

This account shows us two important aspects of our adversary. First, it reveals to us Satan's activity. Second, it reveals to us Satan's philosophy and thinking.

What is Satan's activity? He roams the earth, going up and down and all around, looking for someone to attack and undermine. This picture of satanic activity is consistent with what Peter tells us: "Be of sober spirit, be on the alert. Your adversary, the devil, prowls around like a roaring lion, seeking someone to devour" (1 Peter 5:8 NASB).

Satan prowls the earth, seeking someone to pounce on and consume. He's always looking for vulnerable souls. He's always alert to the weak points in our spiritual armor. This is an apt and instructive image of the spiritual forces that are arrayed against us. In Ephesians 4, Paul warns us not to give Satan an opportunity to invade our lives: "'In your anger do not sin': Do not let the sun go down while you are still angry, and do not give the devil a foot-hold" (vv. 26–27).

When do we give our adversary an opportunity to attack? When we hold grudges, when we refuse to forgive others, when we nurse our anger and feed our wrath. Satan watches and says, "Aha! There's my chance! Now I have them right where I want them!" Why does our anger give Satan a foothold in our lives? Because when we hold on to bitterness and rage, we are living out the satanic philosophy. We are aligning our thoughts with the thoughts of Satan.

What is Satan's philosophy? "Me first." It is a philosophy of the ego enthroned, the self deified. Selfishness is at the core of all hate, grudge bearing, and revenge. Why did Satan fall? The prophet Isaiah explains:

How you have fallen from heaven,
O morning star, son of the dawn!
You have been cast down to the earth,
you who once laid low the nations!
You said in your heart,
"I will ascend to heaven;
I will raise my throne
above the stars of God;
I will sit enthroned on the mount of assembly,
on the utmost heights of the sacred mountain.
I will ascend above the tops of the clouds;
I will make myself like the Most High" (14:12–14).

Here is Satan's philosophy, a philosophy that sounds much like what many of our contemporaries say today: "I look out for Number One. I bow to no one. I am my own god." Satan believes that the law of serving ourselves is so fundamental and universal that *everyone* must think as he does. He even thinks Job shares his satanic philosophy.

So the adversary tells God, in effect, "The only reason Job loves you is because You shower him with blessing. You protect him from harm. But I'll wager that if You put Job in some really painful circumstances, if You take away all of his blessings, he will choose resentment and bitterness. He'll curse You to Your face. Deep down, Your creatures are all the same, and even though You've condemned me for being prideful and rebellious, Job is really no different from me."

THE RULES OF THE TEST

So the Lord proposes a test of Satan's theory. He says, "Very well, then, everything Job has is in your hands, but on the man himself do not lay a finger." Notice this significant fact: Satan is limited by God. The Lord sets boundaries to Satan's activities toward human beings. He says, "Satan, you can go thus far, but no further."

We must understand that Satan is a rebel. What does he care about God's rules? He'd break them in a heartbeat if he could—*but he can't!* When God makes His decree, there is no hint that Satan would even think of violating it. Satan has no power to go beyond God's control. The Lord is sovereign, and even Satan must acknowledge God's authority to set limits on his activity. Yet

Satan, in his utter brutality and viciousness, makes sure to inflict as cruel and painful a loss on Job as those limits allow:

> One day when Job's sons and daughters were feasting and drinking wine at the oldest brother's house, a messenger came to Job and said, "The oxen were plowing and the donkeys were grazing nearby, and the Sabeans attacked and carried them off. They put the servants to the sword, and I am the only one who has escaped to tell you!"
>
> While he was still speaking, another messenger came and said, "The fire of God fell from the sky and burned up the sheep and the servants, and I am the only one who has escaped to tell you!"
>
> While he was still speaking, another messenger came and said, "The Chaldeans formed three raiding parties and swept down on your camels and carried them off. They put the servants to the sword, and I am the only one who has escaped to tell you!"
>
> While he was still speaking, yet another messenger came and said, "Your sons and daughters were feasting and drinking wine at the oldest brother's house, when suddenly a mighty wind swept in from the desert and struck the four corners of the house. It collapsed on them and they are dead, and I am the only one who has escaped to tell you!" (Job 1:13–18).

Within a short time, four messengers of doom visit Job. Each delivers the message that Job has suffered a catastrophic loss. Not only are Job's possessions stripped from him, but also all ten of his children are dead. Job is left childless, bereft and bereaved.

The cruelty and malignancy of Satan is revealed in that he struck everything Job had, just as God permitted him. Satan dumped everything on Job without warning, without giving Job any time to prepare himself mentally, emotionally, and spiritually. In a single day, probably within a single hour, the hammer blows fell on him, one after the other. With the fourth and final hammer blow, Job numbly realized that everything had been stripped from him, even his family. The only family member left to Job was his wife, and as we shall see (and as Satan may have known in advance), Job's wife would be no comfort to him.

In this account we see that Satan is given power over natural forces. Some people misinterpret this passage as saying that Satan always has such power, that he is the one who controls the wind and the waves. This is not true. In many places in Scripture, we see that God controls the natural world. For example, Psalm 78:26 tells us that the Lord "let loose the east wind from the heavens and led forth the south wind by his power." God is the one who created nature, not Satan. So it seems that Satan must have obtained God's express permission to use these natural forces for his own ends.

When Jesus calmed the storm on the Sea of Galilee, He rebuked the wind and the waves. This doesn't mean that Jesus spoke to air and water. Rather, He spoke to the forces *behind* the wind and waves—the satanic power that stirred up the storm. There are apparently occasions, as we see in this account in Job, when Satan receives God's permission to trouble the weather and the elements.

In 2 Corinthians 4:4, Paul calls Satan "the god of this world" (or, in some translations, "the god of this age"). Disastrous forces such as earthquakes, tornadoes, hurricanes, and droughts are often called "acts of God." Yet we need to realize that Satan, the god of this world, is at times given permission to bring these terrible events about.

DEFENDING GOD

Many atheists like to twist this biblical truth into a libelous statement about God. They say, "Your Bible says that God allows these terrible things to happen, even to innocent people! What kind of a monstrous, unjust God do you believe in?" This kind of thinking was once expressed in a parody of the Christian Doxology:

> Blame God from whom all cyclones blow,
> Blame Him, all creatures here below.
> Blame Him, who knocks down church and steeple,
> Who sends the floods, and drowns the people.

Before we become angry with the infidel who wrote those lines, we have to acknowledge that there is a modicum of truth in them. It *is* God who allows bad things to happen to good people. That is why our faith often trembles and falters. That is why we often come up with superficial answers to difficult and complex problems of human suffering.

There is an entire branch of theology called *theodicy*, which seeks to reconcile the existence of an all-good, all-powerful God with the existence of evil. The term *theodicy* was coined in 1710 by the German philosopher Gottfried Leibniz from two Greek words, *theos* (God) and *dike* (justice). An attempt to defend God from the accusation that He is unjust or unloving is called a theodicy.

This is not to suggest, of course, that God needs our defense. God does not have a fragile ego that is easily bruised by the accusations of atheists. The reason we speak of "defending God" is not to suggest that God is somehow vulnerable to the attacks of human enemies. We speak of "defending God" in a philosophical sense because, in order to advance the Gospel of Jesus Christ, we must sometimes break down the faulty arguments and false ideologies that Satan has planted in unbelieving minds.

The defense of God that we find in these opening pages of Job could be stated this way: Satan is an independent agent with free will. He does what he likes. God has given him areas in which he can operate, and God sometimes permits Satan to initiate a major disaster—a great earthquake, a volcanic explosion, a war, a mass murder. Yes, God is in ultimate sovereign control of the universe, but Satan's free will is the force that instigates evil in the world.

This is why the book of Job was given to us—to show that there is a deeper reason that God permits tragedy than the superficial answers that we often give. This theodicy, this defense of God's love and justice, will be unfolded to us as we press deeper into this book. In the pages of Job, we will see that God is not, as Satan would like us to believe, a cold and impersonal Being who does not care about us. Nor is He a cruel and sadistic God who afflicts us with tortures and disasters for His own twisted pleasure—again, as Satan would have us believe. Rather, God is merciful and compassionate. Out of the pain, loss, and questioning of Job, a picture will emerge of the mercy and compassion of God.

JOB RESPONDS TO HIS PAIN AND LOSS

How would you respond to the incredible loss that Job has just suffered? What if everything you owned and all of your beloved children were taken away from you in a single day of calamity? We see Job's response in the closing verses of chapter 1:

> At this, Job got up and tore his robe and shaved his head. Then he fell to the ground in worship and said:
>
> > "Naked I came from my mother's womb,
> >   and naked I will depart.
> > The LORD gave and the LORD has taken away;
> >   may the name of the LORD be praised."
>
> In all this, Job did not sin by charging God with wrongdoing (vv. 20–22).

Job didn't complain. He didn't blame God. He didn't cry out, "Why did this happen to me? This is so unfair!"

Someone once asked C. S. Lewis, "Why do the righteous suffer?"

He replied, "Why shouldn't the righteous suffer? They're the only ones who can handle it."

Clearly Job demonstrated that he could handle suffering. Instead of raging at the unfairness that everything had been taken from him, he thanked God for the privilege and joy of having had possessions and children. Rather than complaining about his loss, Job recognized God's sovereign right to do as He chose.

Job had no idea that his life was a battleground and that his righteous response had given God the victory over Satan. You and I never know exactly how much is at stake when we suffer pain and loss. Our response to pain and suffering might give the victory to God—or to Satan.

Because of Job's righteous response, God has won the first round and Satan's argument has been answered. Job loves God. Take away his possessions, even take away his children, and Job still loves God. This is a severe test, and I don't know if I could have passed it. Could you?

Yet the testing isn't over. There is more to come—much more. Before this story is over, we will see the layers of Job's life and soul peeled away like the layers of an onion. He will discover truths about God and about himself that he never suspected. Most important, Job will begin to see what God wants to accomplish in his life through loss and suffering. As we walk alongside Job in his pain and questioning, we will see what God wants to accomplish in our lives as well.

You may wonder, *What's happening behind the scenes of my life? Is Satan targeting my life right now? Am I the next battlefield in Satan's cosmic rebellion against God's authority?*

All I can say is this: Don't worry about things you can't control. Live your life a day at a time. It's true—if Satan had his way, he would destroy each of us. He would wreck our joy, slash our faith, and fill us with every grief and pain imaginable. Why does Satan want to hurt us? Is he angry with us? No, he's angry with God. He wants to attack God, whom we serve, and he will carry out his attack through us.

But God's protecting hand is over us, shielding us from Satan's rage. If we can enjoy any peace and security in this life, it's because the hand of God has been around us like a hedge of protection. So our attitude should not be, *Oh, what if God is about to let Satan hurt me!* Rather, our attitude should be, *Oh,*

Lord, thank You for the blessings You've given me. Help me to appreciate them while they are mine and to release them when the time comes to let go. I don't know what the future holds, Lord, but I know You hold the future. Whatever You choose to do or allow in my life, I will never let go of You.

What are the toughest, hardiest plants in a time of drought? The ones that put down the deepest roots. In fact, farmers sometimes stress certain varieties of trees, depriving them of water for weeks after they are planted, in order to force those trees to put their roots down deep into the soil. When those trees are mature and times of drought and hardship come, they will survive, while trees with shallow root systems are scorched to death by heat and drought.

That is what hardship does in our lives: It forces us to put our roots down deep into the soil of God's love. Whenever we are tested by trials of pain and loss, it's helpful to look beyond our momentary suffering and see the eternal implications of this test. This life is a battlefield, and we are warriors who serve the King of the universe. This life is a test, and we win a battle on behalf of our Lord and Master whenever we pass the test.

As the apostle Paul reminds us, "And God is faithful; he will not let you be tempted [tested] beyond what you can bear" (1 Corinthians 10:13). God will not test you beyond your ability to maintain your faith in Him.

THE PRESSURE OF PAIN

D r. Paul Brand was an orthopedic surgeon who specialized in treating leprosy in India and Louisiana. Leprosy (or Hansen's disease) is a disfiguring disease caused by a bacterial infection. Once considered incurable, leprosy can now be cured with antibiotics. One effect of the disease is that it destroys the nerves and causes numbness—a lack of pain sensation—in the limbs.

On one occasion, at a time when the disease was still considered incurable and the antibiotic treatments were still unknown, Dr. Brand was traveling by train in England. As he was getting ready for bed, he removed his shoes and socks and discovered to his horror and dismay that he had no feeling in his heel. He rubbed his heel, and the numbness persisted. He took a pin out of one of the shirts in his suitcase and jabbed it hard into the heel. Blood beaded up from the puncture wound, but still he felt no pain.

His mind awhirl with fear, Dr. Brand spent most of the night lying awake, imagining his new life as a leprosy victim. He would have to live in isolation from his family and suffer the progressive deterioration caused by a then-incurable disease.

In the morning, he sat up in bed and decided to conduct one more test. He took the pin, jabbed it hard into his heel—

And cried out in pain! *It hurt!* Thank God, it hurt!

Then he realized what had caused the numbness the night before. During the long train ride along the English coast, he had hardly gotten up once to stretch his legs. The long period of immobility had numbed the nerve leading to his heel. From then on, Dr. Brand would often speak of what he called "the blessing of pain."

We tend to think of pain as a curse, not a blessing, and that's understandable. Pain hurts. Pain brings pressure to bear upon our bodies, minds, emotions, and spirits. But God sometimes has a purpose in our pain that we cannot see. And He is always present in our pain, even when we can't sense Him there.

This is one of the great lessons of the book of Job. From the beginning of this book, we are confronted by the argument that God is present in the life of every human being, even in the midst of severe and painful trials.

As we have already seen in Job 1, this godly man named Job is being subjected to a severe test. God has permitted Satan to take away all of Job's possessions. Satan's goal in afflicting Job is to prove that when a man's possessions are taken away, he will curse God, no matter how faithful that man seemed while he was prosperous.

But Job confounds Satan. He passes the first cycle of tests. Job is left crushed and broken, yet his faith remains strong and intact. At the end of Job 1, the score was one to zero against Satan.

Job 2 opens with the second round of Satan's test. The first three verses of Job 2 take us back to the courts of heaven, where again we find God debating with Satan:

> On another day the angels came to present themselves before the LORD, and Satan also came with them to present himself before him. And the LORD said to Satan, "Where have you come from?"
>
> Satan answered the LORD, "From roaming through the earth and going back and forth in it."
>
> Then the LORD said to Satan, "Have you considered my servant Job? There is no one on earth like him; he is blameless and upright, a man who fears God and shuns evil. And he still maintains his integrity, though you incited me against him to ruin him without any reason" (vv. 1–3).

This reads much like the first chapter, of course. It is another glimpse behind the scenes into the heavenly realm, where God and Satan hold a conversation about Job. As we move on through later chapters of Job, we should remember the scenes in these opening chapters because they give us a heavenly perspective on our earthly trials.

PERSPECTIVE MAKES ALL THE DIFFERENCE

A friend once told me about a time when he was scheduled to sing at a youth group meeting for high school students at our church. Before he left to go to the meeting, his four-year-old daughter tugged at his sleeve and said, "Daddy, where are you going?"

"I'm going to go sing for some kids at church, honey," he answered.

"Can I come, too?"

"Sure!"

So my friend took his daughter to the youth group meeting. They arrived, and the little girl looked around at all the high school kids. Then she tugged at her father's sleeve and said, "Daddy, you said there would be kids here. Where are they?"

Her father looked around and pointed to the thirty or forty high school students in the room. "Just look!" he said. "There are kids all around you."

The girl put her hands on her hips and scowled. "Daddy!" she said in an exasperated tone. "Those aren't kids! Those are babysitters!"

You see what a difference perspective makes?

Here in Job 2, we are given a perspective on Job and his sufferings—a perspective that Job himself is not permitted to have. It's important to realize that Job's perspective is limited throughout his trials. An understanding of that fact is important because the same principle is true during our times of trial. When we suffer, our perspective is limited just as Job's was. We can't see behind the scenes of our lives during times of pressure and trials. We don't know what transpires between God and Satan when we suffer.

But these glimpses of the heavenly realm in Job 1 and 2 tell us something important: When we are put to the test, God is involved in our suffering. Our affliction is never meaningless; it always has something to do with God's eternal purpose.

"SKIN FOR SKIN!"

God says to Satan, "What do you think of Job now? You moved against him without a cause, and I allowed it to happen; yet Job passed the test. There is none like him on the earth. He is blameless and upright, and he turns away from evil. You haven't moved him an inch." How does Satan respond? He wants to change the rules of the game:

> "Skin for skin!" Satan replied. "A man will give all he has for his own life. But stretch out your hand and strike his flesh and bones, and he will surely curse you to your face."
>
> The LORD said to Satan, "Very well, then, he is in your hands; but you must spare his life" (Job 2:4–6).

What does Satan mean by the phrase "skin for skin"? This is apparently an ancient expression. In its context, we can see that the expression probably means that a man will give his skin to save his skin. A man will give every-thing he has, even his skin, in order to save his life." Again, Satan is claiming that Job loves God only out of self-interest. Strike him, and Job's love will surely turn to cursing. That is the devil's wager.

Satan is using essentially the same argument he used in chapter 1. His philosophy is that human beings are self-centered creatures. They love God only while life goes smoothly. But, Satan says, human love is conditional. As soon as life becomes difficult and painful, they'll give up their faith and love for God.

The Lord answered Satan's argument in chapter 1, which dealt with Job's possessions and his family. Job was tested and he passed the test, remaining steadfast in his integrity, refusing to curse God or accuse Him of wrongdoing. Now, in chapter 2, God allows Satan to test Job not merely in the realm of his wealth and family but even in the realm of Job's own body, his physical and emotional health.

It's a sobering experience to realize that the tests that come into our lives are actually aimed at getting us to curse God to His face, to tell Him He's unjust, to accuse Him of not keeping His promises. Satan wants to use our suffering to convince us that God is not truly God, that He's some kind of cosmic sadist or torturer.

Think back to the times when you have been in pain, under pressure, or experiencing loss. What was the great temptation you felt in such times? Weren't you tempted to cry out in protest to God, saying, "God, why don't You keep Your promises? Why are You being so unfair to me?" That is what Satan always tries to achieve in our lives. He has the same objective for our lives that he had for Job: Satan wants us to curse God.

In Job 2, Satan asks God to change the rules. He says to God, "You didn't go far enough. You put a boundary around Job, and You said that I couldn't touch his body. That's the problem. It's true that a man may give up his pos-sessions, but one thing he will never give up is his health. Just let me get at him, let me destroy his health, and he will give up his faith in You. He'll curse You to your face."

So the Lord agrees to change the rules. He tells Satan, "Job is in your power—only don't do anything that would cause him to die." Once again there is a divine limitation to the power of Satan, but this time God moves the boundaries closer to the limits of Job's endurance.

Notice that Satan uses the phrase "strike his flesh and bones." Here Satan asks God for access to the total humanity of Job. Satan doesn't want to attack

Job merely in his physical body but in his emotional life as well. The word *flesh* speaks of Job's health. The word *bones* speaks of Job's inner man—his thoughts, emotions, and subconscious mind. God grants Satan total access to Job in his body, soul, and spirit.

And Satan proceeds to attack Job in that same order: first, Job's body; next, Job's soul; and finally, Job's spirit. This three-phase assault on Job constitutes the storyline of most of the book of Job.

Satan knows what he is trying to achieve. The evil one is convinced that if he can get at Job in every part of his being, then he can shake Job's faith and cause him to turn away from God. Satan reasons that if he hurts Job deeply enough, he can goad Job into cursing God to His face.

DOES GOD KNOW WHAT HE'S DOING?

Once, after I spoke at church from the book of Job, two young men came up and challenged me. One said, "I can't accept your claim that the story of Job was an actual historical event." The other said, "I can't believe there was ever a man named Job who went through such trials."

"Why not?" I asked.

"Because," said one of them, "if this story is true, then it portrays God as being unconcerned about human life. God allows all of Job's children to be taken from him as if their lives don't even matter!"

"Exactly," said the other. "That's why I just can't accept this book as an historical record. If it's true, then God doesn't care about human beings."

These young men were struggling with the same feelings that have troubled many people over the years. They saw God as nothing more than a man—an all-powerful man—but a man who has no more rights than any other human being. They saw God as being subject to some higher moral law. Because they had such a diminished view of God, they felt that God should be charged with murder for the deaths of Job's ten children.

So I tried to show them a different perspective—a *biblical* perspective on God. I told them, "God can't be charged with murder and cruelty."

"Why not?" they asked.

"Because all of life is in God's hands. He created us and the universe we live in. He gave us life. He can take life away. He determines the length of life for everyone. So how can we say God is guilty of murder when He simply takes back what already belongs to Him—the gift of life?"

They still were not convinced.

"Look at it this way. Suppose Job's children all fell ill and died from a disease. Would you still call God a murderer?"

"I suppose not. That would be death due to natural causes."

"So if a person dies slowly due to an illness, that's natural. But if a person dies suddenly, that seems unfair. But is it unfair?"

The two young men decided they would have to think about it some more. I never found out what they decided, and I truly wish I knew.

A single, individual death can hit us very hard and make us doubt God's goodness. I recall one occasion when Elaine and I received a call telling us that a dear friend had suddenly died. She was a young woman, the mother of five children. She and her husband operated a Christian retreat in the Lake Tahoe area, and they had befriended our daughters.

How had she died? She and her husband were taking a walk beside a mountain stream. She stopped by the stream to rest while her husband went ahead to climb a rock. When he returned, he found her in the stream, drowned. It seemed so senseless. The stream was not dangerous, and they were not taking any extraordinary risks. This woman had so much to live for, and her family loved and needed her. Now she's gone.

We ask, "Why, Lord? Why did You allow that to happen? Are You sure you didn't make a mistake?"

Sometimes, we learn of a death toll that is simply staggering and beyond our comprehension. We wonder, "Why did God allow that war or that terrorist attack?" Or, "Why did God allow that earthquake, that hurricane, that devastating tsunami?" Sometimes, terrible things happen in the world and people die by the thousands or the tens of thousands in a single day, a single event. And we ask, "Why, Lord? Why did You allow tragedy to strike the world on such an unimaginable scale?"

Here again, we need to gain a different perspective—God's perspective— on tragedy, loss, and suffering. We see a disaster unfold on CNN or Fox News, and we think, "Oh, what horrible loss of life!" And it *is* horrible, it truly is. But at the same time, we must acknowledge that our perspective is different from God's perspective.

When we see tragedy on our TV screens, we are only aware of that *one* tragedy. We are aware only of the hundreds or thousands of people who perished in that one event.

God, however, is aware of every single person who suffers and dies, every moment of every day in every part of the world. Did you know that around the world about 154,000 people die every single day? And God knows each of them by name.

You may think that God is unfair when He allows thousands of people to die in a single event, such as a tsunami or an earthquake. But is that really any more unfair than the 154,000 people who die every day from heart attacks, cancer, malaria, AIDS, car crashes, falling in the bathtub, and countless other causes? What makes one death fair and another unfair?

The reason we have the book of Job is so that we can catch a glimpse of what God is doing in the universe. There are reasons for our pain that we cannot see in this life. But God sees and God knows. He is working out His purposes through our lives and in our suffering. Every trial and test we face has a purpose; through our pain, God manifests the plans of His mind and the compassion of His heart.

THE ATTACK OF JOB'S WIFE

In the next section, we see the physical test that comes when God gives Satan access to Job:

> So Satan went out from the presence of the LORD and afflicted Job with painful sores from the soles of his feet to the top of his head. Then Job took a piece of broken pottery and scraped himself with it as he sat among the ashes.
>
> His wife said to him, "Are you still holding on to your integrity? Curse God and die!" (Job 2:7–9).

Here we see Satan's first attack on Job's body. Some Bible scholars believe that this attack involved leprosy. Other scholars suggest that it may have been a form of elephantiasis, a disease that causes extreme enlargement of the limbs and other body distortions, resulting from obstructions in the lymphatic system. The description of "painful sores from the soles of his feet to the top of his head" is generally interpreted as referring to boils—painful, pus-filled eruptions in the flesh usually caused by a staphylococcus infection. Whatever Job's illness was, it turned him into a pitiful, repulsive, horrifying figure.

When I was in my early twenties, I endured a recurring attack of painful boils that lasted almost two years. The boils usually appeared in my skin one or two at a time and were extremely painful. There is almost nothing you can do to relieve the pain of a boil. It throbs day and night, and you must grit your teeth and endure the agony until the boil heals of its own accord. During the limited time I was going through that trial of pain (which doesn't begin to compare with the painful trial of Job), I found that my youthful faith was tested.

Ever since that time, I've had a deep sympathy for dear old Job. Here he is, covered with agonizing sores. He's not only physically afflicted, but he's also painfully humiliated. He ends up sitting in the ashes, scraping the pus from his sores with a broken piece of pottery.

As if his pain isn't already at the limit of human endurance, his wife—who should be a source of comfort and emotional support—says to him, "Are you still holding on to your integrity? Curse God and die!" Her faith has already been shattered by Satan's attacks against Job. Remember that she, too, has lost wealth and all of her children. In her own pain and grief, she has lost her ability to see God as loving, good, and just. She sees her own suffering and Job's as proof that God has forsaken His promises, that God's Word is not true.

Over the years, I have counseled many people who were going through trials and who had reached the same point as Job's wife. They said to me, "I tried trusting God's promises. I tried believing in God and His love, but it doesn't work; it isn't true. God can't be trusted."

That's the viewpoint Job's wife expresses when she says, "Are you still holding on to your integrity? Curse God and die!" And notice this: What Job's wife wants him to do is exactly what Satan is trying to get Job to do—curse God and die. Clearly, Satan is using Job's wife as his instrument against Job, just as Satan used Eve as his instrument against Adam in the Garden of Eden. I am not saying here that either Eve or Job's wife were possessed by the devil; but these two women did permit themselves to be used by Satan when they yielded to the temptation to disobey God.

What two things is Satan saying to Job through Job's wife? First, Satan urges Job to give up his faith, to become an apostate and an enemy of God: "Curse God," Job's wife says. Second, Satan urges Job to commit suicide. "Curse God *and die!*" she says. So Satan, through Job's wife, clearly suggests to Job that it would be better for him to take his own life than to go on living like this.

Job is already drowning in pain, loss, disfigurement, and humiliation. Now his suffering is intensified because he has been emotionally abandoned and spiritually abused by his own wife.

If you are a wife, you may not fully understand how much your husband depends on you for his emotional, mental, and spiritual well being. Husbands typically draw much more emotional and spiritual strength from their wives than either they or their wives realize. Whenever you are tempted to say something that might wound your husband or make him feel abandoned or rejected, remember Job and his wife.

Remember that Job's wife was doing the bidding of Satan and carrying out his plan. As husbands and wives, we owe it to our spouses and to God to make sure that everything we say to each other serves to further God's plan, not Satan's.

JOB'S GENTLE REBUKE

In Job 2:10, we see the results of the second round of tests that Satan has inflicted on Job:

> He replied, "You are talking like a foolish woman. Shall we accept good from God, and not trouble?"
>
> In all this, Job did not sin in what he said.

Job's rebuke is gentle. He does not attack his wife. He does not say, "You foolish woman!" Rather, he gently says, "You are talking like a foolish woman." He points out that her words represent a temporary lapse of faith on her part, and they are no different from the words of foolish women who do not know God, but he does not attack her personally.

Moreover, he goes on to speak words of grace to his wife, encouraging her to return to the faith she once embraced: "Shall we accept good from God, and not trouble?" Job saw that his wife had fallen prey to a false philosophy that is still common today—a belief that life ought to always be pleasant, and if it is not, then we should give up on God and life.

Though God, in His love and grace, has provided many blessings in this life, He did not create us merely to spend our lives having a good time and pursuing pleasure. Even in times of pain and loss, our lives were meant to have meaning and purpose. An outlook that abandons life and faith as soon as living becomes difficult is a shallow and distorted view of living.

In the midst of his pain, Job reaffirms his faith in God: "Shall we accept good from God, and not trouble?" In other words, we should enjoy life's pleasures and blessings with gladness and gratitude. And when hard times come, we should continue to trust God and love Him. Don't abandon faith in God when hardships come, because *that is exactly what Satan wants us to do*. Our adversary wants us to resent God and give up on our faith. If we surrender our love for God in times of trial, then we are giving Satan the victory he seeks.

This we must not do.

THE MOST DEVASTATING ASSAULT

Job has won round two. The score is now two to zero in favor of Job, but Satan is not finished. Remember, he obtained permission from God to assault this man in every area of his being. He has not only taken Job's children and all of his possessions, but he has also taken away Job's health. What's more, Satan has also assaulted Job's soul by making him feel abandoned by his wife.

Now Satan proceeds to assault the innermost stronghold of Job's being: his spirit. The human spirit is, after all, the ultimate reality of a human life. At this point, Satan aims his heavy artillery at Job's spirit and his faith:

> When Job's three friends, Eliphaz the Temanite, Bildad the Shuhite and Zophar the Naamathite, heard about all the troubles that had come upon him, they set out from their homes and met together by agreement to go and sympathize with him and comfort him (Job 2:11).

This verse sets the stage for the major argument of this book. The most devastating attack on Job's faith doesn't come through his physical trials, as painful as those have been. They come through an attack on his spiritual relationship with God Himself. Ironically, this attack comes through Job's well-meaning but misguided friends. These friends are sincere, and they want to help. But the truth is that they are actually Satan's instruments of assault against the castle of Job's faith. So devastating is this attack that they nearly cause his faith to collapse.

From the text we can see that these men had to travel from distant places, so a certain amount of time must have elapsed while Job was suffering. It took time for word to reach these friends and time for them to agree to meet at an appointed time and set off to visit Job. Probably weeks, if not months, passed while Job was undergoing this intense trial of suffering. When his friends arrived, they were shocked at the sight of him:

> When they saw him from a distance, they could hardly recognize him; they began to weep aloud, and they tore their robes and sprinkled dust on their heads. Then they sat on the ground with him for seven days and

seven nights. No one said a word to him, because they saw how great his suffering was (Job 2:12–13).

These friends were astonished to find that their old friend had become a thing of horror, a repulsive and sickening sight. When they saw Job, this man they had known and laughed with and prayed with, sitting in a heap of ashes, scraping himself raw with broken pieces of pottery, they responded with the same intensity of grief as if Job had died. When they wept, tore their robes, covered their heads with dust, and then observed silence for seven days, they were, in effect, holding a funeral service for him. These were the ancient rites that were reserved for the dead.

As these friends sat quietly for seven days, their minds were not idle. They were thinking. And the thoughts they were thinking will be revealed to us in detail in the next section of the book. For now, however, we can summarize their thoughts in a few words: Job's friends concluded that he was suffering under the hand of God because of *sins* he had committed. They felt he *deserved* his sufferings.

Job was innocent! God had chosen him from among all men on earth as the ultimate example of faith, righteousness, and love for God. There couldn't be a more unjust accusation than that of Job's friends. They had unfairly hardened their hearts against Job. Though they had come far from home to comfort him, they changed their minds about him while they sat in silence with him. They came to him as friends, but they became his adversaries.

Why were they silent for seven days? At first, perhaps, their silence was the silence of mourning. But as they pondered the reasons for Job's suffering, they probably wondered, "How do we tell Job what he needs to hear? Where do we begin? How do we get him to listen to us? How do we confront him and tell him, 'The reason you're suffering is that you have unconfessed sin in your life'?"

At the end of those seven days, Job's friends break their silence. They argue against Job, and Job defends his own innocence. As we listen to the debate between them, we discover how much of our own philosophy and worldview is reflected in the misguided words of Job's friends.

We should always remember what we saw in Job 1 and 2: God is the one who is in control of Job's life, including his sufferings. Though it was Satan who afflicted Job, God gave Satan permission, and He did so because He had a plan for Job's sufferings. God never tells Job what this plan is, and that is instructive to you and me because we usually don't know what God has planned for our sufferings either. So we empathize with Job. We understand his feelings because we, too, have experienced the anguish and desolation and questioning that suffering brings.

But there is an answer. God does have a reason. He has a plan that encompasses not only all of time but all of eternity, and our trials and sufferings are a part of that plan. Sooner or later, we all experience times of trial and testing. To be faithful to the truth of Scripture, we must recognize that God Himself allows these trials in our lives. They come to us by His permission. If you are going through a trial right now, the book of Job will give you a glimpse behind the scenes of your pain and show you that God is at work, even in your suffering.

Even though God permits us to suffer, He does not delight in our suffering. Satan is the one who takes pleasure in our pain. If Satan had his way, we would all suffer and perish. But God guards and keeps us. Even if He temporarily permits hardship and affliction in our lives, we have the promise of God's Word that it will never be more than we can handle. Job proved that.

True, we sometimes feel that our pain is more than we can bear, that God is pushing us beyond human endurance. But that He will not do. Instead, God teaches us that we are stronger in Him than we ever imagined, and His life and power are strong in us. That is the message of the book of Job whenever we find ourselves under the pressure of pain.

IS IT BETTER TO DIE?

Most people knew James as a caring friend with a positive, can-do attitude. He had a successful career in sales and also served in the army reserves. His closest friends knew he had gone through a painful experience as a child, having been sexually molested by a priest. But he seemed to have put it behind him, dealing with his painful memories in a healthy and redemptive way.

In his thirties, James became involved with an organization of abuse survivors. There, he counseled abuse victims, telling them, "Remember, you're not a victim. You're a survivor." He also spoke to law enforcement groups about ways to protect children from sexual predators.

Everyone thought James was doing fine. No one knew that James had his good days and his bad days, including days when he was horribly depressed. Early one Sunday morning, when he was not coping well with his bad memories, James went for a walk along the train tracks near his home. He heard the train coming, and he stepped into the middle of the tracks and ended his life.

Like James, many people today are dealing with so much pain in their lives that they ask themselves, "Is it better to die?" That, in fact, is the question Job asks as we come to the third chapter of Job.

JOB'S ONLY ALTERNATIVE

Job has undergone severe testing, unaware that he is the subject of a challenge between God and Satan. All he knows is that he has experienced one devastating calamity after another. He has lost his possessions and his ten children. He has lost his health and been afflicted with a disfiguring disease. His wife has turned against him, urging him to curse God and commit suicide. Despite these pressures, Job still trusts in God's mercy and love. He steadfastly resists the will of Satan, who wants Job to curse God and die.

The book of Job is a rebuke to me. I have often responded with far less trust and faith than Job has, even though my problems didn't begin to compare with Job's. How many times have we railed in anger and resentment toward God because of some minor setback in our lives? How many times have we ranted and cursed because we can't find our car keys or we burned a pan of brownies?

God is good. His love endures forever. If He allows pain or problems to come into our lives, He does so for reasons that are good, perfect, and loving. We need to learn that our only righteous response is one of blessing God and acknowledging His goodness.

At this point in the story of Job, we see that Satan uses three of Job's friends to turn up the heat. Job 3 begins the dialogue between Job and his friends, which becomes the major part of the book of Job. The chapter opens with Job's bitter lament. Weeks have gone by since he was first afflicted with this horrible disease, and God does not explain to Job what He is doing. Job knows nothing of the dialogue between God and Satan. He is baffled, and his suffering seems like a random and meaningless catastrophe. In the opening lines of Job 3, he opens his mouth in a cry of despair, longing for death:

After this, Job opened his mouth and cursed the day of his birth.

He said:
    "May the day of my birth perish,
        and the night it was said, 'A boy is born!'
    That day—may it turn to darkness;
        may God above not care about it;
        may no light shine upon it.
    May darkness and deep shadow claim it once more;
        may a cloud settle over it;
        may blackness overwhelm its light.
    That night—may thick darkness seize it;
        may it not be included among the days of the year
        nor be entered in any of the months.
    May that night be barren;
        may no shout of joy be heard in it.
    May those who curse days curse that day,
        those who are ready to rouse Leviathan.
    May its morning stars become dark;
        may it wait for daylight in vain
        and not see the first rays of dawn,

for it did not shut the doors of the womb on me
    to hide trouble from my eyes" (vv. 1–10).

Those are extreme emotions, the result of extreme pain. Have you ever felt that way? I know there have been times I wished I could drop out of the scene entirely and go home to heaven.

Once, while my wife Elaine and I were going through a time of intense trial, I received a card of encouragement from a dear friend who understood the extremes of our pain and emotions. She wrote:

> You may feel helpless right now. The fact is, you *are* helpless. There is little you can do but simply persevere through these circumstances. I believe God sometimes leads us into these places of pain and helplessness.
>
> When we are there, hurting and unable to change our circumstances, the crutches we always relied on are stripped from us, one by one. At that point, God's words and His love stand out to us in a way they never could when we had those crutches to lean on. We begin to see Him as constant and unchanging, and His love becomes irresistible to us.
>
> Finally, Jesus becomes our only alternative. Otherwise, death would be the only logical relief.

That's the place where we find Job in chapter 3. All the crutches of his life have been stripped away. Death seems to be the only logical relief for his pain. So he cries out for death, cursing the day he was born. He hopes his birthday will be forgotten and wiped out of all memory. It used to be a happy day, a day of celebration. Now he says, in effect, "Let the day I was born be darkened, and let no one rejoice in it. May it be a day of cursing, not blessing." Though Job speaks of the day of his birth, he is actually expressing his longing for death.

While Job comes close to cursing God, he never crosses that line. Instead, Job curses the day of his birth, and he curses what God has allowed to happen. You can see how the pressure of his pain is increasing, and Job is beginning to break under that pressure.

Few things are harder to bear than meaningless suffering. If we could see some reason for what we have to go through, we could more easily endure it. But pointless trouble is corrosive to our souls.

That's what Job experiences at this stage in his life. So he cries out, "Why was I ever born? Why can't I simply die and be done with it?" The only relief Job sees for his pain is death.

A PRIMITIVE VIEW OF DEATH

Job goes on to a second despairing question: "If I had to be born at all, why couldn't I have died at birth? Why should I have to live if living involves so much pain? My life is totally meaningless! It would have been better to have died when I was born!" He laments:

> Why did I not perish at birth,
> and die as I came from the womb?
> Why were there knees to receive me
> and breasts that I might be nursed? (Job 3:11–12).

Next, Job goes on to give us his view of death. This is revealing, because Job has a much more primitive view of death than that found in the New Testament. It's the view of those who have no knowledge of the Bible. He says:

> For now I would be lying down in peace;
> I would be asleep and at rest
> with kings and counselors of the earth,
> who built for themselves places now lying in ruins,
> with rulers who had gold,
> who filled their houses with silver.
> Or why was I not hidden in the ground like a stillborn child,
> like an infant who never saw the light of day?
> There the wicked cease from turmoil,
> and there the weary are at rest.
> Captives also enjoy their ease;
> they no longer hear the slave driver's shout.
> The small and the great are there,
> and the slave is freed from his master (3:13–19).

Job views death as a time of rest, a period of solitude and quiet after the tumult and trouble of life. I think many people see death that way.

In Thornton Wilder's play *Our Town*, there is a vivid segment that describes a visit to a cemetery where the dead talk among themselves. The dead form a community of souls who simply lie at peace in their coffins, free from the toil and troubles that plagued them during life. Ironically, the dead pity the living. A young woman named Emily has just died, and she reflects on the living, saying, "They're sort of shut up in little boxes"—as if the life of the living is more confining than a coffin in the ground.

These verses indicate that Job's understanding of life after death is limited. In fact, one of the reasons for his suffering is that he needs to be enlightened about the afterlife. We will see, by the end of this story, that Job's view of life, death, and the afterlife undergoes a radical transformation from the beginning to the end of this book.

Next, Job approaches a question many hurting people ask today: "Why shouldn't I die right now? Since I didn't die when I was born, why can't I at least die now and end my sufferings?"

> Why is light given to those in misery,
>> and life to the bitter of soul,
> to those who long for death that does not come,
>> who search for it more than for hidden treasure,
> who are filled with gladness
>> and rejoice when they reach the grave?
> Why is life given to a man
>> whose way is hidden,
>> whom God has hedged in?
> For sighing comes to me instead of food;
>> my groans pour out like water.
> What I feared has come upon me;
>> what I dreaded has happened to me.
> I have no peace, no quietness;
>> I have no rest, but only turmoil (3:20–26).

Job is saying, "What is the purpose of my life? What use is a life that is so full of misery and anguish? Why not end it now?" Many people feel that way. Even if you have never felt suicidal, you can imagine being in such pain that you would not want to go on living.

I don't think that Job is contemplating suicide. If he were truly speaking of suicide, I think he would have said so plainly. Yes, he wishes that his body would simply collapse in death. Yes, he wishes that God would take him home. There is nothing about life that seems meaningful or enjoyable, so why go on living? But Job is not about to take his own life.

As Job has been lamenting the pain and pointlessness of life, his three friends have been listening. In Job 4, they offer the first of several replies to Job's lament.

JOB'S FRIENDS RESPOND

Job's three friends are named Eliphaz, Bildad, and Zophar. They all come with the same solution to the problem, but they approach it in three distinct ways, each according to his own personality. As I read through this passage, I have noticed the three distinct confrontational styles of these individuals, and I have dubbed these men "Eliphaz the Elegant," "Bildad the Brutal," and "Zophar the Zealous."

Eliphaz is the first speaker. He is evidently the oldest, for he speaks with an elegant smoothness and a polished courtesy (at least at the beginning), suggesting that he has some experience in saying unpleasant things in a gracious way.

Bildad is brutally frank and plainspoken. He lays his thoughts and accusations before Job, not caring what effect his words will have on Job.

Zophar is passionate and emotional. He speaks with a great deal of impact and tries to move Job with emotional appeals.

The argument of Eliphaz the Elegant breaks down into six main points. When you hear what he has to say, you will have a good idea what these three friends will say throughout the rest of the book. Eliphaz starts out by saying to Job, "Follow your own advice." As Eliphaz begins, notice how elegant and polished his words sound:

> If someone ventures a word with you, will you be impatient?
>> But who can keep from speaking?
> Think how you have instructed many,
>> how you have strengthened feeble hands.
> Your words have supported those who stumbled;
>> you have strengthened faltering knees.
> But now trouble comes to you, and you are discouraged;
>> it strikes you, and you are dismayed.
> Should not your piety be your confidence
>> and your blameless ways your hope? (Job 4:2–6).

Eliphaz is saying, "Job, you've been a counselor to many people, and you've been able to help them solve their problems. You've helped them face the truth about their own hurts. Now follow your own advice. You've been caught in the same kind of problem you've helped others with. You've been struck down by trouble, and now you're discouraged. If you're really innocent and blameless, you shouldn't feel so bad. You should take confidence in your own innocence!"

Next, Eliphaz goes on to state plainly Job's problem as he sees it. In the next few verses, Eliphaz states his own view of life:

> Consider now: Who, being innocent, has ever perished?
>   Where were the upright ever destroyed?
> As I have observed, those who plow evil
>   and those who sow trouble reap it.
> At the breath of God they are destroyed;
>   at the blast of his anger they perish.
> The lions may roar and growl,
>   yet the teeth of the great lions are broken.
> The lion perishes for lack of prey,
>   and the cubs of the lioness are scattered (Job 4:7–11).

Eliphaz uses lions to describe the natural strength of human beings. An evil man may appear strong, but in God's judging hands his power is broken. In other words, Eliphaz argues that the righteous are never punished; only the unrighteous suffer. He asks, "Did you ever see an innocent man perish? Or an evil man succeed?" Notice the smooth subtlety of this argument. Without coming out and bluntly saying so, Eliphaz accuses Job of hiding sin in his life. If Job is suffering, he must have sinned, because these things don't happen to upright, innocent people.

This, in fact, is the basic argument of all three of Job's so-called friends throughout the book: "There's something wrong with your life, Job. Your suffering is all your own fault. Admit your sin, and you will be healed."

Some years ago, I picked up a magazine that claimed to be Christian, yet it seemed that its primary reason for existing was to attack men who were in public Christian ministry. In this particular issue, the magazine took up its cudgel against Dr. Billy Graham. The editor of the magazine noted that Dr. Graham had recently come down with an illness. He opined that Dr. Graham's illness was God's judgment against him for associating with the wrong kinds of people.

A few weeks later, another issue of the magazine came out, and in this issue, the editor talked about how he had fallen down a flight of stairs. In falling, he had broken his leg and was left hobbling around on crutches. His explanation for his injury was that Satan was attacking him and trying to stop his ministry for God.

This magazine editor is typical of human beings. We can all see clearly that the suffering of *others* is caused by their *sin*—but *our* suffering could only have been caused by Satan, who is trying to halt the wonderful work we are doing for the Lord. This is a dangerous form of self-deception.

A DISTURBING PASSAGE

Eliphaz the Elegant goes on to tell Job that if he will fear God and admit his sin, things will be all right. He begins by relating a message he received in a strange visitation at night. I think you'll agree that this is a disturbing section of Eliphaz's argument:

> A word was secretly brought to me,
>   my ears caught a whisper of it.
> Amid disquieting dreams in the night,
>   when deep sleep falls on men,
> fear and trembling seized me
>   and made all my bones shake.
> A spirit glided past my face,
>   and the hair on my body stood on end.
> It stopped,
>   but I could not tell what it was.
> A form stood before my eyes,
>   and I heard a hushed voice:
> "Can a mortal be more righteous than God?
>   Can a man be more pure than his Maker?" (Job 4:12–17).

Here Eliphaz says that he was visited in the middle of the night by a spirit. Though he says that this spirit came to him "amid disquieting dreams in the night," Eliphaz does not say that the spirit was something he saw in a dream. Rather, the spirit appears to have interrupted his dreams and awakened him from sleep. The description of this spirit is like something from a horror film. This strange and frightening entity actually glided close to his face, filling him with fear and trembling, making the hair on his body stand up straight, and causing his bones to shake. The entity was visible yet vague and formless, and it spoke in a hushed and whispery voice.

This visiting spirit clearly wanted to create the impression that it spoke for God, saying, "Can a mortal be more righteous than God? Can a man be more pure than his Maker?" Significantly, however, this spirit doesn't specifically say that it was sent from God. Eliphaz believes—and would have Job believe—that this spirit is an angel, but this strange entity doesn't behave in the same way as other angels in Scripture.

When angels appear in Scripture, they usually appear as men, not vague and formless spirits. In Genesis 18, Abraham welcomed three angels who appeared to be human travelers. The two angels who went to Sodom in Genesis 19 were assumed by the people of Sodom to be human visitors. The angel at the tomb of Jesus in Mark 16 was described as "a young man dressed in a white robe." Clearly the spirit that visited Eliphaz does not fit this description.

The sudden appearance of an angel was often startling, but when people were frightened by an angel, the angel always allayed their fears by saying, "Do not be afraid." These reassuring words were spoken by the angel who visited Hagar in Genesis 21:17; Elijah in 2 Kings 1:15; Joseph, Mary's betrothed, in Matthew 1:20; the Virgin Mary in Luke 1:30; Zechariah, the father of John the Baptist, in Luke 1:13; the shepherds in Luke 2:10; and the women at the garden tomb in Mark 16:6. God never sent angels to terrify, disturb, or alarm those who loved Him. The frightening nature of the spirit that visited Eliphaz and the fact that the spirit says nothing to allay this man's fears strongly suggest that this spirit was not sent from God and did not speak for God.

Next, let's look at the message the spirit spoke to Eliphaz, and let's ask ourselves: Is this the kind of message God would send through one of His angels? Eliphaz recalls the spirit's words:

> Can a mortal be more righteous than God?
>> Can a man be more pure than his Maker?
> If God places no trust in his servants,
>> if he charges his angels with error,
> how much more those who live in houses of clay,
>> whose foundations are in the dust,
>> who are crushed more readily than a moth!
> Between dawn and dusk they are broken to pieces;
>> unnoticed, they perish forever.
> Are not the cords of their tent pulled up,
>> so that they die without wisdom? (Job 4:17–21).

Notice the metaphor describing human beings as "those who live in houses of clay, whose foundations are in the dust." The "houses" are our bodies. This spirit speaks of the fact that human bodies are impermanent and made from the dust of the earth. This use of metaphorical language is intended to demean human beings.

The spirit asks Eliphaz, "Does a human being have a right to question God? Certainly not! A human being is not more righteous than God, so humanity has no right to ask God anything. Human beings are insignificant to God because they are made of dust, and they are as weak and fragile as moths. God, who accuses angels of error and sin, has even less regard for mortal humans—creatures who live from dawn to dusk, then die without ever knowing what their lives were about. Humanity is beneath God's notice. He is completely indifferent to human beings. Shall an insignificant man question Almighty God? What a laughable idea!"

Now there can be no doubt. The spirit that visited Eliphaz was an *evil* spirit pretending to be an angel of God. A true messenger of the Lord would never portray God as being indifferent to people, considering humanity to be unworthy of His notice. Everywhere else in Scripture we see that God loves His people and takes care of them. In Luke 12:7, Jesus tells us that God loves us so much that He has even numbered the hairs on our heads. We see God's love and concern vividly described for us in such passages as Psalm 23 or in Psalm 33, which tells us:

> From heaven the LORD looks down
> > and sees all mankind;
> from his dwelling place he watches
> > all who live on earth—
> he who forms the hearts of all,
> > who considers everything they do (vv. 13–15).

Notice, too, that the spirit that visited Eliphaz seems to complain about God's judgment against the fallen angels, the demons who followed Satan in his rebellion. The spirit says that God "places no trust in his servants" and that He "charges his angels with error." This sounds like the sort of complaint Satan himself might make against God. The demons undoubtedly are baffled and resentful over the fact that God actually loves these miserable little creatures who live from dusk to dawn and whose bodies are made of dust. These clearly sound like the words of Satan or one of his demons, not the words of our loving God.

Yet Eliphaz thinks that he has been privileged to receive an oracle from God. He has no clue that this message was given to him by the evil one as a means of attacking and undermining Job. So Eliphaz repeats the evil spirit's argument: God is infinite; human beings are nothing. If God is so pure that even the angels are sinful compared to Him, then human beings don't stand a chance before God.

The most effective lies usually contain at least a kernel of truth, and that is certainly the case with this lie. There is a little nugget of good theology at the heart of the false theology expressed here by Eliphaz: Human beings truly are fallen, and human righteousness truly is worthless before God. That's correct. But here's the lie: The spirit, quoted by Eliphaz, claims that human beings are also *worthless* before God, and that's utterly false.

Moreover, in applying this false message to Job, Eliphaz argues that because human beings are worthless and human righteousness is worthless, then Job's claim to be innocent is worthless, because no one is innocent. God is just, Eliphaz reasons, and all human beings are like dust beneath His feet. Job is sinful and worthless. So the reason Job is suffering is because God is punishing him for being a worthless sinner.

Eliphaz sees God only as a God of justice. He sees nothing of the love, compassion, forgiveness, and patience of God. So because of his unbalanced and incomplete theology, even the limited truth that Eliphaz speaks becomes a lie. Eliphaz speaks the truth when he says, in effect, that all humans are sinners and fall short of the holy standards of a righteous God. But when Eliphaz applies that broad truth to Job, claiming that Job's suffering is due to his utter sinfulness, it becomes a lie that blasphemes the character of God.

That is how a lot of error creeps into our interpretation of Scripture. We evangelical Christians readily cite Scripture in support of our doctrinal beliefs, and our beliefs may be perfectly true, but when we try to apply them from a false or incomplete premise, we end up turning God's truth into an ugly falsehood.

SLY ACCUSATIONS

Next, Eliphaz the Elegant becomes even more pointed and personal in his attack on Job's character:

> Call if you will, but who will answer you?
>> To which of the holy ones will you turn?
> Resentment kills a fool,
>> and envy slays the simple.

I myself have seen a fool taking root,
> but suddenly his house was cursed.

His children are far from safety,
> crushed in court without a defender (Job 5:1–4).

What a low blow! Without directly pointing a finger at Job, Eliphaz has insulted Job by calling him a fool. When he says, "I myself have seen a fool taking root," he is speaking of the fact that Job, like a plant taking root in good, well-watered soil, became wealthy and prosperous (roots, in the Bible, generally refer to strength, health, wealth, and a flourishing life). Perhaps there is a suggestion here that when Job was so prosperous, Eliphaz may have envied his success.

Eliphaz then makes a cruel reference to the calamity that befell all Job's children in one day. He notes that the house of this fool was cursed, his children exposed to danger, and then crushed—just as Job's children were crushed in the tornado and collapse of their house. Why did all of these things happen? Eliphaz can point to only one reason: sin in Job's life.

The hungry consume his harvest,
> taking it even from among thorns,
> and the thirsty pant after his wealth.

For hardship does not spring from the soil,
> nor does trouble sprout from the ground.

Yet man is born to trouble
> as surely as sparks fly upward (Job 5:5–7).

Trouble doesn't just spring from the ground or come out of nowhere, says Eliphaz. Yet because man is born to trouble, we know that trouble must have a cause. In these verses, Eliphaz only *hints* at the cause—but it's clear he's hinting at an accusation against Job, an accusation of hidden sin.

THE FLAWED THEOLOGY OF ELIPHAZ

In the next section of his argument, Eliphaz suggests to Job that there is no point in playing games with God because God knows all things:

But if it were I, I would appeal to God;
> I would lay my cause before him.

He performs wonders that cannot be fathomed,
> miracles that cannot be counted.

He bestows rain on the earth;
>   he sends water upon the countryside.
The lowly he sets on high,
>   and those who mourn are lifted to safety.
He thwarts the plans of the crafty,
>   so that their hands achieve no success.
He catches the wise in their craftiness,
>   and the schemes of the wily are swept away.
Darkness comes upon them in the daytime;
>   at noon they grope as in the night.
He saves the needy from the sword in their mouth;
>   he saves them from the clutches of the powerful.
So the poor have hope,
>   and injustice shuts its mouth (Job 5:8–16).

God is in control, Eliphaz argues. He is so wise that He cannot be deceived. "You can't hide from Him, Job," he says. "He'll catch you and uncover your sin. You might as well get it out in the open!" Eliphaz goes on to urge Job to surrender to God, and then God will bless him:

Blessed is the man whom God corrects;
>   so do not despise the discipline of the Almighty.
For he wounds, but he also binds up;
>   he injures, but his hands also heal.
From six calamities he will rescue you;
>   in seven no harm will befall you.
In famine he will ransom you from death,
>   and in battle from the stroke of the sword.
You will be protected from the lash of the tongue,
>   and need not fear when destruction comes.
You will laugh at destruction and famine,
>   and need not fear the beasts of the earth.
For you will have a covenant with the stones of the field,
>   and the wild animals will be at peace with you.
You will know that your tent is secure;
>   you will take stock of your property
>   and find nothing missing.
You will know that your children will be many,
>   and your descendants like the grass of the earth.

You will come to the grave in full vigor,
   like sheaves gathered in season.
We have examined this, and it is true.
   So hear it and apply it to yourself (Job 5:17–27).

Eliphaz argues from a simplistic and unrealistic theology: If you just cast yourself on God's mercy, He will restore you and everything will be fine. Do that, and God will protect you and keep you safe from trouble.

This, of course, is not the way the universe works. If you have lived long at all, you know that godly people are not immune from trouble. In fact, many people go through trial and suffering precisely *because* they live godly lives. Their righteous lifestyle is the direct cause of their suffering. As the apostle Paul told his spiritual son Timothy, "In fact, everyone who wants to live a godly life in Christ Jesus will be persecuted" (2 Timothy 3:12). Those who think godly living makes them invulnerable to trouble are living in a fantasy world.

The book of Job was written to correct such errors in our theology. It was written to show us that there are deeper reasons for suffering than sin alone. Yes, sin produces consequences, including suffering. But sometimes we suffer even though we are living for God.

JOB'S REPLY TO ELIPHAZ

In Job 6 and 7, Job responds to the accusations of Eliphaz. His response is divided into two parts. In Job 6, he rebukes his friends, speaking to all three of them. In Job 7, he addresses his complaint to God. He begins:

If only my anguish could be weighed
   and all my misery be placed on the scales!
It would surely outweigh the sand of the seas—
   no wonder my words have been impetuous (Job 6:2–3).

First, Job says he has a right to complain. He admits he has spoken strongly, but he says, "If you were where I am, you'd understand. My sorrow is so terrible it gives me good reason to complain."

The arrows of the Almighty are in me,
   my spirit drinks in their poison;
   God's terrors are marshaled against me.

Does a wild donkey bray when it has grass,
> or an ox bellow when it has fodder?
Is tasteless food eaten without salt,
> or is there flavor in the white of an egg?
I refuse to touch it;
> such food makes me ill (Job 6:4–7).

You never hear an animal complain when it is well fed and taken care of—only when it's ill fed. That's why Job is complaining. You can't eat food that is tasteless and loathsome without trying to improve it with salt. So Job says his complaining helps him to cope with his troubles.

Many people talk that way. They feel that if God sends them tribulation, then they have a right to tribulate! And most of them do. Job felt that way: "What I'm going through is so bad I have to complain!"

Job then speaks of his inability to bear any further suffering:

Oh, that I might have my request,
> that God would grant what I hope for,
that God would be willing to crush me,
> to let loose his hand and cut me off!
Then I would still have this consolation—
> my joy in unrelenting pain—
> that I had not denied the words of the Holy One.
What strength do I have, that I should still hope?
> What prospects, that I should be patient?
Do I have the strength of stone?
> Is my flesh bronze?
Do I have any power to help myself,
> now that success has been driven from me? (Job 6:8–13).

In other words, Job says, "What does God think I'm made of—stone or bronze? Doesn't He know I've reached the limits of my endurance?"

Have you ever felt that way? Have you ever said, "Lord, You promised You would never push me beyond what I can bear, but Lord, we passed that point weeks ago!" God knows us better than we know ourselves. He knew how much Job could take, and He had a reason and a plan for all of Job's sufferings.

As Job's cry goes unanswered, he turns to his friends, rebuking their lack of empathy and understanding:

A despairing man should have the devotion of his friends,
>   even though he forsakes the fear of the Almighty.
But my brothers are as undependable as intermittent streams,
>   as the streams that overflow
when darkened by thawing ice
>   and swollen with melting snow,
but that cease to flow in the dry season,
>   and in the heat vanish from their channels.
Caravans turn aside from their routes;
>   they go up into the wasteland and perish.
The caravans of Tema look for water,
>   the traveling merchants of Sheba look in hope.
They are distressed, because they had been confident;
>   they arrive there, only to be disappointed.
Now you too have proved to be of no help;
>   you see something dreadful and are afraid (Job 6:14–21).

Job tells his three friends, "You fellows are like a mountain brook that's full of water in the wintertime when nobody needs it. But when the hot summer sun comes out, and you long for some refreshing water, there's nothing available but a dry, gravel-filled streambed. You said you came to comfort me, and all you've given me is trouble."

Have I ever said, "Give something on my behalf,
>   pay a ransom for me from your wealth,
deliver me from the hand of the enemy,
>   ransom me from the clutches of the ruthless?" (Job 6:22–23).

In other words, "Did I ask you to help me? I didn't send for you! I didn't ask you to come and 'comfort' me, so don't do me any 'favors'!"

Teach me, and I will be quiet;
>   show me where I have been wrong.
How painful are honest words!
>   But what do your arguments prove?
Do you mean to correct what I say,
>   and treat the words of a despairing man as wind?
You would even cast lots for the fatherless
>   and barter away your friend.

But now be so kind as to look at me.
  Would I lie to your face?
Relent, do not be unjust;
  reconsider, for my integrity is at stake.
Is there any wickedness on my lips?
  Can my mouth not discern malice? (Job 6:24–30).

Job is saying, "If there is something wrong with my life, then tell me specifically what it is! If you know something I don't know, what is it?"

Job's dilemma is plain: This man knows that God has allowed this pain in his life, but he can't understand why. Job knows there is no sin in his life that he has not already confessed and dealt with. He's not claiming to be sinless. He's saying that he has kept short accounts of his sin with God. Yet God has chosen to allow him to suffer horrible affliction. Why?

JOB ADDRESSES GOD

Finally, Job turns to God and complains about the hardness of his present experience:

Does not man have hard service on earth?
  Are not his days like those of a hired man?
Like a slave longing for the evening shadows,
  or a hired man waiting eagerly for his wages,
so I have been allotted months of futility,
  and nights of misery have been assigned to me.
When I lie down I think, "How long before I get up?"
  The night drags on, and I toss till dawn.
My body is clothed with worms and scabs,
  my skin is broken and festering.
My days are swifter than a weaver's shuttle,
  and they come to an end without hope (Job 7:1–6).

Job speaks to God about the hard toil of his life, the pointlessness and misery of it all, and the physical suffering of the boils and worms in his festering flesh. Finally, he takes a look at the overall span of life and finds it dismally brief:

Remember, O God, that my life is but a breath;
  my eyes will never see happiness again.

The eye that now sees me will see me no longer;
    you will look for me, but I will be no more.
As a cloud vanishes and is gone,
    so he who goes down to the grave does not return.
He will never come to his house again;
    his place will know him no more (Job 7:7–10).

Job has given up. He thinks he will never see any relief, that suffering will mark his life till the end. Out of his meaningless suffering, he cries out in honest despair:

Therefore I will not keep silent;
    I will speak out in the anguish of my spirit,
    I will complain in the bitterness of my soul.
Am I the sea, or the monster of the deep,
    that you put me under guard?
When I think my bed will comfort me
    and my couch will ease my complaint,
even then you frighten me with dreams
    and terrify me with visions,
so that I prefer strangling and death,
    rather than this body of mine.
I despise my life; I would not live forever.
    Let me alone; my days have no meaning.
What is man that you make so much of him,
    that you give him so much attention,
that you examine him every morning
    and test him every moment?
Will you never look away from me,
    or let me alone even for an instant?
If I have sinned, what have I done to you,
    O watcher of men?
Why have you made me your target?
    Have I become a burden to you?
Why do you not pardon my offenses
    and forgive my sins?
For I will soon lie down in the dust;
    you will search for me, but I will be no more (7:11–21).

Have you ever felt that way? "Lord, leave me alone! I've had enough! I can't take any more! Why are You so intent on making life miserable for me? Why do You have to test and try me this way? What have I done to offend You so much? Can't You just forgive me and let me be?" This is the cry of Job in his pain and bafflement.

Remember, Job does not know what we know. We have caught a glimpse into the purposes for Job's sufferings that he hasn't seen. Here's an important principle to remember every time you go through a time of trial and suffering: In every trial there are two purposes in view: Satan has his purpose, and God has His purpose. Our sufferings occur at the point of conflict between God's purpose and Satan's.

What is Satan's purpose in Job's suffering? First, Satan uses Job's pain and illness to torment Job's body. Second, Satan uses the well-intentioned but misguided "comfort" of Job's three friends to afflict his soul. Third, Satan uses God's silence to assault Job's spirit and break his faith.

But God has two purposes that we can see in the book of Job.

First, He has a plan for using Job's suffering in Job's own life. He wants to use this trial of pain and loss to teach Job some truths that he has never grasped before. God wants to deepen Job's theology and help Job to know and understand Him in a more real and profound way.

Second, God plans to use Job's suffering to answer Satan in the eyes of all the principalities and powers of the whole universe and to prove Satan wrong in his philosophy of life. That is God's larger purpose in Job's sufferings, and that is still His purpose in the life of believers today. As Paul wrote to the believers in Ephesus, "His intent was that now, through the church, the manifold wisdom of God should be made known to the rulers and authorities in the heavenly realms [that is, all of the angels, including Satan and his fallen angels], according to his eternal purpose which he accomplished in Christ Jesus our Lord" (Ephesians 3:10–11).

Our suffering is woven into this vast eternal purpose of God, which He has accomplished through our Lord Jesus. When we are afflicted, God provides a demonstration before all of the heavenly powers and before each of us that God's judgment is just, His ways are perfect, and He knows what He is doing. As the book of Job unfolds, we'll see how these truths are gradually brought to light.

Suffering is not always the result of sin, as Eliphaz would have us believe. Suffering, in fact, is sometimes the result of righteousness and of God's eternal plan for our lives. Satan has his reasons for *wanting* us to suffer, but God has His reasons for *allowing* us to suffer, and His reasons will ultimately bring perfection out of our pain.

When we experience trials and sufferings, it is good to take a look behind the curtain of God's purposes. There we can see that great and eternal events hang upon the outcome of our day-to-day struggles. Our hurts are not meaningless events that serve no purpose. Rather, they are wounds suffered in battle during a cosmic war between good and evil, and God is weaving our wounds into a vast plan for ultimate victory.

FOOLISH PLATITUDES

In 1940, C. S. Lewis published his first popular book on Christian doctrine, *The Problem of Pain*. The book examined the question of why we suffer, yet it did so from a theological and theoretical point of view. The book is aimed at our intellect, not our emotions.

Around the time *The Problem of Pain* was published, Lewis became acquainted with a Christian poet and novelist named Charles Williams. They became good friends, and Lewis invited Williams to join a literary discussion group, the Inklings, which included such authors and scholars as J. R. R. Tolkien, Owen Barfield, and Hugo Dyson.

On one occasion, C. S. Lewis and Charles Williams engaged in a lively discussion of the book of Job. During their talk, Williams pointed out that God permitted Job to boldly, even angrily, question Him. Though He did point out to Job that his human understanding was flawed and limited, God never reprimanded Job or punished him for asking tough, painful questions about suffering. Instead, God's displeasure was reserved for Job's so-called comforters, three people who try to provide simplistic answers to life's tough questions—"the sort of people," Williams added with an accusing stare, "who write books on 'the problem of pain.'"

Williams was joking with Lewis, needling him in a good-natured way, but he was also making a serious point: Suffering is much more than an intellectual problem. It's an experience that engulfs the body, mind, and soul of the sufferer. Those who provide neat theoretical and theological answers to the "problem of pain" are of no help to people who suffer.

I'm not suggesting that C. S. Lewis was a "Job's comforter" when he wrote *The Problem of Pain*. The point of that book was not to comfort people in their sufferings. Rather, it was a Christian defense against the atheist charge (still commonly heard today) that the reality of suffering proves that God doesn't exist. It's an excellent book, and I commend it to you.

But twenty years after *The Problem of Pain*, C. S. Lewis wrote another book—a book filled with painful, angry questions. That book, called *A Grief*

Observed, reads a lot like the book of Job. It opens with intense questioning, it offers no pat answers, and it shows the author moving through a terrible time of pain and loss with his faith bruised but intact. Lewis wrote *A Grief Observed* after watching his wife of three years, Joy Davidman Lewis, die of bone cancer.

A Grief Observed was so raw and honest in its questioning that Lewis was afraid to publish it under his own name; instead, he used a pen name, N. W. Clerk. He allowed it to be published under his own name only after a number of well-meaning friends offered him copies of the book, thinking it would help him work through his own grief.

It's easy to be a "Job's comforter." It's easy to offer simplistic answers to our suffering friends. But it takes courage and honesty to admit that there are no easy answers to the problem of pain. It takes genuine love to stand by people when they are suffering, to simply be present with them instead of offering a lot of empty platitudes or self-righteous accusations about hidden sin.

As we come to Job 8, we find Job surrounded by a trio of do-gooders who have no "comfort" to offer but plenty of trite sayings. They are intent on forcing Job to confess his sin, though they have no evidence of sin in his life. There are few experiences more difficult for the human spirit to bear than being misunderstood and falsely accused. So after all Job has suffered, from the loss of his children to the loss of his health, he now faces the trial of being misjudged and mistreated by those he has called friends.

BILDAD THE BRUTAL

In the midst of Job's calamities, these three men get up on their soapboxes. They harangue and bloviate, trying to force Job into admitting his sin. Their arguments seem logical: God is just. If you suffer, then you must deserve to suffer.

Of course there are many biblical examples of innocent people who suffer injustice. Adam's son Abel, whose offering pleased God, was murdered by his brother Cain, whose offering was rejected by God. Joseph, the son of Jacob, did no harm to his brothers, yet his brothers became jealous of him, threw him in a pit, and sold him into slavery. As a slave, Joseph served his Egyptian master faithfully and honestly, yet his master's wife falsely accused him and had him thrown into prison.

And then there was Jesus, the most innocent human being who ever lived—and He was falsely accused, beaten and flogged, then crucified between two thieves. Clearly, even though God is just and loving, the innocent do suffer. That is the way this fallen world works. This is a truth that Job's three "comforters" seem unable to understand.

Eliphaz the Temanite, the oldest, has spoken first, but his eloquent and lofty arguments only leave Job angry and depressed, crying out for relief from his pain and from the miserable "comfort" of his friends. Later, we will hear from Zophar the Naamathite. But here in Job 8, we hear from Bildad the Shuhite, the "comforter" who is generally considered the most hurtful and least consoling of the three. I call him Bildad the Brutal. His discourse is fairly short, and he begins by attempting to break down Job's defenses with logic:

> How long will you say such things?
>   Your words are a blustering wind.
> Does God pervert justice?
> Does the Almighty pervert what is right?
> When your children sinned against him,
> he gave them over to the penalty of their sin" (Job 8:2–4).

Bildad's style is to ask questions that focus on the logic of the argument. He is a cold, intellectual thinker and a hard-nosed debater. His first question is, "Can God do wrong?" That's a good question to ask. Logically, of course, the answer is, "No, God can't do wrong." After all, our ideas of right and wrong derive from the nature and character of God. Rightness is being like God; wrongness is being unlike God. So obviously, God can't do wrong.

Bildad then proceeds from this basic premise to draw a logical conclusion for Job: "If your children have sinned against God, then He has delivered them over to the consequences of their sin. When your children died, when the tornado blew down the house and killed them all, it must have been the just penalty for some sin they committed against God." Bildad follows the line of reasoning that all three of Job's friends pursue in this discussion: Tragedy is God's punishment for sin, especially hidden sin.

Next, Bildad presses his argument by appealing to the past:

> But if you will look to God
>   and plead with the Almighty,
> if you are pure and upright,
>   even now he will rouse himself on your behalf
>   and restore you to your rightful place.
> Your beginnings will seem humble,
>   so prosperous will your future be.

Ask the former generations
>and find out what their fathers learned,
for we were born only yesterday and know nothing,
and our days on earth are but a shadow (Job 8:5–9).

There is much truth in what Bildad and the other two men say to Job.
Bildad reminds Job that the experience of the past confirms the fact that God
blesses those who turn to Him, and He rebukes and punishes those who turn
away. All of that is true, but it doesn't apply to Job. His pain is not a punishment for sin. Bildad supports his argument with various common sayings of
the day:

Will they not instruct you and tell you?
Will they not bring forth words from their understanding?
Can papyrus grow tall where there is no marsh?
Can reeds thrive without water?
While still growing and uncut,
they wither more quickly than grass.
Such is the destiny of all who forget God;
so perishes the hope of the godless.
What he trusts in is fragile;
what he relies on is a spider's web.
He leans on his web, but it gives way;
he clings to it, but it does not hold.
He is like a well-watered plant in the sunshine,
spreading its shoots over the garden;
it entwines its roots around a pile of rocks
and looks for a place among the stones.
But when it is torn from its spot,
that place disowns it and says, "I never saw you."
Surely its life withers away,
and from the soil other plants grow (Job 8:10–19).

He argues that man, by nature, must have God's blessing in order to
prosper. If man is cut off from God's blessing, he will perish as the reed withers without water. The things man has built his life upon will collapse like a
flimsy spider web. Bildad continues:

Surely God does not reject a blameless man
>or strengthen the hands of evildoers.

> He will yet fill your mouth with laughter
>   and your lips with shouts of joy.
> Your enemies will be clothed in shame,
>   and the tents of the wicked will be no more (Job 8:20–22).

Here Bildad states that God always cuts off those who seem to prosper because of evil. He says in short, "If you don't want to be utterly destroyed, Job, repent of your sin!" This is a heartfelt and earnest exhortation to Job. When you read these arguments, you wonder, "What's wrong with what Bildad says? It sounds so right and true. It's a logical argument, supported by experience and the testimony of Scripture. Why, then, is Bildad considered a 'miserable comforter'?"

Because Bildad is speaking out of a wrong spirit, and he is leaving out some important truths. An incomplete truth is often no better than a lie, and that's the case with Bildad's words. There are, in fact, three major problems with the approach Bildad the Brutal and the other two friends use. Let's look at each of these three problems in turn.

THREE FLAWS IN THE THINKING OF JOB'S "COMFORTERS"

First flaw: Bildad and the other two "comforters" answer Job's words without trying to find out the truth of Job's situation. They zero in on what he says without understanding his agony. Job himself admits that he speaks rashly, but he does so because of his incredible pain and grief. Anyone who has undergone deep, unrelenting pain knows how suffering can grind down the human spirit. When Job speaks out about his pain, his friends should listen to his emotions and understand his torment; instead, they argue and attack.

This is a common problem today, especially in marriage. Husbands are often coldly analytical when their wives are pressured, weary, or anxious about circumstances. Often husbands hear only their wives' words and try to analyze those words, pointing out inconsistencies or flaws in their wives' statements. That's a good way to destroy communication and a relationship.

When people are hurting, they need someone who can identify with their hurt. They need someone to listen and empathize, not criticize. When we focus on logic instead of feelings with hurting people, we are no more helpful than Bildad the Shuhite—a cold, analytical, and unfeeling debater, not a true friend.

Second flaw: Bildad and his two friends may have had correct theology—as far as it went—but it was an incomplete theology. They spoke as if their views were the final word on the subject. They seemed unaware that there might be dimensions to God and His plans that they couldn't even imagine. According to their limited view of life, suffering is always caused by sin. It's true, of course, that sin does have consequences in our lives, but trials are not always the result of sin. Their theology was narrow and incomplete.

They were like the men in the story of the blind men and the elephant. Sightless, they felt the various parts of the elephant and tried to describe what the huge animal was like. One, grasping the trunk, said, "An elephant is like a snake." Another, feeling the leg, said, "An elephant is like a tree." Another, running his hands across the side of the animal, said, "An elephant is like a wall." Still another, grabbing the tail, said, "An elephant is like a rope." Thus they argued back and forth. All were right and all were wrong because none could see the whole picture.

Third flaw: Job's three friends never ask God for help in understanding Job's problem. They never pray with Job. They never ask God for open minds, sensitive hearts, or an enlightened understanding so that they can truly help their friend. The book of Job is filled with prayers, but they are all prayers of Job crying out to God in the midst of his sufferings. Job's "comforters" never feel any need for God's help and illumination. What a testimony this is to us of the need to approach our suffering friends with an attitude of humble prayer, always seeking to *authentically* understand and comfort them in times of hurt and loss.

WHO CAN JUDGE THE JUDGE?

In Job 9 and 10, Job makes his reply to Bildad. He begins by setting forth his dilemma:

> Indeed, I know that this is true.
>> But how can a mortal be righteous before God?
> Though one wished to dispute with him,
>> he could not answer him one time out of a thousand (Job 9:2–3).

What is Job saying? On the one hand, he is saying that he himself has an inadequate theology, just as his three friends do. He recognizes that mortal human beings are inherently sinful. In fact, he once believed as his three "comforters" believe that suffering is the result of sin. Before going through his own trial of pain and loss, he would have analyzed other people's trials just as they have analyzed his.

On the other hand, having searched his own heart, Job can find no unconfessed sin in his life. He has done what God demanded of him: Whenever he became aware of sin in his life, he made his offerings to God in repentance, and he accepted God's forgiveness. Even though he has done that, his torment continues.

This is Job's dilemma: Since he is not aware of any sin in his life and since he continues to undergo suffering, the problem must not lie with Job; the problem must lie with God. Yet God is perfect, wise, and loving—so the problem cannot lie with God. It's a riddle Job cannot solve. It's unsolvable, Job says, because he has no way to examine and debate God:

> His wisdom is profound, his power is vast.
>   Who has resisted him and come out unscathed?
> He moves mountains without their knowing it
>   and overturns them in his anger.
> He shakes the earth from its place
>   and makes its pillars tremble.
> He speaks to the sun and it does not shine;
>   he seals off the light of the stars.
> He alone stretches out the heavens
>   and treads on the waves of the sea.
> He is the Maker of the Bear and Orion,
>   the Pleiades and the constellations of the south.
> He performs wonders that cannot be fathomed,
>   miracles that cannot be counted (9:4–10).

How can you debate such a God? How can you demand that the creator of the universe give an accounting for your suffering? What makes the problem even more perplexing is the fact that this creator is invisible:

> When he passes me, I cannot see him;
>   when he goes by, I cannot perceive him.
> If he snatches away, who can stop him?
>   Who can say to him, "What are you doing?" (9:11–12).

Next, Job speaks of how this great Creator-God has moved in the affairs of human history:

God does not restrain his anger;
>   even the cohorts of Rahab [Egypt] cowered at his feet.
How then can I dispute with him?
>   How can I find words to argue with him?
Though I were innocent, I could not answer him;
>   I could only plead with my Judge for mercy.
Even if I summoned him and he responded,
>   I do not believe he would give me a hearing.
He would crush me with a storm
>   and multiply my wounds for no reason.
He would not let me regain my breath
>   but would overwhelm me with misery.
If it is a matter of strength, he is mighty!
>   And if it is a matter of justice, who will summon him? (9:13–19).

The essence of this passage is found in the last two lines, which could be restated, "Who can force God to explain Himself? Who can judge the Judge?" Job was frustrated by his powerlessness before an omnipotent and sovereign God. There was no arena, no courtroom, where Job could be on an equal footing with God.

Job is saying to God, in effect, "Do You get some kind of pleasure out of my pain? Is that why You put me through this?" I don't think Job is being sarcastic here. I believe he is honestly asking, "Is God the kind of being who takes pleasure in people's suffering? If that's the explanation, then at least I am contributing to His pleasure by my pain!"

In these lines, Job is doing what almost everyone does in a time of pain and loss: He's looking for *meaning* in his suffering, and the fact that he can find *no* meaning for his pain actually magnifies his suffering.

Even if I were innocent, my mouth would condemn me;
>   if I were blameless, it would pronounce me guilty.
Although I am blameless,
>   I have no concern for myself;
>   I despise my own life.
It is all the same; that is why I say,
>   "He destroys both the blameless and the wicked."
When a scourge brings sudden death,
>   he mocks the despair of the innocent.

When a land falls into the hands of the wicked,
> he blindfolds its judges.
> If it is not he, then who is it?
My days are swifter than a runner;
> they fly away without a glimpse of joy.
They skim past like boats of papyrus,
> like eagles swooping down on their prey.
If I say, "I will forget my complaint,
> I will change my expression, and smile,"
I still dread all my sufferings,
> for I know you will not hold me innocent.
Since I am already found guilty,
> why should I struggle in vain?
Even if I washed myself with soap
> and my hands with washing soda,
you would plunge me into a slime pit
> so that even my clothes would detest me.
He is not a man like me that I might answer him,
> that we might confront each other in court.
If only there were someone to arbitrate between us,
> to lay his hand upon us both,
someone to remove God's rod from me,
> so that his terror would frighten me no more.
Then I would speak up without fear of him,
> but as it now stands with me, I cannot (9:20–35).

Here, Job shows why he remains stuck in his dilemma: Though he believes he is blameless (that is, he has repented of his sins, and they have been forgiven), Job recognizes that no human being is truly sinless. Compared with the righteousness of God, Job's righteousness is as filthy rags. Even so, he believes that his affliction is without cause or justification.

Job longs for an arbitrator, a mediator, to settle this dispute between himself and God. If only there were someone who could remove God's rod of affliction from him so that he would not be terrified of God. Job goes on to ask:

Do you have eyes of flesh?
> Do you see as a mortal sees?
Are your days like those of a mortal
> or your years like those of a man,

that you must search out my faults
    and probe after my sin—
though you know that I am not guilty
    and that no one can rescue me from your hand? (10:4–7).

In this anguished prayer, Job turns to God and asks, "Have You somehow limited Your wisdom so that You see life as a mere mortal does? Have You lost Your ability to act as the wise and loving God You once were? Is that why You put me through this? Have You somehow allowed Yourself to think and act like a man?"

I believe these lines contain hints of the incarnation, the great underlying truth of the New Testament: the fact that God did truly limit Himself and become a man. What Job is not able to understand is that in the incarnation God did not lose His wisdom and compassion, as Job suggests here. When God became a man in the person of Jesus Christ, He identified with us and put Himself in our place. This enabled Him to understand our emotions, our weakness, and our suffering. Because God fully understands our humanity, we can trust His mercy and compassion.

The New Testament writer to the Hebrews said that Jesus shared in our humanity and was "made like his brothers in every way, in order that he might become a merciful and faithful high priest" between us and God (see Hebrews 4:15). Because Jesus is both fully God and fully human, He is able to sympathize with us in our weaknesses and our sufferings.

Your hands shaped me and made me.
    Will you now turn and destroy me?
Remember that you molded me like clay.
    Will you now turn me to dust again?
Did you not pour me out like milk
    and curdle me like cheese,
clothe me with skin and flesh
    and knit me together with bones and sinews?
You gave me life and showed me kindness,
    and in your providence watched over my spirit.
But this is what you concealed in your heart,
    and I know that this was in your mind (Job 10:8–13).

Here Job asks, "How can it be rational and reasonable for me to go through such intense suffering? You made me, you formed me, you gave me life and showed me kindness, and then you turned on me and ripped me apart. That isn't a logical thing for a rational God to do!"

Job continues:

> If I sinned, you would be watching me
>> and would not let my offense go unpunished.
> If I am guilty—woe to me!
>> Even if I am innocent, I cannot lift my head,
> for I am full of shame
>> and drowned in my affliction.
> If I hold my head high, you stalk me like a lion
>> and again display your awesome power against me.
> You bring new witnesses against me
>> and increase your anger toward me;
>> your forces come against me wave upon wave (10:14–17).

In these verses, Job's baffled complaint to God is, "What can I do? What recourse do I have? How can I please you? How can I change myself so that you will stop afflicting and punishing me?"

JOB'S VIEW OF DEATH

As we read through Job's cry to God, we realize that Job gives voice to the anguished arguments that have occurred to suffering saints. Job explores the nuances of affliction, whether mental or physical, to the utmost in his prayers. He asks the questions, describes the dilemmas, and articulates the shades of doubt, fear, hurt, and bitterness that we all express in times of suffering.

Are Job's questions answered? Not here, not yet. God remains silent at this point of the book. Oppressed by God's silence, Job cries out:

> Why then did you bring me out of the womb?
>> I wish I had died before any eye saw me.
> If only I had never come into being,
>> or had been carried straight from the womb to the grave!
> Are not my few days almost over?
>> Turn away from me so I can have a moment's joy
> before I go to the place of no return,
>> to the land of gloom and deep shadow,

to the land of deepest night,
>   of deep shadow and disorder,
>   where even the light is like darkness" (10:18–22).

Here we catch a fascinating insight into Job's mindset. He says, "Leave me alone, God! Life is useless and meaningless. Death is but darkness from which there is no return, but at least death is better than suffering. I would rather go into the darkness and nothingness of death than continue living in pain."

At this point in his spiritual journey, Job does not believe in an afterlife. Many liberal Bible scholars read this passage and mistakenly conclude that Job and other Old Testament people had no conception of, or belief in, the afterlife. That is not true. There are references to heaven throughout the Old Testament. Though Job does not believe in heaven and the resurrection while he is in the throes of his affliction, there comes a time, later in this discourse, when Job says:

> I know that my Redeemer lives,
>   and that in the end he will stand upon the earth.
> And after my skin has been destroyed,
>   yet in my flesh I will see God;
> I myself will see him
>   with my own eyes—I, and not another.
>   How my heart yearns within me! (19:25–27).

Other Old Testament passages reflect this same assurance of life after death in the presence of the Lord. For example, David closes the beloved Twenty-Third Psalm with the words, "I will dwell in the house of the Lord forever." The phrase "the house of the Lord" does not refer to the temple or the tabernacle, places of worship, but to God's eternal dwelling place. And in Psalm 133:3, the psalmist David tells us that God bestows His blessing to us, "even life forevermore." The Old Testament prophet Daniel put it this way:

> Multitudes who sleep in the dust of the earth will awake: some to everlasting life, others to shame and everlasting contempt. Those who are wise will shine like the brightness of the heavens, and those who lead many to righteousness, like the stars for ever and ever (Daniel 12:2–3).

Another Old Testament prophet, Isaiah, spoke plainly of the resurrection—of being raised by God to a new and eternal life:

But your dead will live;
their bodies will rise.
You who dwell in the dust,
wake up and shout for joy.
Your dew is like the dew of the morning;
the earth will give birth to her dead (Isaiah 26:19).

Eternal life has always been God's plan for His redeemed children. Though Job does not believe in an afterlife with God at this point in his sufferings, he will come to such a belief later in his journey.

ZOPHAR THE ZEALOUS

In Job 11, Zophar the Naamathite steps forward. He is the man I call "Zophar the Zealous." He opens with a scorching rebuke of what he sees as Job's sinful folly:

Then Zophar the Naamathite replied:
"Are all these words to go unanswered?
    Is this talker to be vindicated?
Will your idle talk reduce men to silence?
    Will no one rebuke you when you mock?
You say to God, 'My beliefs are flawless
    and I am pure in your sight.'
Oh, how I wish that God would speak,
    that he would open his lips against you
and disclose to you the secrets of wisdom,
    for true wisdom has two sides.
Know this: God has even forgotten some of your sin" (vv. 1–6).

You can almost see Zophar shaking his fist in Job's face. He accuses Job of wordiness, foolishness, mockery, and self-righteous arrogance. He says that Job's punishment is richly deserved. How would you like to have Zophar as your friend and comforter? This man goes on to contrast God's wisdom against the supposed ignorance of Job:

Can you fathom the mysteries of God?
    Can you probe the limits of the Almighty?
They are higher than the heavens—what can you do?

They are deeper than the depths of the grave
    —what can you know?
Their measure is longer than the earth
    and wider than the sea.
If he comes along and confines you in prison
    and convenes a court, who can oppose him?
Surely he recognizes deceitful men;
    and when he sees evil, does he not take note?
But a witless man can no more become wise
    than a wild donkey's colt can be born a man" (Job 11:7–12).

Zophar is piling on many harsh and heavy words to express what should be a simple concept: "Job, you are stupid and deceitful, and God knows it. Your chances of gaining wisdom and finding relief from God's judgment are exactly zero! You can no more gain wisdom than the colt of a wild donkey can be born a human being! Job, you're a hopeless fool!"

Then, Zophar appears to contradict himself. Immediately after stating that Job is beyond hope of repentance and redemption, Zophar appeals to Job to repent and be redeemed. He says:

Yet if you devote your heart to him
    and stretch out your hands to him,
if you put away the sin that is in your hand
    and allow no evil to dwell in your tent,
then you will lift up your face without shame;
    you will stand firm and without fear.
You will surely forget your trouble,
    recalling it only as waters gone by.
Life will be brighter than noonday,
    and darkness will become like morning.
You will be secure, because there is hope;
    you will look about you and take your rest in safety.
You will lie down, with no one to make you afraid,
    and many will court your favor.
But the eyes of the wicked will fail,
    and escape will elude them;
        their hope will become a dying gasp (Job 11:13–20).

Zophar displays no more compassion than the previous two "comforters." These three men do nothing but compound Job's suffering. They analyze his affliction in cold, analytical terms. They approach Job's problems from a purely theological point of view.

That's the difference between theology and the experience of a man taught by the Spirit. Theology can be very clear and right, but it is all in the head. When you deal with the pain of a human life, you must add a deeper dimension, a dimension of compassion and Christlike empathy. You must authentically *love* the afflicted person. Christlike love opens the door of the human soul to receive the light of God's Spirit.

Paul expressed this same principle when he wrote, "Rejoice with those who rejoice; mourn with those who mourn" (Romans 12:15). If we learn nothing else from the book of Job, I hope we learn this and learn it well: We should be careful and prayerful in our approach to the suffering of others so that we do not add to it.

Suffering people do not need judgmental "friends" who mouth foolish platitudes and heartless accusations. They need true friends who will listen—and love.

THE PRISONER PLEADS HIS CASE

Michael spent thirteen years in prison for a crime he didn't commit. How did it happen?

In 1988, Michael was a twenty-two-year-old black man living in Ohio. A functionally illiterate sixth-grade dropout, Michael never envisioned much of a future for himself. He had committed a few petty crimes and been involved in a few street fights, but he'd never been accused of a violent crime. He and his girlfriend had a two-year-old daughter, and he was trying to provide for her by working at a minimum-wage job.

One day Michael ran into a friend he hadn't seen in months. "Say, Michael," the friend said, "did you know the police are looking for you? They say you attacked a white woman at a hotel."

Michael was stunned. "That's crazy! I never attacked anybody!"

He didn't own a car, so he walked two miles to the police station. He told the police who he was and that he'd heard they were looking for him. The police told him that a black man who said his name was Tony had attacked a white woman. Michael's real first name was Anthony, but he never went by that name, and he never called himself Tony. It was a case of mistaken identity.

But that didn't matter. He was indicted and tried. In court, a woman Michael had never seen before pointed at him and said, "That's the man." Though there was hardly any evidence presented—no fingerprints, no DNA evidence, and no other witnesses—the jury convicted Michael of the crime.

"But I didn't do it!" Michael protested. He would repeat his claim of innocence throughout the next thirteen years.

While Michael was in prison, his daughter became a teenager, and he didn't get to see her once in all that time. His health, eyesight, and hearing deteriorated. He became embittered and suicidal.

But during his time in prison, he met a man named Arthur, a prisoner who spent a lot of time in the prison library. Arthur told him, "Everybody here says he's innocent. If you want to *prove* you're innocent, you have to learn about the law." Arthur told Michael about several inmates who had used the library to study the law and win their freedom.

Michael said, "But I can't read."

"Then it's time you learn," Arthur replied.

So Arthur helped Michael learn how to read and how to use the law library. By learning how the law is supposed to work, Michael was able to obtain a new trial and prove his innocence. After thirteen years in prison for a crime he didn't commit, Michael walked out a free man.

As we come to Job 12 and 13, we see Job preparing his defense. He is like a prisoner studying in the prison library, getting ready to defend himself in court, preparing to prove his innocence before God. Listen with me as Job, a man imprisoned by his own pain and loss, prepares to make his case before the Judge of the universe.

GOD CANNOT BE BOXED IN

Job has listened to the accusations and rationales of his three friends, Eliphaz, Bildad, and Zophar, and now he replies:

> Doubtless you are the people,
>   and wisdom will die with you!
> But I have a mind as well as you;
>   I am not inferior to you.
>   Who does not know all these things?" (Job 12:2–3).

Job's response drips with sarcasm. He is saying, "Oh, you men have all the answers, don't you? Why, when you die, all the world's wisdom will die with you—you bunch of know-it-alls! Everything you've said may be true in a limited sense, but these are elementary truths. Everybody knows these things. Your thinking is shallow and incomplete. You haven't helped me at all. You haven't added anything to my wisdom. You've only added to my pain."

Then Job details the harm they have caused him with their foolish "wisdom" and their accusing words of "comfort." He says:

> I have become a laughingstock to my friends,
>   though I called upon God and he answered—
>   a mere laughingstock, though righteous and blameless!
> Men at ease have contempt for misfortune
>   as the fate of those whose feet are slipping.

The tents of marauders are undisturbed,
    and those who provoke God are secure—
those who carry their god in their hands (Job 12:4–6).

In other words, "Even though I am blameless before God, my own 'friends' treat me with scorn. You three treat me with contempt while I am suffering, telling me I deserve my fate. How easy it is for you to treat me this way, because you've never been in my shoes. You've never felt what I feel! You think that the only people who suffer are evildoers, yet marauders and idol worshippers live secure lives while I suffer. You speak about things you know nothing about!"

Then Job goes on to tell them that they simply haven't faced the facts about how the universe works:

But ask the animals, and they will teach you,
    or the birds of the air, and they will tell you;
or speak to the earth, and it will teach you,
    or let the fish of the sea inform you.
Which of all these does not know
    that the hand of the LORD has done this?
In his hand is the life of every creature
    and the breath of all mankind (Job 12:7–10).

In other words, nature affirms that God deals as He pleases. There is no way of predicting His actions. God cannot be boxed in by the neat little platitudes of these three "comforters." The life of every creature and every human being is in God's hands.

Finally, in a moving and beautiful passage, Job asserts that he understands God as well as his three friends.

Does not the ear test words
    as the tongue tastes food?
Is not wisdom found among the aged?
    Does not long life bring understanding?
To God belong wisdom and power;
    counsel and understanding are his.
What he tears down cannot be rebuilt;
    the man he imprisons cannot be released.
If he holds back the waters, there is drought;
    if he lets them loose, they devastate the land.

To him belong strength and victory;
   both deceived and deceiver are his.
He leads counselors away stripped
   and makes fools of judges.
He takes off the shackles put on by kings
   and ties a loincloth around their waist.
He leads priests away stripped
   and overthrows men long established.
He silences the lips of trusted advisers
   and takes away the discernment of elders.
He pours contempt on nobles
   and disarms the mighty.
He reveals the deep things of darkness
   and brings deep shadows into the light.
He makes nations great, and destroys them;
   he enlarges nations, and disperses them.
He deprives the leaders of the earth of their reason;
   he sends them wandering through a trackless waste.
They grope in darkness with no light;
   he makes them stagger like drunkards (Job 12:11–25).

This is a glowing tribute to the majesty, might, and wisdom of God. No one can resist the will and power of God. What He tears down cannot be rebuilt. The greatest kings and warriors fall trembling in His presence. By God's sovereign will, nations rise and fall. In this passage, Job does not utter a single word of complaint against God—only praise.

THE WISEST THING YOU CAN SAY TO A HURTING PERSON

Next Job continues his defense by confronting his three friends for attacking him instead of seeking to support him and authentically comfort him in his pain:

My eyes have seen all this,
   my ears have heard and understood it.
What you know, I also know;
   I am not inferior to you.
But I desire to speak to the Almighty
   and to argue my case with God.

You, however, smear me with lies;
>   you are worthless physicians, all of you!
If only you would be altogether silent!
>   For you, that would be wisdom.
Hear now my argument;
>   listen to the plea of my lips.
Will you speak wickedly on God's behalf?
>   Will you speak deceitfully for him?
Will you show him partiality?
>   Will you argue the case for God?
Would it turn out well if he examined you?
>   Could you deceive him as you might deceive men?
He would surely rebuke you
>   if you secretly showed partiality.
Would not his splendor terrify you?
>   Would not the dread of him fall on you?
Your maxims are proverbs of ashes;
>   your defenses are defenses of clay (Job 13:1–12).

Job's comforters think they are spiritually superior to him, but Job says that they have not said anything he doesn't already know. As "physicians" of his soul, they are worthless; they are committing spiritual malpractice. They claim to speak for God, yet they speak wickedly and hurtfully on His behalf. So Job warns them that if God judges him, He will also judge them; if God overwhelms him, He will overwhelm them as well. They are in the same boat.

"If only you would be altogether silent!" he says. "For you, that would be wisdom." These words, expressed another way, reveal an important truth: "What is the wisest thing you could have said to me? Nothing at all!"

This is a principle you and I need to remember whenever we are called to minister to a suffering, grieving friend: Silence is often golden. Yes, long silences make us feel uncomfortable. We think we should have something to say to make it all better. But the truth is that words ring hollow in a heart pierced by pain. Sometimes the greatest wisdom can be found in simply being quietly present alongside a hurting person.

Paul tells us that God "comforts us in all our troubles, so that we can comfort those in any trouble with the comfort we ourselves have received from God" (2 Corinthians 1:4). As someone once said, "God comforts us to make us comforters, not to make us comfortable." It's uncomfortable to be a true comforter. It means we have to listen, not just talk. It means we have to be sensitive, not selfish.

Hurting people are rarely in a receptive frame of mind to hear platitudes, Bible verses, or theological explanations. Sometimes they will ask why. That doesn't mean they want you to give them a simplistic theological answer. When a friend asks why, have the grace to say, "I don't know why, but I am praying for you and I'm hurting with you. I'll be here with you for as long as you need me."

When your friends are grieving, show them you care. Bring them a meal. Mow their lawn. Do some cleaning around the house. Do the things that they can't do right now because of their pain and sorrow. But don't feel you have to do a lot of talking. When your friend is hurting, there's great wisdom in simply being there and being quiet.

A FINAL PLEA

Job's final plea to his three friends is a plea that they would leave him alone so that he might come before God and debate the matter:

> Keep silent and let me speak;
> > then let come to me what may.
> Why do I put myself in jeopardy
> > and take my life in my hands?
> Though he slay me, yet will I hope in him;
> > I will surely defend my ways to his face.
> Indeed, this will turn out for my deliverance,
> > for no godless man would dare come before him! (Job 13:13–16).

The NIV version of verse 15 is, I believe, a mistranslation. It sounds like a beautiful and pious statement of Job's faith in God: "Though He slay me, yet will I hope in Him." But I don't believe Job, in the midst of his suffering, feels that pious, and a close look at the original Hebrew language of this verse suggests otherwise. I think a more accurate translation would be that of the Revised Standard Version: "Behold, he will slay me; I have no hope; yet I will defend my ways to his face."

Job is expressing the fact that his pain and loss have been corrosive to his faith. He doesn't expect God to rescue him; rather, He believes God is killing him. But even if God is determined to kill him, even if he has no hope of surviving his ordeal, Job insists on defending himself before God.

Job concludes:

Listen carefully to my words;
    let your ears take in what I say.
Now that I have prepared my case,
    I know I will be vindicated.
Can anyone bring charges against me?
    If so, I will be silent and die (Job 13:17–19).

Job asks his friends to stop arguing and start listening to what he is saying. Notice his words: "Now that I have prepared my case, I know I will be vindicated." A prisoner of his own suffering, Job has spent time in the library, preparing the case he will take before the Lord. Now he's ready to stand before God and defend himself. Beginning with Job 13:20 and continuing on through Job 14, he will present his defense before God.

JOB'S TWO-PART REQUEST

Now Job lifts his eyes to God and makes a two-part request of the court. He asks his Judge for two conditions he feels must be met before he can make his case:

Only grant me these two things, O God,
    and then I will not hide from you:
Withdraw your hand far from me,
    and stop frightening me with your terrors (Job 13:20–21).

C. S. Lewis has well said that to argue with God is to argue with the very power that makes it possible to argue at all. And Job knows that. He understands that he must have mercy from God before he can even stand before Him. So Job asks that two conditions be granted him: that God lift the pain and anguish he is going through so that he does not have to speak out of this state of constant torment; and (2) that God would veil His presence so that Job would not be terrified by God's awesome and intimidating majesty.

Job never forsakes his awareness of the greatness and goodness of God. Though Job experiences doubt over what God is doing, though he feels misunderstood and mistreated, he respects the majesty of God.

Next, Job cries out for knowledge and understanding. He says:

> Then summon me and I will answer,
>   or let me speak, and you reply.
> How many wrongs and sins have I committed?
>   Show me my offense and my sin (Job 13:22–23).

In any court of law, a prisoner has the right to know the charges against him. Job has searched his heart but can find no hidden sin in his life. His three friends have accused him of harboring sin, and he has approached their accusations with an open mind. He is genuinely, sincerely asking God, "What have I done? How have I offended You?"

Next, Job protests the silence of God, and we catch a glimpse of Job's anger toward God:

> Why do you hide your face
>   and consider me your enemy?
> Will you torment a windblown leaf?
>   Will you chase after dry chaff?
> For you write down bitter things against me
>   and make me inherit the sins of my youth.
> You fasten my feet in shackles;
>   you keep close watch on all my paths
>   by putting marks on the soles of my feet.
> So man wastes away like something rotten,
>   like a garment eaten by moths (Job 13:24–28).

In trying to understand why God has subjected him to such unrelenting pain, Job wonders if God still blames him for past sins, even the sins of his youth.

CHAPTER ONE OF THE GREAT STORY

In Job 14, Job addresses the helplessness and hopelessness of a man before God. First, a man is helpless to control his affairs:

> Man born of woman
>   is of few days and full of trouble.
> He springs up like a flower and withers away;
>   like a fleeting shadow, he does not endure (vv. 1–2).

Human beings, says Job, are victims of their circumstances. Their lives are amazingly brief and filled with problems and pain. Despite the helplessness and limitations of the human condition, God seems to judge human beings for failings that are beyond human control. That is Job's opening argument. He goes on to say:

> Do you fix your eye on such a one?
>> Will you bring him before you for judgment?
> Who can bring what is pure from the impure?
>> No one!
> Man's days are determined;
>> you have decreed the number of his months
>> and have set limits he cannot exceed (14:3–5).

Again, Job expresses his perception that human beings are victims of forces they cannot control. He says, in effect, "I was born into this fallen world with these fallen traits. I can't help sinning because I come from sinful parents and I live in a sinful world. You can't expect a pure man to arise from impure circumstances and an impure heritage. You can't expect me to be perfect when I was born into an imperfect world. Just as there are limits to the span of my life, there are limits to the kind of life I can live."

This is the expression of Job's heart, and you can probably identify with his feelings. I have certainly felt this way. We can't help it that we were born into a fallen world, so what can we do? Doesn't God expect too much of us? That is the basis of Job's plea. He continues:

> At least there is hope for a tree:
>> If it is cut down, it will sprout again,
>> and its new shoots will not fail.
> Its roots may grow old in the ground
>> and its stump die in the soil,
> yet at the scent of water it will bud
>> and put forth shoots like a plant.
> But man dies and is laid low;
>> he breathes his last and is no more.
> As water disappears from the sea
>> or a riverbed becomes parched and dry,
> so man lies down and does not rise;
>> till the heavens are no more, men will not awake
>> or be roused from their sleep (Job 14:7–12).

Here again, Job expresses humanity's sense of hopelessness and regret. A tree can sprout again after being cut down, but human beings can't live their lives over again. We learn from our mistakes, but we can't go back and undo them. At one time or another, we have all wished we could live our lives over again and avoid the mistakes we made the first time. We wish God would give us a second chance at life, but we live only once. Then life disappears as water evaporates from a dry riverbed.

In his pain, Job has come to a pessimistic view of life. Though there is much truth in what he says, it's a one-sided and distorted view. Because of his pain, he's unable to see the goodness of life and the blessings of God's grace. We should not fall into the trap of Job's pessimism, nor should we judge Job for feeling this way. This is the kind of thinking that pain and loss produce in human lives. Job goes on: "If only you would hide me in the grave and conceal me till your anger has passed! If only you would set me a time and then remember me!" (14:13).

Here Job describes the joy a human being would feel to stand before God *after God's wrath was already past*! Understand, Job doesn't think this is possible. He longs for relief from God's anger, but he believes he will never find it. He is voicing the inarticulate longings of the human heart to be freed from guilt and judgment for sin.

As Christians, we know that we truly can experience what Job longed for. Through the sacrificial death of Jesus on the cross, we have peace with God. We can stand before God, knowing His wrath is already past. This is what Paul writes about to the Christians at Rome:

> Therefore, since we have been justified through faith, we have peace with God through our Lord Jesus Christ, through whom we have gained access by faith into this grace in which we now stand. And we rejoice in the hope of the glory of God. Not only so, but we also rejoice in our sufferings, because we know that suffering produces perseverance; perseverance, character; and character, hope. And hope does not disappoint us, because God has poured out his love into our hearts by the Holy Spirit, whom he has given us (Romans 5:1–5).

Paul says we "rejoice in our sufferings" because we have peace with God, and we know that suffering has a purpose in our lives. But Job could not rejoice in his sufferings because he felt that God was at war with him. Job could see no meaning or purpose for the suffering in his life, only judgment, condemnation, and wrath.

That's why Job says, "If only you would hide me in the grave and conceal me till your anger has passed! If only you would set me a time and then remember me!" Job is expressing a desire for a place that, in Roman Catholic theology, is called purgatory. Roman Catholics believe that purgatory is a place or condition that follows death but precedes heaven in which the souls of those who died in grace must be purged of their sins.

Evangelical Christians do not believe in purgatory because there is no reference to purgatory in the Protestant canon of the Scriptures and because the Scriptures make it clear that Jesus died for all of our sins. So there is no need for the believer to suffer any further for the purging of guilt and sin.

Job, with his limited, pre-Christian theology, wishes that he could spend time in a form of purgatory after his death. He wishes he could hide in the grave until a time when God gets over His anger. Then he can stand before God and be accepted by Him. What Job expresses, of course, is not accurate theology but simply the limited viewpoint of an ancient man suffering extreme fear, pain, and loss.

Despite his limited understanding, Job has a glimmer of insight. Though Job can't imagine how God plans to deal with the sin problem through the sacrifice of His own Son, he makes this amazing statement:

If a man dies, will he live again?
All the days of my hard service
I will wait for my renewal to come.
You will call and I will answer you;
you will long for the creature your hands have made.
Surely then you will count my steps
but not keep track of my sin.
My offenses will be sealed up in a bag;
you will cover over my sin (Job 14:14–17).

Job is saying, "If only you would hide me from your anger, then remember me after your anger passes, then You would call for me and I would answer You. We would have fellowship together because You would treasure me as the creature made by Your hands. You would keep track of everything I do and everywhere I go, but you would not keep track of my sins. All my sins would be out of sight, as if sealed up in a bag. If only you could shield me from your anger, my sins would be covered and forgotten."

You and I experience that reality today as Christians. God has shielded us from His wrath through the sacrifice of Jesus. Our sins are sealed up in a bag and removed from us forever. God treasures us and keeps track of our steps, but He keeps no record of our sins. So we experience renewal in our lives as we walk with Him.

Job closes chapter 14 with a description of the hopelessness of the human condition:

> But as a mountain erodes and crumbles
>   and as a rock is moved from its place,
> as water wears away stones
>   and torrents wash away the soil,
>   so you destroy man's hope.
> You overpower him once for all, and he is gone;
>   you change his countenance and send him away.
> If his sons are honored, he does not know it;
>   if they are brought low, he does not see it.
> He feels but the pain of his own body
>   and mourns only for himself (vv. 18–22).

Here is a vivid expression of what is wrong with our view of life. In this passage, Job looks at life from the natural person's viewpoint. According to this view, all that matters is the present moment, so let's live for today. Let's forget about tomorrow—and about eternity. This is the view that is hammered into us by the world around us, and it's a false view. It's not God's view of reality.

This live-for-today mentality is one reason many marriages—even Christian marriages—end in divorce after twenty-five or thirty years. One partner or the other thinks, "I'm getting into middle age, and I haven't really lived! I've been trapped with one person all these years. Before I know it, life will have passed me by. I need to start living for today! I need to start experiencing more pleasure and enjoyment in life. So I'm going to leave this marriage, leave my kids, and start my life all over again." People call this a midlife crisis, but it's really a failure to see life from God's perspective.

By the end of the book of Job, we will find that God has been teaching Job throughout his troubles. He has been guiding Job out of this faulty and limited view of life so that Job can discover what life is all about. This life is but a schooling process, a time of preparation designed to make us ready for the real life that lies ahead.

Compare Job's view of life and the afterlife with the view we find in the New Testament. What a stark contrast! The New Testament writers all looked forward to an afterlife that is so beautiful, grand, and glorious that they could hardly wait to seize it. Paul, for example, writes:

> For the perishable must clothe itself with the imperishable, and the mortal with immortality. When the perishable has been clothed with the imperishable, and the mortal with immortality, then the saying that is written will come true: "Death has been swallowed up in victory" (1 Corinthians 15:53–54).

And the apostle Peter wrote about a "living hope" of heaven:

> Praise be to the God and Father of our Lord Jesus Christ! In his great mercy he has given us new birth into a living hope through the resurrection of Jesus Christ from the dead, and into an inheritance that can never perish, spoil or fade—kept in heaven for you (1 Peter 1:3–4).

And the apostle John recorded this beautiful and comforting picture of the life that awaits us after death:

> Never again will they hunger;
>   never again will they thirst.
> The sun will not beat upon them,
>   nor any scorching heat.
> For the Lamb at the center of the throne will be their shepherd;
>   he will lead them to springs of living water.
> And God will wipe away every tear from their eyes (Revelation 7:16–17).

This life is not all there is; there is a life to come, beyond this life. The meaning of life is not merely that we should "grab all the gusto" we can before we die. This life is a school for the soul, where we become prepared for life in eternity with God. The sufferings and testings of this life are meant to prepare us for the *real* life to come.

C. S. Lewis pictured this coming reality for us in the closing lines of the final book of his Chronicles of Narnia, a book called *The Last Battle*:

> And for us this is the end of all the stories, and we can most truly say that they all lived happily ever after. But for them it was only the beginning of the real story. All their life in this world and all their adventures in Narnia had only been the cover and the title page: now at last they were beginning Chapter One of the Great Story, which no one on earth has read: which goes on for ever: in which every chapter is better than the one before.

Job didn't understand it, but Chapter One of the Great Story still lay ahead of him, after his death. That same Chapter One still lies ahead of you and me. That is our joy and our hope. That is our eternity with God.

God's suffering servant Job has gone to the library of his prison and has prepared his case. He has presented his petitions and arguments before the Judge of the universe. A verdict is coming.

But first, Job's accusing friends intend to have their say once more.

HELP FROM ON HIGH

Job 15–19

William Tyndale was a sixteenth-century Bible scholar with a passion for making the Scriptures available to the English-speaking masses. He translated the Bible from the original Hebrew and Greek into the language of the common people. Because the Church of England did not approve Tyndale's translation, King Henry VIII banned it. In 1524, Tyndale fled to Belgium to avoid being arrested.

In 1535, Tyndale met a student from England named Henry Philips. Young Philips said he wanted to know everything he could about Bible translation, so the two men became close friends. One evening, Tyndale and Philips went out to have dinner at an inn down the street. As they reached the door of the inn, Philips stepped back and let Tyndale enter. As Tyndale stepped through the doorway, two men seized him—agents of the king of England. Only then did William Tyndale realize that his friend, Henry Philips, had betrayed him to his enemies.

For sixteen months Tyndale was imprisoned in the castle of Vilvorde, Belgium. During his imprisonment, he had conversations with his guard, the guard's daughter, and several others in the castle, and all of them converted to faith in Jesus Christ. He was tried and condemned to death as a heretic. On October 6, 1536, Tyndale was led to the place of execution. His last words, as he was tied to the stake, were, "Lord! Open the king of England's eyes!" Then he was strangled to death and his body was consumed by fire.

Just three years after Tyndale's death, God answered the martyr's dying prayer. Henry VIII dropped his opposition to a Bible translation for the masses, and the English Great Bible was published in 1539, based almost entirely on Tyndale's translation.

Friends may betray us, as Henry Philips betrayed William Tyndale. But God can accomplish His will even through the betrayal of a friend. God brought good out of the sin of Judas Iscariot, who betrayed his Lord; and God brought good out of the sin of Henry Philips, who betrayed William Tyndale. Though Tyndale was imprisoned and condemned to die, he continued living for Christ, witnessing to his jailors, and praying that the king of England would allow God's Word to go out to the people. God answered this martyr's dying prayer, and history was changed.

Job is a man who would identify with William Tyndale. His own friends—men he had known and trusted for years—have now turned on him. He used to invite them into his home to break bread with him. Now they have become Job's chief accusers and tormentors. Yet we will see God achieve His good and perfect will, even through the sin of these false friends, Eliphaz, Bildad, and Zophar.

These three men have taken their shots at Job in the first debate, Job chapters 3 through 14. That was round one. Now we come to round two, the second debate, Job chapters 15 through 21. Job's friends have no sympathy for his suffering and no ear to hear his arguments. Instead of asking themselves if there is any merit to Job's position, they sharpen their verbal weapons and attack him even more fiercely.

Though Job may seem defenseless against the accusations and attacks of his friends, he is about to discover that he has help from on high.

THE ARROGANCE OF ELIPHAZ

Here, in the second debate, Job's three friends speak in the same order as before, beginning with the man I call Eliphaz the Elegant. In Job 15, Eliphaz accuses Job of speaking presumptuously:

> Would a wise man answer with empty notions
>   or fill his belly with the hot east wind?
> Would he argue with useless words,
>   with speeches that have no value?
> But you even undermine piety
>   and hinder devotion to God.
> Your sin prompts your mouth;
>   you adopt the tongue of the crafty.
> Your own mouth condemns you, not mine;
>   your own lips testify against you.
> Are you the first man ever born?
>   Were you brought forth before the hills?
> Do you listen in on God's council?
>   Do you limit wisdom to yourself?

What do you know that we do not know?

What insights do you have that we do not have? (vv. 2–9).

In the first debate, Eliphaz began with a courteous and lofty tone. But here, in the opening lines of the second debate, he drops all show of courtesy toward Job. His verbal thrust is deep, sharp, and cutting. He says, "Job, your talk is empty and foolish—a lot of hot air. You attack religious piety and devotion. Your words are sly and prompted by a sinful heart. I don't have to condemn you; your own words condemn you. You think you have an inside track on God's wisdom. You think you're so smart—smarter than we are!"

Eliphaz has let his pride get in the way of his reason and compassion for Job. He's more interested in proving himself right and proving Job wrong than he is in finding the truth and comforting a friend. So he resorts to a rigid and narrow-minded theology:

The gray-haired and the aged are on our side,
    men even older than your father.
Are God's consolations not enough for you,
    words spoken gently to you?
Why has your heart carried you away,
    and why do your eyes flash,
so that you vent your rage against God
    and pour out such words from your mouth?
What is man, that he could be pure,
    or one born of woman, that he could be righteous?
If God places no trust in his holy ones,
    if even the heavens are not pure in his eyes,
how much less man, who is vile and corrupt,
    who drinks up evil like water! (Job 15:10–16).

Eliphaz, of course, is accusing Job of being vile and corrupt, a man who drinks up evil like water. Job is the man of whom God said, "There is no one on earth like him; he is blameless and upright, a man who fears God and shuns evil" (1:8). Truly, there could be no more false and unjust accusation than the one Eliphaz has leveled at Job.

Eliphaz is not completely wrong in everything he says. His theology is essentially correct. He says, "What is man, that he could be pure, or one born of woman, that he could be righteous?" Eliphaz speaks here of the general nature of fallen and depraved human beings. He is correct in saying that no one is righteous and sinless before God, including Job.

But Eliphaz is mixing two different concepts. He starts with the general and universal truth expressed by the apostle Paul in Romans 3:23: "For all have sinned and fall short of the glory of God." But then he jumps to Job's specific situation and accuses Job of living a vile, corrupt, and evil lifestyle, and he makes this accusation without any evidence to back up the charge. While all human beings are sinners, we know that some human beings are fallen but faithful servants of God while others are rebellious and corrupt enemies of God. Job is God's servant; Eliphaz has falsely accused him of being God's enemy.

Yes, Job is a sinner, but he has repented of every sin he can recall, and God has forgiven his sin. Job's life provides the evidence against all the charges lodged against him by his so-called friends. More to the point, his friends are themselves guilty of the very sins they accuse Job of committing because they, too, are part of the fallen human race.

There is a profound lesson for all of us in this scene. When we talk to somebody who is in trouble or in pain or suffering or even caught in a sin, we should never be arrogant or accusing. As Paul wrote to the Galatians:

> Brothers, if someone is caught in a sin, you who are spiritual should restore him gently. But watch yourself, or you also may be tempted. Carry each other's burdens, and in this way you will fulfill the law of Christ. If anyone thinks he is something when he is nothing, he deceives himself (6:1–3).

Eliphaz violates every principle expressed in this passage. He goes to Job with harsh accusations, not gentleness. He points out Job's sinfulness while ignoring his own failings. Instead of carrying Job's burden, he increases that burden. He thinks he is something and that Job is nothing—and he deceives himself. May we be strong in God's wisdom, compassion, and humility so that we never fall into the sin of Eliphaz.

"BLAME-THE-VICTIM" THEOLOGY

Eliphaz goes on to argue from his own life experience and observation. This passage reinforces the impression that Eliphaz is arrogant and impressed with his own "wisdom."

Listen to me and I will explain to you;
>   let me tell you what I have seen,
what wise men have declared,
>   hiding nothing received from their fathers
(to whom alone the land was given
>   when no alien passed among them):
All his days the wicked man suffers torment,
>   the ruthless through all the years stored up for him.
Terrifying sounds fill his ears;
>   when all seems well, marauders attack him.
He despairs of escaping the darkness;
>   he is marked for the sword.
He wanders about—food for vultures;
>   he knows the day of darkness is at hand.
Distress and anguish fill him with terror;
>   they overwhelm him, like a king poised to attack,
because he shakes his fist at God
>   and vaunts himself against the Almighty,
defiantly charging against him
>   with a thick, strong shield.
Though his face is covered with fat
>   and his waist bulges with flesh,
he will inhabit ruined towns
>   and houses where no one lives,
>   houses crumbling to rubble.
He will no longer be rich and his wealth will not endure,
>   nor will his possessions spread over the land.
He will not escape the darkness;
>   a flame will wither his shoots,
>   and the breath of God's mouth will carry him away.
Let him not deceive himself by trusting what is worthless,
>   for he will get nothing in return.
Before his time he will be paid in full,
>   and his branches will not flourish.
He will be like a vine stripped of its unripe grapes,
>   like an olive tree shedding its blossoms.
For the company of the godless will be barren,
>   and fire will consume the tents of those who love bribes.

They conceive trouble and give birth to evil;
    their womb fashions deceit (Job 15:17–35).

Eliphaz says, in effect, "I know what I'm talking about, so listen up, Job. A wicked man like you should expect nothing but torment and trouble in his life. The older you get, the worse your troubles will be. Every little noise will spook you, and the moment you think you're safe, some enemy will attack you!

"You'll wander aimlessly, never knowing when you'll drop dead, and your bones will be picked clean by the vultures. Because you insist on defying God, you will live in constant fear. You'll have no home; you'll hide in the rubble of ghost towns. Nothing will go right for you. You're only deceiving yourself, Job, and your lies will leave you empty.

"All the riches you once had were undoubtedly amassed with bribery and dishonesty. That's why your home and possessions have been consumed by fire. People like you can't bring forth anything good. You're like a woman who gives birth to a monster, whose womb brings forth only lies."

That's quite an accusation! Again, I think you can hear the pettiness and jealousy in the voice of Eliphaz. He thinks there is only one way Job could have gotten as rich as he was: bribery and lies. Having envied Job's former success, Eliphaz says, "Job, you finally got what you deserved. You keep saying you're innocent, but an honest man couldn't become as wealthy as you were. Your suffering just proves what I've been saying: God won't let a man get away with wickedness. Sinners like you always get what's coming to them."

It's the same old "blame-the-victim" theology: If you're suffering, then you must be sinning. This view is as wrong today as it was in the day of Job and Eliphaz.

A PROPHETIC DIMENSION

Now we come to Job 16. Here this suffering man answers his friends a second time, rebuking their lack of understanding:

Then Job replied:
"I have heard many things like these;
    miserable comforters are you all!
Will your long-winded speeches never end?
    What ails you that you keep on arguing?

I also could speak like you,
    if you were in my place;
I could make fine speeches against you
    and shake my head at you.
But my mouth would encourage you;
    comfort from my lips would bring you relief.
Yet if I speak, my pain is not relieved;
    and if I refrain, it does not go away" (vv. 1–6).

These words drip with sarcasm, anger, and pain. They come from a man who has been tortured and tried beyond our ability to comprehend. He rightly refers to his so-called friends as "miserable comforters." What a weight of irony is contained in those two words. These men came to comfort Job; instead, they increased his misery. When a person is suffering, there is no more unwelcome visitor than a "miserable comforter," a person who brings misery and calls it comfort.

Notice that by this point in the story of Job, Satan has faded from the scene; his name is not mentioned. He's still there—make no mistake—but he's in the background. He's using Job's three friends as vehicles for delivering what the apostle Paul calls "the flaming arrows of the evil one" (Ephesians 6:16). In the book of Revelation, Satan is called "the accuser of our brothers, who accuses them before our God day and night" (12:10). It is tragic indeed that Eliphaz, Bildad, and Zophar allowed themselves to be used as channels for Satan's accusations against an innocent, suffering man.

Next, Job goes on to state the facts, as he understands them. First he says, "All I can conclude from what I am suffering is that God must hate me."

Surely, O God, you have worn me out;
    you have devastated my entire household.
You have bound me—and it has become a witness;
    my gauntness rises up and testifies against me.
God assails me and tears me in his anger
    and gnashes his teeth at me;
    my opponent fastens on me his piercing eyes.
Men open their mouths to jeer at me;
    they strike my cheek in scorn
    and unite together against me.
God has turned me over to evil men
    and thrown me into the clutches of the wicked.

All was well with me, but he shattered me;
    he seized me by the neck and crushed me.
He has made me his target;
his archers surround me.
Without pity, he pierces my kidneys
    and spills my gall on the ground.
Again and again he bursts upon me;
    he rushes at me like a warrior (16:7–14).

Job charges God with all that is wrong in his life, from the death of his children to the loss of his health to the fact that his supposed friends have turned against him. God, who is wonderfully patient, does not reply against Job, nor does He retaliate in anger.

God knows Job's heart. He knows Job's faith and love for Him. But He also understands that Job has his breaking point. In this passage, the natural view of life has broken into Job's faith. This suffering man now sees his life in a different light. I believe the main point of this passage is to teach us that God sometimes has to translate theory and theology into painful experience before we can truly grasp what God is saying to us.

This passage may also have a prophetic dimension. When Job says that men jeer and strike him, that God has turned him over to evil men, this sounds very much like what Jesus experienced during the crucifixion. And when Job speaks of being crushed, pierced without pity, and having his gall spilled on the ground, he again reminds us of what Jesus endured when He was beaten and crucified. The prophetic nature of this passage is suggested again a few verses later, as we shall see.

Next, Job protests his innocence once more:

I have sewed sackcloth over my skin
    and buried my brow in the dust.
My face is red with weeping,
    deep shadows ring my eyes;
yet my hands have been free of violence
    and my prayer is pure (16:15–17).

Then, breaking into Job's consciousness, we again glimpse a faint reflection of what God is trying to show him:

O earth, do not cover my blood;
    may my cry never be laid to rest!

Even now my witness is in heaven;
> my advocate is on high.
My intercessor is my friend
> as my eyes pour out tears to God;
on behalf of a man he pleads with God
> as a man pleads for his friend.
Only a few years will pass
> before I go on the journey of no return (16:18–22).

Moments before, Job charged God with causing all of his suffering and loss. Now, however, faith breaks through once more. Job concludes that he still has a witness in heaven, an advocate on high, an intercessor, a friend who will plead with God. Job expects help from on high as he wrestles with his pain and his sense of separation and alienation from God.

Who is this witness, this advocate on high? If we go to 1 John 2:1, we find a striking New Testament parallel to Job's words: "My dear children, I write this to you so that you will not sin. But if anybody does sin, we have one who speaks to the Father in our defense [an Advocate]—Jesus Christ the Righteous One."

Who is this Advocate, this Intercessor, who pleads Job's case with God? Again, the New Testament provides a clue in a parallel passage: "But because Jesus lives forever, he has a permanent priesthood. Therefore he is able to save completely those who come to God through him, because he always lives to intercede for them" (Hebrews 7:24–25).

Though Job's theological understanding is limited because he lives in Old Testament times, God seems to have revealed to him a partial glimpse of the spiritual reality that has been revealed to us in full: Jesus Christ, the Son of the Living God, the God-Man who was crucified and rose again, is our Advocate on high, our Intercessor, our Friend. He has broken down the wall of separation between humanity and God.

Though Job can't possibly grasp the length and breadth and depth of this truth, faith has broken through to his struggling heart, enabling him to lay hold of the fact that God has provided help from on high. Job had no name for that help, but you and I do: Jesus Christ the Lord. He is the One God wants us to lean on in times of pain and loss.

Every now and then, I talk to someone who is going through an intense trial. That person will ask the same question Job asks: "Why is this happening to me?" The answer I find most often in Scripture is that God has sent this trial to wean us from dependence on people and things. He wants us to find our resources in God alone. He sometimes has to separate us from the crutches we lean on so that we will find our strength solely in Him.

Job is learning that the Lord alone can sustain him. God Himself can answer the searching questions of a suffering heart.

HOPE CRUMBLES TO DUST

In Job 17, Job prays that God will set him free and give him a measure of relief—and especially some relief from his friends. He says:

> My spirit is broken,
>> my days are cut short,
>> the grave awaits me.
> Surely mockers surround me;
>> my eyes must dwell on their hostility.
> Give me, O God, the pledge you demand.
>> Who else will put up security for me?
> You have closed their minds to understanding;
>> therefore you will not let them triumph
> If a man denounces his friends for reward,
>> the eyes of his children will fail (vv. 1–5).

Job has had enough of these friends, so he asks God to defend him against them. Then he discusses how other people have responded to him in his pain and suffering:

> God has made me a byword to everyone,
>> a man in whose face people spit.
> My eyes have grown dim with grief;
>> my whole frame is but a shadow.
> Upright men are appalled at this;
>> the innocent are aroused against the ungodly.
> Nevertheless, the righteous will hold to their ways,
>> and those with clean hands will grow stronger (17:6–9).

Next, he issues a challenge to his three "miserable comforters," Eliphaz, Bildad, and Zophar: "But come on, all of you, try again! I will not find a wise man among you" (17:10).

Job has heard all their arguments, and he knows these judgmental accusations are foolish, they're cruel, and they do not help him in his suffering. After issuing this challenge, Job sinks into the pit of despair:

My days have passed, my plans are shattered,
    and so are the desires of my heart.
These men turn night into day;
    in the face of darkness they say, "Light is near."
If the only home I hope for is the grave,
    if I spread out my bed in darkness,
if I say to corruption, "You are my father,"
    and to the worm, "My mother" or "My sister,"
where then is my hope?
    Who can see any hope for me?
Will it go down to the gates of death?
    Will we descend together into the dust? (17:11–16).

Job's spirit has reached a low point. He views corruption and death as his family; he sees the grave as his home, the darkness of death as his only comfort. Job's hope is crumbling into dust, just as a body crumbles into dust in the tomb.

At this point, at least, you would think that Job's friends would finally agree that he has had enough. You'd think they would give this poor man a break from their accusations, their finger pointing, and their tongue wagging. But no, they are relentless in their effort to force Job to admit to hidden sins he has never committed.

Why are Job's "comforters" so determined to find sin in the life of this blameless man? Perhaps part of the reason is that Job's affliction makes them feel anxious and insecure about their own lives. They see Job and think, "If *he* can be stricken with calamity, then it could happen to me, too!"

Job's suffering disrupts their neat and tidy theological worldview, which says, "If you do good, you'll be rewarded; only evil people suffer." If good people can suffer pain and loss (and these three men certainly see themselves as good), then where is their security in life? If the innocent can suffer, then any one of them could end up just like Job.

So Job and his three friends are locked in conflict. Job knows he is innocent, and he will not lie by admitting to sin he never committed. Yet his three friends feel they *must* force Job to admit his sin or their whole worldview comes apart. The longer Job asserts his own innocence, the more desperate his friends become to obtain his confession. It's a case of three relentless forces versus one immovable object.

BILDAD GETS MAD

Job 18 opens with Bildad's retort. This is the man I call Bildad the Brutal because he is brutally frank and plainspoken. He lobs his accusations at Job as if they were hand grenades, not caring what devastation he causes. This "miserable comforter" clearly feels stung by Job's words, so he defends himself by attacking Job.

In the first debate, Bildad gave the appearance of a logician, the coldly analytical intellectual. Here, in the second debate, Bildad is still coldhearted toward Job and analytical in his argument—but with a difference. Now Bildad is clearly angry with Job because Job has not admitted his own sin. Bildad is frustrated with what he sees as Job's stubbornness and dishonesty, and he's upset that Job's replies have been blunt and strongly worded. In short, Bildad gets mad:

> When will you end these speeches?
>   Be sensible, and then we can talk.
> Why are we regarded as cattle
>   and considered stupid in your sight?
> You who tear yourself to pieces in your anger,
>   is the earth to be abandoned for your sake?
>   Or must the rocks be moved from their place? (18:2–4).

In Job 17:10, Job said to his three tormentors, "I will not find a wise man among you." Bildad, who is very proud of his intellectual prowess, clearly takes offense at Job's statement. So he counterattacks and demands that Job "be sensible," adding, "Why are we regarded as cattle and considered stupid in your sight?" He then compares his own intellect and wisdom to the bedrock of the earth. He tells Job, "In order for you to be innocent, as you claim, the rocks that form the foundation of the earth would have to be overthrown. In order for you to be innocent, everything that is true about reality would have to stand on its head."

Bildad then goes on at length to restate the same tired argument he made in the first debate:

The lamp of the wicked is snuffed out;
    the flame of his fire stops burning.
The light in his tent becomes dark;
    the lamp beside him goes out.
The vigor of his step is weakened;
    his own schemes throw him down.
His feet thrust him into a net
    and he wanders into its mesh.
A trap seizes him by the heel;
    a snare holds him fast.
A noose is hidden for him on the ground;
    a trap lies in his path.
Terrors startle him on every side
    and dog his every step.
Calamity is hungry for him;
    disaster is ready for him when he falls.
It eats away parts of his skin;
    death's firstborn devours his limbs.
He is torn from the security of his tent
    and marched off to the king of terrors.
Fire resides in his tent;
    burning sulfur is scattered over his dwelling.
His roots dry up below
    and his branches wither above.
The memory of him perishes from the earth;
    he has no name in the land.
He is driven from light into darkness
    and is banished from the world.
He has no offspring or descendants among his people,
    no survivor where once he lived.
Men of the west are appalled at his fate;
    men of the east are seized with horror.
Surely such is the dwelling of an evil man;
    such is the place of one who knows not God (18:5–21).

Bildad's long harangue boils down to this: "It is the evil that suffer, not the righteous. Job, you are suffering because of sin. We all know it. Now, admit it! You complain about your pain, loss, and terror, but that's what happens to people who do evil. You complain that your children have all been killed, but it's the wicked that have no offspring or descendents, no survivors where they once lived. Job, you complained that God has made you a byword to everyone, a man in whose face people spit. But it's the wicked that suffer mistreatment, not the innocent. Complain all you want, deny it if you will—but we all know that you are an evil man, and your suffering is God's punishment for wrongdoers."

"MY REDEEMER LIVES!"

In chapter 19, Job responds with a plea that should break the heart of anyone who has any compassion for a suffering soul. He pleads with his friends to stop tormenting him with their accusations:

> How long will you torment me
>   and crush me with words?
> Ten times now you have reproached me;
>   shamelessly you attack me.
> If it is true that I have gone astray,
>   my error remains my concern alone.
> If indeed you would exalt yourselves above me
>   and use my humiliation against me,
> then know that God has wronged me
>   and drawn his net around me (vv. 2–6).

Job rightly says that if he has sinned, it is now his concern alone. Even if Eliphaz, Bildad, and Zophar are right about Job, they have already done all they can do. What purpose is served by continuing to attack him? He's also correct in pointing out the unrighteous motives behind their attack: At the same time they are accusing Job of unconfessed sin, they are exalting themselves over him. They cannot accuse Job of being an "evil man" (to use Bildad's words) without setting themselves up as good men. They have used Job's pain and humiliation against him. In the process, they have elevated themselves over him.

Job wants them to know that if the world truly works as they say—if only the wicked suffer and the innocent are always blessed—then something is terribly wrong. If that's the case, then God has treated Job unfairly, because he knows in his heart of hearts that he is innocent of the accusations of his three so-called "comforters." And this, he goes on to say, is what continues to baffle him about God's silence:

Though I cry, "I've been wronged!" I get no response;
    though I call for help, there is no justice.
He has blocked my way so I cannot pass;
    he has shrouded my paths in darkness.
He has stripped me of my honor
    and removed the crown from my head.
He tears me down on every side till I am gone;
    he uproots my hope like a tree.
His anger burns against me;
    he counts me among his enemies.
His troops advance in force;
    they build a siege ramp against me
    and encamp around my tent.
He has alienated my brothers from me;
    my acquaintances are completely estranged from me.
My kinsmen have gone away;
    my friends have forgotten me.
My guests and my maidservants count me a stranger;
    they look upon me as an alien.
I summon my servant, but he does not answer,
    though I beg him with my own mouth.
My breath is offensive to my wife;
    I am loathsome to my own brothers.
Even the little boys scorn me;
    when I appear, they ridicule me.
All my intimate friends detest me;
    those I love have turned against me.
I am nothing but skin and bones;
    I have escaped with only the skin of my teeth.
Have pity on me, my friends, have pity,
    for the hand of God has struck me.
Why do you pursue me as God does?
    Will you never get enough of my flesh? (19:7–22).

Job feels bewildered, isolated, and rejected by family, friends, and God Himself. There are few experiences in life more baffling and painful than being rejected by those who should understand us. Job is still reeling from his physical pain—still scraping his boils with pieces of broken pottery. He's reeling from his emotional pain—still grieving the deaths of his children and the loss of all his material possessions. And along with all of this suffering, he must endure the misjudgment and rejection of family and friends. How much can this poor man take?

Yet here, in the depths of Job's darkness, a ray of golden light breaks through:

> Oh, that my words were recorded,
>   that they were written on a scroll,
> that they were inscribed with an iron tool on lead,
>   or engraved in rock forever!
> I know that my Redeemer lives,
>   and that in the end he will stand upon the earth.
> And after my skin has been destroyed,
>   yet in my flesh I will see God;
> I myself will see him
>   with my own eyes—I, and not another.
>   How my heart yearns within me! (19:23–27).

Amid all of his suffering and the accusations from his supposed friends, something wonderful happens: Job experiences a vision of faith. I believe God gave Job this vision to sustain him—a glimpse of glorious light at the end of a very dark tunnel of pain. This vision refines and expands upon a previous insight God gave to Job—a promise of help from on high. You'll recall that in chapter 16, Job said:

> Even now my witness is in heaven;
>   my advocate is on high.
> My intercessor is my friend
>   as my eyes pour out tears to God;
> on behalf of a man he pleads with God
>   as a man pleads for his friend (vv. 19–21).

Job already knows that he has a witness in heaven, an advocate on high, an intercessor and friend who will plead his case before God. As we have seen, God partially revealed to Job a truth that has been revealed to us in full: Jesus Christ is our advocate on high. Now an even greater truth breaks through:

> I know that my Redeemer lives,
>   and that in the end he will stand upon the earth.

And after my skin has been destroyed,
>   yet in my flesh I will see God (19:25–26).

This Old Testament saint has been granted a glimpse into a profound New Testament truth: Job's advocate in heaven is also the Redeemer. This Redeemer was alive in Job's time and would one day stand upon the earth. Job fully expected that even after his death and the destruction of his flesh he would rise from the grave and see God. This is a vivid and unmistakable expression of an Old Testament confidence in the resurrection of the dead through Jesus Christ. As Job ponders this vision, he exclaims, "How my heart yearns within me!"

This is one of the most triumphant statements of faith in all the Scriptures. It may well be the earliest written intimation of the resurrection to be found in the Word of God. Gradually, out of the anguish and despair of this man's heart, a realization has dawned: God is working out a great and mighty purpose in human history. A day will come when God Himself—a God whom Job has consistently viewed as the epitome of majesty and power—shall become visibly present before humanity. He shall appear on the earth and vindicate all that He does.

In this statement, Job looks ahead by faith to the incarnation of the Lord Jesus. Job calls him "my Redeemer"—that is, his vindicator, the one who will defend him, ransom him, and resurrect him from the dust of death. Praise God, Job's Redeemer is my Redeemer and yours as well if we place our trust in Him.

GOD KNOWS WHAT HE'S ABOUT

One of the central themes of the book of Job is that life is a mystery. Though we would love to reduce this life to a few simple principles (do good and you'll be blessed; do evil and you'll be punished), life doesn't work that way. Life is complicated, not simple. The ways of God are beyond us. As the Lord said through the prophet Isaiah,

>   "For my thoughts are not your thoughts,
>   neither are your ways my ways,"
>   declares the LORD.
>   "As the heavens are higher than the earth,
>   so are my ways higher than your ways
>   and my thoughts than your thoughts" (Isaiah 55:8–9).

Job is gradually learning to believe that God is working out His eternal purpose in a way that is consistent with His unchanging love.

I once heard Elisabeth Elliot, author of *Through Gates of Splendor,* speak at a Christian conference. She was married to missionary Jim Elliot, one of the five brave men who were killed in 1956 by Auca Indians in South America as they sought to bring the gospel to that tribe. Jim's death left Elisabeth a widow with a one-year-old baby. She later lived with the tribe and was instrumental in completing the work her husband began, bringing the good news of Jesus Christ to the Aucas (now called Waoranis).

In 1963, Elisabeth Elliot returned to the United States. After thirteen years as a widow, she married Addison H. Leitch, a professor of philosophy and religion at Tarkio College in Missouri. They had a wonderful life together until 1973, when Professor Leitch passed away, taken by cancer. Again, Elisabeth Elliot was a widow.

At the time I heard her speak, just a few years after Professor Leitch died, she said, "I have spent six-sevenths of my life single, though I have been married twice. I did not choose the gift of widowhood, but I accepted it as the sphere in which I am to live to the glory of God."

Elisabeth Elliot was learning a lesson you and I need to learn: Whether we experience blessing or trials, God is working out His purpose in our lives. If tragedy comes into our lives, it is not necessarily related to a specific sin (though, as we will see, Job learns much about the depravity of his own nature before this book is over). Suffering is a normal part of the human condition. We cause great harm to hurting people when we judge and accuse them. In doing so, we risk the judgment of God.

Job has gone through pain and loss, and now his three so-called friends have falsely accused him. Yet amid his trials and troubles, Job has been blessed by God. He has received a vision of help from on high, a vision of a coming Redeemer. In light of this vision, Job warns his "miserable comforters":

> If you say, "How we will hound him,
>   since the root of the trouble lies in him,"
> you should fear the sword yourselves;
>   for wrath will bring punishment by the sword,
>   and then you will know that there is judgment (Job 19:28–29).

Job is warning these three men that they are unjustly persecuting an innocent man, and by accusing him falsely, they are storing up judgment for themselves. This is a warning we should take seriously whenever we are tempted to harshly judge our Christian brothers and sisters.

Years ago, I ran across these words by an unknown poet—words that beautifully express this lesson from the book of Job:

When God wants to drill a man,
And thrill a man,
And skill a man;
When God wants to mold a man
To play the noblest part;
When He yearns with all His heart
To create so great and bold a man
That all the world shall be amazed,
Watch His methods, watch His ways!

How He ruthlessly perfects
Whom He royally elects!
How He hammers him and hurts him,
And with mighty blows, converts him
Into trial shapes of clay
Which only God understands;
While his tortured heart is crying,
And he lifts beseeching hands!

How He bends but never breaks
When his good He undertakes.
How He uses whom He chooses,
And with every purpose fuses him;
By every act, induces him
To try His splendor out.
God knows what He's about.

That's the message of Job to us. You may be going through pain, loss, and disappointment. You may ask, as Job did, "Why, Lord? Why did You allow this to happen?" God's answer is that He knows what He's about. He has a purpose for your pain. In eternity that purpose will be plain for you to see. In the meantime, rest in the confidence that your Redeemer lives. Help is coming from on high.

WHY DOESN'T GOD INTERVENE?

Job 20–26

In her book *Miracles of Courage*, Monica Dickens tells of two-year-old David, who was being treated for leukemia at Massachusetts General Hospital in Boston. The physician in David's case, Dr. John Truman, had given the child only a fifty-fifty chance of surviving the illness.

David underwent numerous painful treatments and blood tests, and his mother, Deborah, found it hard to watch her boy suffer. Although David always cried during the painful treatments, he never cried in the waiting room. He knew that when he went into the clinic, Dr. Truman would stick him with needles and hurt him, yet whenever his name was called, he would hurry in ahead of his mother and greet the nurses with a smile. He had trouble pronouncing the letter *r*, so when he saw the doctor, he'd wave and say, "Hi, Dr. Tooman!"

Soon after he turned three, David had to undergo a painful spinal tap—the removal of fluid from the lumbar region of the spinal cord. David was scared but put on a brave front. His mother told him, "Dr. Truman has to do this to make you well, honey. I know it hurts, but Dr. Truman only does this because he loves you."

The procedure was horribly painful. Deborah was in agony watching her son squirm and scream. Three nurses had to hold the boy down. When it was over, the boy was soaked in sweat and tears. He looked up at the doctor with trusting eyes and said, "Thank you, Dr. Tooman, for my hurting."

The spirit of this boy reminds me of the spirit of Job, a man who has suffered for reasons he cannot understand. In his pain he has squirmed, sobbed, and screamed to God. Yet his eyes, though full of tears, are still eyes of trust, eyes of faith, eyes of a blameless and upright servant. As we come to Job 20, Job's faith is about to be tested to the breaking point as he confronts the ultimate question: Why doesn't God intervene?

PHARISEES OF JOB'S DAY—AND OURS

Job's three friends represent a worldview now known as pharisaism. The Pharisees were a party or sect within Judaism at the time of Christ; they were some of the harshest critics and enemies of our Lord. Pharisaism may be defined as "orthodoxy without true godliness." It makes an appearance of being orthodox, correct in theology, and righteous in outward behavior, yet the heart of a Pharisee is proud, self-righteous, rigid, hateful, and opposed to true godliness, compassion, and humility. Pharisees see themselves as superior because of their strict adherence to rules and rituals.

Though the Pharisees did not emerge as an organized movement until centuries after Job was written, Eliphaz, Bildad, and Zophar represent three subtly different forms of pharisaism. These three forms of pharisaism are still with us today. In many places, the church has fallen into pharisaism—an outward rightness combined with an inward wrongness. The book of Job was written in part to show us how wrong these three friends were and to warn us against treating people the way they treated Job.

ZOPHAR'S IMPASSIONED SPEECH

We come now to a second encounter with the man I call Zophar the Zealous. He tends to be hotheaded and passionate in his speeches. He represents the type of pharisaism that is expressed with impassioned words and emotional outbursts. Zophar appeals more to the emotions than to the intellect. In Job 20, we find Zophar's second and last appearance in the book of Job:

> Then Zophar the Naamathite replied:
> "My troubled thoughts prompt me to answer
>   because I am greatly disturbed.
> I hear a rebuke that dishonors me,
>   and my understanding inspires me to reply" (vv. 1–3).

Zophar seems insulted and annoyed by Job's stubborn insistence on his own innocence. He confesses that he is disturbed because Job has rebuked him. Zophar sees Job as a sinful man, and he feels that being rebuked by a sinful man is a stain on his honor. So Zophar launches into an angry attack on Job's integrity. He doesn't have any new arguments to offer; he merely restates what he has already said. The wicked do not prosper for long, and the joy of the godless is short-lived:

Surely you know how it has been from of old,
> ever since man was placed on the earth,
that the mirth of the wicked is brief,
> the joy of the godless lasts but a moment.
Though his pride reaches to the heavens
> and his head touches the clouds,
he will perish forever, like his own dung;
> those who have seen him will say, "Where is he?"
Like a dream he flies away, no more to be found,
> banished like a vision of the night.
The eye that saw him will not see him again;
> his place will look on him no more.
His children must make amends to the poor;
> his own hands must give back his wealth.
The youthful vigor that fills his bones
> will lie with him in the dust (Job 20:4–11).

He goes on to say that the punishment of the wicked is certain; there's no way to avoid it. God will surely bring judgment upon them:

Though evil is sweet in his mouth
> and he hides it under his tongue,
though he cannot bear to let it go
> and keeps it in his mouth,
yet his food will turn sour in his stomach;
> it will become the venom of serpents within him.
He will spit out the riches he swallowed;
> God will make his stomach vomit them up.
He will suck the poison of serpents;
> the fangs of an adder will kill him.
He will not enjoy the streams,
> the rivers flowing with honey and cream.
What he toiled for he must give back uneaten;
> he will not enjoy the profit from his trading (Job 20:12–18).

Zophar declares that the evil deeds of the wicked will always be exposed. He suggests that Job has acquired his wealth by oppressing the poor, and that while Job was enjoying his wealth, disaster and ill health (including an outbreak of boils) overtook him. Zophar sees Job's suffering as proof that his evil has been brought to light:

For he has oppressed the poor and left them destitute;
> he has seized houses he did not build.
Surely he will have no respite from his craving;
> he cannot save himself by his treasure.
Nothing is left for him to devour;
> his prosperity will not endure.
In the midst of his plenty, distress will overtake him;
> the full force of misery will come upon him (Job 20:19–22).

Next, Zophar describes the terrible fate of the wicked:

When he has filled his belly,
> God will vent his burning anger against him
> and rain down his blows upon him.
Though he flees from an iron weapon,
> a bronze-tipped arrow pierces him.
He pulls it out of his back,
> the gleaming point out of his liver.
Terrors will come over him;
total darkness lies in wait for his treasures.
A fire unfanned will consume him
> and devour what is left in his tent.
The heavens will expose his guilt;
> the earth will rise up against him.
A flood will carry off his house,
> rushing waters on the day of God's wrath.
Such is the fate God allots the wicked,
> the heritage appointed for them by God (Job 20:23–29).

All that Zophar says is true, in a real sense. The prosperity of the wicked will be cut off, and their evil deeds will be exposed, judged, and punished. But only God can say when that will happen, and it is presumptuous and arrogant to point a finger at a suffering person and say, without evidence, "Your suffering is a punishment for sin."

Zophar has finished his impassioned speech. It's Job's turn to reply.

JOB'S REASONED RESPONSE

As we have already seen, there are times when Job speaks sharply, even angrily and sarcastically, to his three friends. At other times—perhaps when his pain is less intense—he uses a more calm and dispassionate tone. In Job 21, he responds to Zophar's emotion-charged arguments in a thoughtful and reasoned way:

> Listen carefully to my words;
>> let this be the consolation you give me.
> Bear with me while I speak,
>> and after I have spoken, mock on.
> Is my complaint directed to man?
>> Why should I not be impatient?
> Look at me and be astonished;
>> clap your hand over your mouth.
> When I think about this, I am terrified;
>> trembling seizes my body (vv. 2–6).

Job says, in effect, "If you can't offer me any consolation, at least listen to me. It will be some consolation to me if you'll just hear me out. My argument isn't with you; it's with God. The things I'm about to say will shock you, and it frightens me to contemplate the argument I'm about to make. But I have to say this. If you still want to mock me when I've said my piece, then feel free. But for now, please have the decency to sit quietly and listen to what I have to say."

What does Job want to say that's so shocking and frightening, even to himself? Simply this: The facts contradict his friends' theology, a theology Job himself once held. The facts show that many wicked people live their entire lives without trouble, without being punished for their evil works. He says:

> Why do the wicked live on,
>> growing old and increasing in power?
> They see their children established around them,
>> their offspring before their eyes.
> Their homes are safe and free from fear;
>> the rod of God is not upon them.
> Their bulls never fail to breed;
>> their cows calve and do not miscarry.
> They send forth their children as a flock;
>> their little ones dance about.
> They sing to the music of tambourine and harp;
>> they make merry to the sound of the flute.

They spend their years in prosperity
and go down to the grave in peace (Job 21:7–13).

What is the life of the wicked? It's a life of prosperity, contentment, and ease. Nothing ever seems to trouble them. They are outwardly, openly wicked, and they seem to get away with their sins. It almost seems that God favors the wicked over the righteous.

Most of us have probably thought this way at some time. We see people committing evil acts, and they are rewarded. They prosper, and they're happy. The world applauds them. Job goes on to say:

Yet they say to God, "Leave us alone!
We have no desire to know your ways.
Who is the Almighty, that we should serve him?
What would we gain by praying to him?"
But their prosperity is not in their own hands,
so I stand aloof from the counsel of the wicked (21:14–16).

Job says, "The ungodly toss God out of their lives, they refuse to serve Him, they neglect to pray to Him and thank Him for all they have. They think they made themselves prosperous without God's help, and they do not acknowledge Him. This kind of thinking is foolish and I'll have nothing to do with it, but this is the way the ungodly think."

Every observation Job makes is as true today as it was in those ancient times. The ungodly defy God, yet they are not punished. We think God should judge them, yet they seem untroubled. The ungodly ridicule and resist God, yet He lets them be. God does not strike them down. In fact, they prosper, and their success makes them all the more arrogant.

Job goes on to ask:

Yet how often is the lamp of the wicked snuffed out?
How often does calamity come upon them,
the fate God allots in his anger?
How often are they like straw before the wind,
like chaff swept away by a gale?
It is said, "God stores up a man's punishment for his sons."
Let him repay the man himself, so that he will know it!
Let his own eyes see his destruction;
let him drink of the wrath of the Almighty.

For what does he care about the family he leaves behind
>   when his allotted months come to an end?
Can anyone teach knowledge to God,
>   since he judges even the highest?
One man dies in full vigor,
>   completely secure and at ease,
his body well nourished,
>   his bones rich with marrow.
Another man dies in bitterness of soul,
>   never having enjoyed anything good.
Side by side they lie in the dust,
>   and worms cover them both (21:17–26).

There is a basic unfairness at the root of life. Some say, "Well, when the evil man goes unpunished, God is simply storing up punishment to inflict on the evil man's descendents." To this argument, Job says, "What good does that do? Let God punish the evildoer himself, not future generations. If God is just, then let the evildoer himself experience destruction. The present state of life is unfair! One man lives well, enjoys all that life has to offer, and dies at peace; another man lives in poverty and bitterness, knowing nothing but suffering, and dies desolate. How can God allow such unfairness yet claim to be just and holy?"

The psalmist Asaph makes the same observation in Psalm 73:

For I envied the arrogant
>   when I saw the prosperity of the wicked.
They have no struggles;
>   their bodies are healthy and strong.
They are free from the burdens common to man;
>   they are not plagued by human ills.
Therefore pride is their necklace;
>   they clothe themselves with violence.
From their callous hearts comes iniquity;
>   the evil conceits of their minds know no limits.
They scoff, and speak with malice;
>   in their arrogance they threaten oppression.
Their mouths lay claim to heaven,
>   and their tongues take possession of the earth.

Therefore their people turn to them
>   and drink up waters in abundance.
They say, "How can God know?
>   Does the Most High have knowledge?"
This is what the wicked are like—
>   always carefree, they increase in wealth.
Surely in vain have I kept my heart pure;
>   in vain have I washed my hands in innocence . . .
When I tried to understand all this,
>   it was oppressive to me
till I entered the sanctuary of God;
>   then I understood their final destiny (Psalm 73:3–13, 16–17).

Asaph has seen what Job has seen—that the wicked prosper while the godly suffer. For a while, Asaph felt that it was a mistake to live a pure and righteous life. If evil is rewarded and good is punished, why be good? Trying to understand why a just and holy God would create such an unfair world only made Asaph's head spin; it was oppressive to him. Only when Asaph went into God's sanctuary and saw reality from God's perspective did he realize that a final destiny awaits the wicked, a destiny of judgment and punishment for the sins they have committed in this life. The scales of justice will be balanced.

Meanwhile, we live in an unfair world—a world in which the righteous suffer and the wicked prosper. If we do not understand this truth, we will become rigid Pharisees like Job's "miserable comforters," accusing innocent people of harboring hidden sin.

GOD IN A BOX

Job then examines his friends and points out the falseness of their friendship:

> I know full well what you are thinking,
>   the schemes by which you would wrong me.
> You say, "Where now is the great man's house,
>   the tents where wicked men lived?" (Job 21:27–28).

Job says, "You say to yourselves, 'Ah! Where is all the wealth of this man? It's gone! Here's proof that what we say is true!' You call yourselves friends, yet you take pride in my pain and humiliation. You are actually pleased and gratified over my suffering!" He goes on:

> Have you never questioned those who travel?
>> Have you paid no regard to their accounts—
> that the evil man is spared from the day of calamity,
>> that he is delivered from the day of wrath?
> Who denounces his conduct to his face?
>> Who repays him for what he has done?
> He is carried to the grave,
>> and watch is kept over his tomb.
> The soil in the valley is sweet to him;
>> all men follow after him,
>> and a countless throng goes before him (21:29–33).

Job tells his friends, "Just ask around among those who travel the world and see life as it is. They'll support what I've said all along: The wicked go unpunished—not just here, but everywhere. The ungodly live above the law, and they die highly honored. There is no justice in this life."

Then Job closes with devastating conclusion: "So how can you console me with your nonsense? Nothing is left of your answers but falsehood!" (21:34).

If you wish to argue with Job, you'd better have your arguments well thought out. This man is able to see through your faulty logic and false assumptions. The fundamental flaw in the arguments of Job's three friends is that their theology does not square with real human experience.

These three friends represent people who try to put God in a box. They think they have God figured out so that they can predict exactly how He is going to act. But when God acts in a way they don't expect, they can't account for it. Instead of re-shaping their theology to fit reality, they keep trying to re-shape God and force Him into their little theological box. Instead of having faith in God Himself, they have faith in religious dogma.

Job's suffering has taught him that God can't be boxed in. Job once thought he knew what God was about, but his limited conception of God was demolished by painful experience. Job learned he had to discard many of his old ideas about God because they didn't fit the reality of his life.

Someone once said, "A man with a true experience is never at the mercy of a man with an argument." Job's friends are unable to answer him because his experience rings true, and their theology rings hollow.

THE THIRD DEBATE BEGINS

The second debate is concluded. In Job 22, we begin the third debate, the final round between Job and his three "comforters." In this third round, only two of the three friends speak: Eliphaz and Bildad.

Again, we begin with Eliphaz the Temanite, whom I call Eliphaz the Elegant. Until now, we have seen that Eliphaz speaks smoothly, with well-crafted sentences. His arguments are like brass knuckles covered in soft velvet. They are beautiful to look upon, but when they hit you, they bruise.

A change comes over Eliphaz, however, as we begin the third debate. Eliphaz has begun to lose his cool. He starts to take off the velvet gloves so that we can see the brutal power of his verbal brass knuckles. In Job 22, Eliphaz piles accusation and invective onto poor Job. He accuses Job of wrong motives. He invents false charges. He resorts to insult in his arguments:

> Can a man be of benefit to God?
>   Can even a wise man benefit him?
> What pleasure would it give the Almighty
>   if you were righteous?
> What would he gain if your ways
>   were blameless? (vv. 2–3).

Eliphaz is trying to peer into Job's hidden motives. He argues that Job thinks that by defending himself, he is defending God's honor and integrity. He thinks Job is claiming that God's reputation depends on Job's own ability to appear righteous.

But that's a false charge. That's not Job's intent at all. Throughout this account, Job has consistently viewed God as holy and righteous, even though Job can't understand God's actions. Job never thinks for a moment that his own circumstances reflect on God's attributes in any way.

Eliphaz goes on to say: "Is it for your piety that he rebukes you and brings charges against you?" (22:4).

Eliphaz suggests that Job feels that God is unfairly punishing him. Again, Job never said that. Had Job done so, he would be doing exactly what Satan wanted Job to do: accuse and blaspheme God. True, Job questioned God and wondered why God allowed him to suffer, but Job never says, "God, You're unjust! You're acting unrighteously!" That is what Eliphaz suggests here, and it's a false charge.

Here is one of the crucial lessons from the book of Job: In our own times of testing and trial, Satan wants us to do what Eliphaz falsely accuses Job of doing. Satan wants us to blame God and accuse Him of being unfair and unjust. If Satan succeeds in wringing such a cry from our lips, then we have succumbed to the satanic strategy. At that moment, we become guilty of making an accusation against the God of righteousness. If we do that in our times of pain and loss, we need to go to God, confess our fault, and ask His forgiveness and for the strength and the faith not to do so again.

Job never yields to Satan. He comes close, but he refuses to cross that brink. Frustrated by Job's resistance to his accusations, Eliphaz goes on to invent a series of wild and unsupported charges against Job:

Is not your wickedness great?
    Are not your sins endless?
You demanded security from your brothers for no reason;
    you stripped men of their clothing, leaving them naked.
You gave no water to the weary
    and you withheld food from the hungry,
though you were a powerful man, owning land—
    an honored man, living on it.
And you sent widows away empty-handed
    and broke the strength of the fatherless.
That is why snares are all around you,
    why sudden peril terrifies you,
why it is so dark you cannot see,
    and why a flood of water covers you (Job 22:5–11).

Here we see the depths of Eliphaz's anger and frustration toward Job. Not one of these accusations is true. Eliphaz simply invents lies. He claims that Job's sins are "endless," that he has extorted, stolen, mistreated the poor, and abused widows and orphans.

In these accusations, Eliphaz displays a second form of pharisaism. You will recall that Zophar's pharisaism, the first form, involved appealing to the emotions instead of the intellect—that is, making impassioned speeches instead of pointing people to the sweet reason of God's Word. Here, Eliphaz's pharisaism seeks to intimidate and browbeat people into agreement. If you do not agree with a Pharisee, he will subject you to insult, accusation, and name-calling.

When my wife, Elaine, was relatively new in the faith, she attended a church led by a demanding and authoritarian pastor. During this time, she began listening to a radio Bible teacher who, in a clear and logical way, taught the truth of the Scriptures. Elaine noticed that what her pastor taught often conflicted with the plain sense of Scripture, as taught by the radio Bible teacher.

When Elaine asked her pastor about these contradictions, he became angry and upset with her. A reasonable person, confident of his position, would have calmly opened his Bible and explained the truth to her. But Elaine's pastor didn't do this. Instead, he accused her of things she had never done. He threatened to charge her with heresy before the church. It was a horrible and frightening experience for Elaine, but she was convinced of what the Scriptures said. In fact, this pastor's hysterical and threatening response convinced her that he didn't have a biblical leg to stand on.

If the Word of God is on your side, don't be intimidated by the threats and accusations of the Pharisees. Trust in God. Stand firmly on His Word.

A CHILDISH LEVEL OF DISCOURSE

Eliphaz goes on to make an insulting, childish charge against Job:

> Is not God in the heights of heaven?
>   And see how lofty are the highest stars!
> Yet you say, "What does God know?
>   Does he judge through such darkness?
> Thick clouds veil him, so he does not see us
>   as he goes about in the vaulted heavens" (22:12–14).

Here Eliphaz twists Job's words and accuses Job of saying something he never said. He says, "The trouble with you, Job, is that you think God is such a limited being that He can't even see what you're doing. You think He's up in heaven, and the clouds get in the way so He can't see all the sins you commit!"

This is an absurd accusation. Job has already demonstrated that he has a clear and exalted concept of God's might and majesty. Job knows there is nothing hidden from God's sight. Eliphaz can't answer Job's arguments, so he twists them and pretends that Job holds childish misconceptions of God.

Next, Eliphaz mocks Job's own words—hardly a gracious way to make a point. He says:

Will you keep to the old path
    that evil men have trod?
They were carried off before their time,
    their foundations washed away by a flood.
They said to God, "Leave us alone!
    What can the Almighty do to us?"
Yet it was he who filled their houses with good things,
    so I stand aloof from the counsel of the wicked (Job 22:15–18).

Compare the words of Eliphaz above to these words of Job, which we just read in Job 21:

Yet they say to God, "Leave us alone!
    We have no desire to know your ways.
Who is the Almighty, that we should serve him?
    What would we gain by praying to him?"
But their prosperity is not in their own hands,
    so I stand aloof from the counsel of the wicked (vv. 14–16).

Eliphaz is mimicking and ridiculing Job. He tells Job, in effect, "You say, 'I stand aloof from the counsel of the wicked,' but you don't fool me! Job, you're just as wicked as the rest of the ungodly." He's mocking Job, much as a child will mock you by repeating your words in a bratty voice. Though Eliphaz began the first debate with elegant words and high-sounding logic, his frustration with Job has brought him to a child's level.

Eliphaz concludes with a wearying and repetitive demand that Job confess his sin and turn to God to be restored and blessed:

The righteous see their ruin and rejoice;
    the innocent mock them, saying,
"Surely our foes are destroyed,
    and fire devours their wealth."
Submit to God and be at peace with him;
    in this way prosperity will come to you.
Accept instruction from his mouth
    and lay up his words in your heart.
If you return to the Almighty, you will be restored:
    If you remove wickedness far from your tent
and assign your nuggets to the dust,
    your gold of Ophir to the rocks in the ravines,

> then the Almighty will be your gold,
> the choicest silver for you.
> Surely then you will find delight in the Almighty
> and will lift up your face to God.
> You will pray to him, and he will hear you,
> and you will fulfill your vows.
> What you decide on will be done,
> and light will shine on your ways.
> When men are brought low and you say, "Lift them up!"
> then he will save the downcast.
> He will deliver even one who is not innocent,
> who will be delivered through the cleanness
> of your hands (Job 22:19–30).

Job has heard this argument before. It has no effect on him. He knows that while he is a fallen human being, there is no rebellion in his heart, no hidden sin in his life.

THE FIRST QUESTION

This brings us to Job 23 and 24, where Job expresses the depths of his dilemma. Here, Job quits trying to answer the arguments of his friends. He simply cries out from the depths of his troubled heart. Though his three friends are present, his cry is not directed at them but to God Himself. Here, Job asks two questions, one in Job 23 and one in Job 24. These are the two great unanswered questions human beings still ask today.

The first question, which Job asks in chapter 23, is this: Why is God seemingly absent from human affairs? Why does He seem to disappear from our lives just when we need Him most? Job opens chapter 23 with an expression of his heartfelt longing for God:

> Even today my complaint is bitter;
> his hand is heavy in spite of my groaning.
> If only I knew where to find him;
> if only I could go to his dwelling!
> I would state my case before him
> and fill my mouth with arguments.
> I would find out what he would answer me,
> and consider what he would say (vv. 1–5).

Job is honest about his pain and frustration. He can't find any way to contact God. He can't argue his case before God and hear God's answers to his questions. Yet, in the very depths of his pain and darkness, Job still expresses an unshaken confidence in God:

Would he oppose me with great power?
    No, he would not press charges against me.
There an upright man could present his case before him,
    and I would be delivered forever from my judge (23:6–7).

Job is confident that if he could lay out his case before God, who is just and fair, then God would judge Job to be right. Job goes on to describe his search for God in the midst of his suffering:

But if I go to the east, he is not there;
    if I go to the west, I do not find him.
When he is at work in the north, I do not see him;
    when he turns to the south, I catch no glimpse of him (Job 23:8–9).

Have you ever felt that way? Have you ever felt abandoned by God? Unable to find Him? Unable to get any answers for your deepest questions? That's how Job feels. And here, once more, Job declares his own righteousness and faith that God will see him through at last: "But he knows the way that I take; when he has tested me, I will come forth as gold"(Job 23:10).

Job expresses complete confidence that God is just and fair. He says, in effect, "I don't understand what I am going through or why I'm being tested so severely. I've searched my heart, and I know that I have no hidden or unconfessed sin in my life, yet this torment goes on. But I know God will explain it to me some day. He knows the kind of man I am, the kind of life I've lived. He knows my heart. When God has tested and tried me, when He has taken me safely through this time of incredible pain and loss, He will know that my heart and my character are as gold."

Job goes on to restate his innocence and his bafflement over the loss he has suffered:

My feet have closely followed his steps;
    I have kept to his way without turning aside.
I have not departed from the commands of his lips;
    I have treasured the words of his mouth more
    than my daily bread.

But he stands alone, and who can oppose him?
    He does whatever he pleases.
He carries out his decree against me,
    and many such plans he still has in store.
That is why I am terrified before him;
    when I think of all this, I fear him.
God has made my heart faint;
    the Almighty has terrified me.
Yet I am not silenced by the darkness,
    by the thick darkness that covers my face (23:11–17).

Embedded in this passage is Job's first question, the question we all ask in times of pain and suffering: Why does God seem absent just when I need Him most? Where is God when my pain is at its worst?

THE SECOND QUESTION

In Job 24, Job raises the second question that people still ask today: Why is God silent? Why doesn't He judge evil? In the opening verses of this chapter, Job describes some of the evil deeds that seem to go unpunished:

Why does the Almighty not set times for judgment?
    Why must those who know him look in vain for such days?
Men move boundary stones;
    they pasture flocks they have stolen.
They drive away the orphan's donkey
    and take the widow's ox in pledge.
They thrust the needy from the path
    and force all the poor of the land into hiding (vv. 1–4).

While thieves and scoundrels flourish, Job says, the poor and defenseless suffer injustice and hardship:

Like wild donkeys in the desert,
    the poor go about their labor of foraging food;
    the wasteland provides food for their children.
They gather fodder in the fields
    and glean in the vineyards of the wicked.
Lacking clothes, they spend the night naked;
    they have nothing to cover themselves in the cold.

> They are drenched by mountain rains
>> and hug the rocks for lack of shelter.
> The fatherless child is snatched from the breast;
>> the infant of the poor is seized for a debt.
> Lacking clothes, they go about naked;
>> they carry the sheaves, but still go hungry.
> They crush olives among the terraces;
>> they tread the winepresses, yet suffer thirst.
> The groans of the dying rise from the city,
>> and the souls of the wounded cry out for help.
>> But God charges no one with wrongdoing (24:5–12).

The rich exploit the poor, Job says. They work for next to nothing in the fields and groves of wealthy oppressors. The children of the poor are stolen and sold into slavery. People are forced to work hard to produce wealth for the rich, yet they are never allowed to share in the wealth that their labor creates. Finally, as they lay dying, the poor and exploited cry out to God.

And God does nothing. He does not punish the oppressor. He does not avenge the oppressed.

This is a common complaint today. As a pastor, I often hear people say, "I've been mistreated, I've been oppressed, I've been abused, and I cry out to God, yet He doesn't answer. I don't know what's wrong with me, but God doesn't seem to listen to my prayers. He just ignores me."

Job goes on to describe how wicked people do their crimes in the dark, and God does nothing to shine a light on their sins:

> There are those who rebel against the light,
>> who do not know its ways
>> or stay in its paths.
> When daylight is gone, the murderer rises up
>> and kills the poor and needy;
>> in the night he steals forth like a thief.
> The eye of the adulterer watches for dusk;
>> he thinks, "No eye will see me,"
>> and he keeps his face concealed.
> In the dark, men break into houses,
>> but by day they shut themselves in;
>> they want nothing to do with the light.

For all of them, deep darkness is their morning;
>   they make friends with the terrors of darkness (24:13–17).

Is it true that the wicked never face God's justice? No. It may seem that way for a time. But Job concludes that God's justice is not denied; it is merely delayed. The wicked flourish now, but judgment is coming:

Yet they are foam on the surface of the water;
>   their portion of the land is cursed,
>   so that no one goes to the vineyards.
As heat and drought snatch away the melted snow,
>   so the grave snatches away those who have sinned.
The womb forgets them,
>   the worm feasts on them;
>   evil men are no longer remembered
>   but are broken like a tree.
They prey on the barren and childless woman,
>   and to the widow show no kindness.
But God drags away the mighty by his power;
>   though they become established, they have
>   no assurance of life.
He may let them rest in a feeling of security,
>   but his eyes are on their ways.
For a little while they are exalted, and then they are gone;
>   they are brought low and gathered up like all others;
>   they are cut off like heads of grain.
If this is not so, who can prove me false
>   and reduce my words to nothing? (24:18–25).

Job has asked two great questions that people ask in every generation: Why is God absent when we need Him? And why is He silent when He should speak and judge?

In answer to these questions, Job says that the wicked will not always prosper. They are like foam that floats on the surface of the water and soon dissolves away. The grave snatches them, and they pass out of memory. God takes them out of this life, and they must face Him at last.

The New Testament reveals why God delays in sending the wicked and the oppressors to their fate. Paul wrote, "Or do you show contempt for the riches of his kindness, tolerance and patience, not realizing that God's kindness leads you toward repentance?" (Romans 2:4). And Peter similarly wrote, "The Lord is not slow in keeping his promise, as some understand slowness. He is patient with you, not wanting anyone to perish, but everyone to come to repentance" (2 Peter 3:9).

If it seems that the wicked go unpunished, it's only because God withholds His hand, giving them a chance to repent. That is why God seems to delay. If He judged every sin the moment it was committed, who would escape judgment? I wouldn't, and neither would you.

YOU ARE NOT A "WORM"!

Next, in Job 25, we hear from Bildad the Shuhite—or, as I have dubbed him, Bildad the Brutal—once more. He is the final speaker in the third debate—a cold intellectual, a theorist who has his theology worked out to the last decimal point. He is unmoved by Job's appeals, just as he is unmoved by Job's pain. His comments are brief, consisting of two arguments we've heard before. First, Bildad tells us that God is all-powerful: "Dominion and awe belong to God; he establishes order in the heights of heaven" (25:2).

In other words, there is no point in fighting God. His power, wisdom, and might are more than a match for any man. What Bildad says is true, of course. What is not true is Bildad's suggestion that Job has opposed God. Like Job's other two friends, Bildad clings to his false premise, which is that Job is suffering because of hidden sin in his life. Bildad continues:

> Can his forces be numbered?
>> Upon whom does his light not rise?
> How then can a man be righteous before God?
>> How can one born of woman be pure?
> If even the moon is not bright
>> and the stars are not pure in his eyes,
> how much less man, who is but a maggot—
>> a son of man, who is only a worm! (25:3–6).

No fallen human being, born of the line of Adam, can ever be righteous before God. That much is true.

But Job never claimed to be sinless. He only claimed to be forgiven. Job had confessed his sin and made the sacrifices God demanded—sacrifices that pointed to the ultimate sacrifice of Jesus on the cross.

I have said that Bildad's second point—that no one is righteous before God—is true. But there is something about the way Bildad makes this point that is totally untrue. Bildad refers to a human being as the equivalent of a maggot or a worm. God's Word never demeans human beings in such terms. Yes, the Bible quotes Bildad's demeaning words, but God Himself never makes such a statement anywhere in Scripture.

God views us as creatures of worth and value, made in His own image, so precious that He would send His only Son to die in our place. God never treats us as maggots or worms, even when we are in the depths of our own sin and rebellion. When Bildad refers to human beings in such ugly terms, he reflects a narrow theology that does not fit the facts.

You are not a worm. You are a precious and lovely child of the King. That is your identity in the eyes of your loving Father.

THE GRAND PERHAPS

Job has finally had enough of his three "miserable comforters." In Job 26, he figuratively slams the door on them and stuffs his ears with cotton. They have their minds made up, and it's no use talking to them any more. Job responds to Bildad with heavy irony and utter finality:

> How you have helped the powerless!
>   How you have saved the arm that is feeble!
> What advice you have offered to one without wisdom!
>   And what great insight you have displayed!
> Who has helped you utter these words?
>   And whose spirit spoke from your mouth? (26:2–4).

These three men left their homes, traveled far, sat with Job in silence for seven days, and finally opened a lengthy dialogue with him. On some level, at least at first, they must have cared for him. They came to comfort him, but in the end, they judged, accused, and bullied him. They tried to get Job to admit to a laundry list of sins he never committed.

After Job told them that their diagnosis was wrong, that he had no hidden sin to confess, his friends became his enemies. His comforters became his tormentors. So his words drip with sarcasm as he says, "What a help you've been in my weakness! What great advice you've given me in my ignorance! Tell me, you three geniuses, who made you so smart?"

Though Job has every reason to resent these three "comforters," it will soon become clear that Job has much to learn from his trials and from his "miserable comforters." Oswald Chambers, author of *My Utmost for His Highest*, once observed that you can't make wine without crushing grapes. God can never bring forth the wine of maturity in our lives if we resist the fingers He uses to crush us. If we resist the crushing pressure He brings into our lives, our suffering becomes meaningless pain, no more. But if we cooperate with the pressure of suffering, then God can turn our suffering into a pleasing vintage of character and Christlike maturity.

Job doesn't see that God is using these three "miserable comforters" to bring forth His vintage in Job's life. Satan may have sent them, but God is using them for His purpose in Job's life. We have already seen the pain they've caused Job; soon, we will see the deepened faith and proven character God has produced in Job's life through the crushing pressure of their insensitive arguments and hurtful accusations.

After speaking sarcastically to his three "comforters," Job takes a more reverent tone in describing the power and wisdom of God:

> The dead are in deep anguish,
>> those beneath the waters and all that live in them.
> Death is naked before God;
>> Destruction lies uncovered.
> He spreads out the northern skies over empty space;
>> he suspends the earth over nothing.
> He wraps up the waters in his clouds,
>> yet the clouds do not burst under their weight.
> He covers the face of the full moon,
>> spreading his clouds over it.
> He marks out the horizon on the face of the waters
>> for a boundary between light and darkness.
> The pillars of the heavens quake,
>> aghast at his rebuke.
> By his power he churned up the sea;
>> by his wisdom he cut Rahab to pieces.
> By his breath the skies became fair;
>> his hand pierced the gliding serpent (26:5–13).

There is fascinating insight in these words of Job. In their debates, Job's three "comforters" have tried to terrify, intimidate, and humble Job by speaking of God's power and might, but Job shows that he truly appreciates God's greatness. The power of the Almighty, Job says, is manifested in the deep realm of the dead. It is manifested in the skies and among the clouds. The limitless might of God is manifested in the beauty of the sea, which stretches from horizon to horizon. It is manifested in space, in the heavens, and among the moon and stars.

Job shows an extraordinary level of understanding for a man of his times when he says that God "suspends the earth over nothing." The ancient Hebrew conception of the universe was that the world was a flat land mass supported on pillars that God had sunk into the depths of a vast ocean. It's unlikely that Job understood, as we do today, that the earth is a ball-shaped planet spinning in space around a sun that is part of the Milky Way galaxy. But on some level, God allowed Job to understand that the world was suspended over nothing, not supported on pillars. This knowledge only increased the awe and reverence that Job already had for God.

That is why Job, after describing the height, depth, width, and breadth of God's greatness, ultimately confesses that words are inadequate to convey a true sense of the Almighty's power and wisdom:

> And these are but the outer fringe of his works;
> how faint the whisper we hear of him!
> Who then can understand the thunder of
> his power? (Job 26:14).

There are mysteries of God that no human mind can plumb. We can catch a glimpse of His omnipotence and omniscience, but our theology can never fully grasp or contain Him. Our infinite God will never fit into the finite little box of human understanding.

I don't think Job had this understanding of God's greatness before he was forced to cling to God through his time of pain and loss. Job's sufferings have magnified his image of God. That is why we need to study the life of Job and learn from the sufferings he endured. Oswald Chambers observed:

> It is men like Job and the apostle Paul who bring us to the basis of things . . . We must get hold of the great souls, the men who have been hard hit and have gone to the basis of things, and whose experiences have been preserved for us by God, that we may know where we stand . . .

It is our Lord Himself, and men like Job in the Old Testament and Paul in the New, who give us the indication of where we are to look for the foundation of our faith when it is being shaken.

The poet Robert Browning once described how a young man, in the arrogance of his youth, once thought he had answered all of life's questions. He had worked out a philosophy in which he had no need of God. When this young man went to an old bishop and explained his view of life, the bishop replied that life has a way of breaking down our neat answers. Pain, suffering, loss, tragedy—these things crash into our lives and make a mess of our theological and philosophical niceties. The old bishop concluded:

> Just when we are safest, there's a sunset-touch,
> A fancy from a flower-bell, some one's death,
> A chorus-ending from Euripides—
> And that's enough for fifty hopes and fears
> As old and new at once as nature's self,
> To rap and knock and enter in our soul,
> Take hands and dance there, a fantastic ring,
> Round the ancient idol, on his base again—
> The grand Perhaps!
> —From *"Bishop Blougram's Apology"*

These are words that Job would well understand. He knows what it means to feel safe and secure, only to feel the sunset-touch of pain and loss, to discover that he has become a figure of epic suffering, like a character in a tragic Greek play by Euripides. He knows what it means to see all of the well-ordered theological concepts fall by the wayside.

Above all, Job is learning what it means to kneel in awestruck silence before the Grand Perhaps!

THE FOLLY OF SELF-DEFENSE

Polycarp of Smyrna was a Christian bishop in Asia Minor (modern-day Turkey). He lived in the second century and was discipled in the Christian faith by the apostle John himself. While in his late eighties, Polycarp had a vision of dying a martyr's death, burned at the stake.

A short time later, the authorities sent soldiers to arrest him. When Polycarp heard that soldiers were searching for him, he refused to flee. Saying, "The will of God be done," he went to meet the soldiers, spoke cordially to them, and had food provided for them. After partaking of Polycarp's hospitality, the soldiers led him away.

After his arrest, two government officials tried to free him by pushing him out of a moving carriage. Polycarp got up, dusted himself off, and followed the carriage on foot into the city. He went to the stadium where a number of Christians had already been martyred that day, torn apart and eaten by wild beasts for the entertainment of the crowd. As the bishop entered the stadium, he was recognized and hauled before the proconsul, who demanded that Polycarp renounce his faith and curse his Lord—or die.

"I have served the Lord Jesus Christ throughout my life," the bishop replied, "and He has never done me any harm. How can I curse my King, the One who saved me?"

The proconsul condemned Polycarp to be burned at the stake, just as he had foreseen in his vision.

When the wood was piled around the stake and ready to be torched, Polycarp removed his outer garments and shoes, and then walked calmly to the stake. An executioner approached him with hammer and nails, intending to nail the bishop's hands to the back of the stake to prevent his escape.

Polycarp said to the executioner, "Put those away. God, who has granted me His peace to endure the fire, will strengthen me to stand at the stake without flinching."

Several men took up torches as Polycarp prayed, "O Lord God, I bless you because you have granted me this day and this hour! I thank you that I am numbered among the martyrs who are privileged to drink the cup of Christ's sufferings. Receive me into Your presence this day!" When he finished his prayer, the woodpile was torched. Witnesses said that when Polycarp's body burned, the smoke smelled as sweet as frankincense.

Polycarp was a man who refused to defend himself against those who sought his blood. He refused to hide from the soldiers; he went out to them and turned himself over to them. He refused to accept the chance to escape. He refused to accept the proconsul's offer of life and freedom if he would renounce his faith and curse his Lord. Polycarp had no interest in defending himself. His one desire was to serve his Lord, whether through life or through a martyr's death.

As we come to Job 27–31, we find that while Job may be a godly man, upright and blameless, there is still an important lesson that God wants to teach him: Job doesn't need to defend himself against false accusations. In the next five chapters of the book of Job, he will learn to let God be his defender.

AN UNYIELDING STANCE

It is said that there are two kinds of people: those who have something to say, and those who have to say something. Job's three friends are the latter kind. They didn't really have much to say, but they had to say something, so they said the same thing over and over again. They kept the dialogue going, chapter after chapter, until it finally ground to a halt.

In Job 27 through 31, Job begins his last defense of himself. He opens with a statement of his resolve to stand fast to the end:

> As surely as God lives, who has denied me justice,
>   the Almighty, who has made me taste bitterness of soul,
> as long as I have life within me,
>   the breath of God in my nostrils,
> my lips will not speak wickedness,
>   and my tongue will utter no deceit.
> I will never admit you are in the right;
>   till I die, I will not deny my integrity.
> I will maintain my righteousness and never let go of it;
>   my conscience will not reproach me as long as I live (27:2–6).

Job's three friends have tried to uncover some sin in his life. He tells them, in effect, "I'll never say that you're right. I will not deny my integrity."

You have to admire the spirit of a man who is determined to tell the truth, even if it costs him everything. I'm reminded of that historic moment at the cathedral in Worms, Germany, when Martin Luther was called before the head of the Holy Roman Empire. All the nobles of the empire and princes of the Roman Catholic Church were on hand to see Luther answer the charge of heresy. On trial for his life, Luther stood his ground, saying,

> Unless I am shown by the testimony of Scripture and by evident reasoning, unless I am overcome by means of the scriptural passages that I have cited, and unless my conscience is taken captive by the words of God, I am neither able nor willing to revoke anything, since to act against one's conscience is neither safe nor honest. Here I stand; God help me, I cannot do otherwise, Amen!

Do you see a difference between the unyielding stance of Luther and the unyielding stance of Job? It's simply this: Luther was defending the Word of God; Job was defending himself. As we shall see throughout Job's final monologue, that is a crucial distinction. Job will defend himself with his dying breath. "I will maintain my righteousness and never let go of it," he says. "My conscience will not reproach me as long as I live."

In Job chapter 27, verses 7 through 13, Job warns these friends that if they are not careful, they may be guilty of a malicious accusation that will merit punishment from God. Under the law of Israel, if someone falsely charged someone else with a crime, the malicious accuser himself could receive the punishment for that crime. So Job says,

> May my enemies be like the wicked,
>   my adversaries like the unjust!
> For what hope has the godless when he is cut off,
>   when God takes away his life?
> Does God listen to his cry
>   when distress comes upon him?
> Will he find delight in the Almighty?
>   Will he call upon God at all times?
> I will teach you about the power of God;
>   the ways of the Almighty I will not conceal.

You have all seen this yourselves.
> Why then this meaningless talk? (Job 27:7–12).

Who are the "enemies" Job refers to here? His three friends!

In the rest of chapter 27, Job repeats the arguments his friends have used. They've told him that the wicked are always punished, so Job says, "Your own words will condemn you. If you have falsely accused me, you will be the ones who are punished!" He says,

> Here is the fate God allots to the wicked,
>> the heritage a ruthless man receives from the Almighty:
> However many his children, their fate is the sword;
>> his offspring will never have enough to eat.
> The plague will bury those who survive him,
>> and their widows will not weep for them.
> Though he heaps up silver like dust
>> and clothes like piles of clay,
> what he lays up the righteous will wear,
>> and the innocent will divide his silver.
> The house he builds is like a moth's cocoon,
>> like a hut made by a watchman.
> He lies down wealthy, but will do so no more;
>> when he opens his eyes, all is gone.
> Terrors overtake him like a flood;
>> a tempest snatches him away in the night.
> The east wind carries him off, and he is gone;
>> it sweeps him out of his place.
> It hurls itself against him without mercy
>> as he flees headlong from its power.
> It claps its hands in derision
>> and hisses him out of his place (vv. 13–23).

Here, Job turns the tables on his three accusers. They have warned him incessantly about the fate of evildoers. Now he warns them because of the evil they have done. He describes how their children will be killed by the sword; how they will heap up wealth and it will disappear in a day; how they will go to bed rich but wake up poor; how terrors will overtake them in a flood, and the east wind will destroy them, and so forth. His message to them: If you continue to be judgmental and hardhearted, accusing the innocent without evidence, you will share the fate of the wicked.

THE TREASURES OF WISDOM

Job 28 is one of the most beautiful chapters in the book. It is Job's meditation on his endless search for an explanation for his suffering, which he frames as a search for wisdom and understanding. The first eleven verses poetically picture the quest for wisdom as a search for hidden treasure:

> There is a mine for silver
> and a place where gold is refined.
> Iron is taken from the earth,
> and copper is smelted from ore.
> Man puts an end to the darkness;
> he searches the farthest recesses
> for ore in the blackest darkness.
> Far from where people dwell he cuts a shaft,
> in places forgotten by the foot of man;
> far from men he dangles and sways.
> The earth, from which food comes,
> is transformed below as by fire;
> sapphires come from its rocks,
> and its dust contains nuggets of gold.
> No bird of prey knows that hidden path,
> no falcon's eye has seen it.
> Proud beasts do not set foot on it,
> and no lion prowls there.
> Man's hand assaults the flinty rock
> and lays bare the roots of the mountains.
> He tunnels through the rock;
> his eyes see all its treasures.
> He searches the sources of the rivers
> and brings hidden things to light (vv. 1–11).

Though this book was written at the very dawn of civilization, its imagery suggests that mining practices have changed very little from Job's time until today. He alludes to the miner's need for light in the darkness in order to locate ore. Today, a miner wears a lamp on his helmet that "puts an end to darkness" in the mines.

Job also refers to the mineshafts men dig and to the scaffolding they set up on the side of a mountain so that the men can get into the mines and find the treasures hidden there. Men will brave great depths and great heights. They will push back the darkness in search of diamonds, rubies, and gold. That's what the search for wisdom is like—a daring and determined quest for hidden treasure.

Job speaks of the beasts and birds that are unaware of the hidden paths deep in the earth where men dig for treasure. Animals do not care about gold or jewels, but men risk their lives for riches. The riches of wisdom are far greater than the riches of the earth. Job continues:

> But where can wisdom be found?
>   Where does understanding dwell?
> Man does not comprehend its worth;
>   it cannot be found in the land of the living.
> The deep says, "It is not in me";
>   the sea says, "It is not with me."
> It cannot be bought with the finest gold,
>   nor can its price be weighed in silver.
> It cannot be bought with the gold of Ophir,
>   with precious onyx or sapphires.
> Neither gold nor crystal can compare with it,
>   nor can it be had for jewels of gold.
> Coral and jasper are not worthy of mention;
>   the price of wisdom is beyond rubies.
> The topaz of Cush cannot compare with it;
>   it cannot be bought with pure gold (Job 28:12–19).

Men search for gold, silver, and jewels, and they find them. But when men search for wisdom, they find it more elusive than treasure. Wisdom can't be found in the sea or purchased with gold. Wisdom is the hardest treasure of all to find—and the most valuable.

THE ANSWER TO THE RIDDLES OF LIFE

I once had dinner with a naval officer in San Diego. On our way into the officer's club, I noticed he walked with a cane. I later learned that he was suffering from cancer that had spread to the bones in his legs. This man had already lost two sons to cancer; both had died at age nineteen. And earlier that very week, he'd received word that his fourteen-year-old son had also been diagnosed with cancer.

My heart went out to this naval officer, who was suffering his own pain and grieving so many losses in his life, yet I also saw that his spirit was strong and triumphant. He never said a word of complaint about his circumstances; I learned these facts from others. But I couldn't help asking God, "Why do these things happen in the lives of godly, upright people?" That's one of the great riddles of life. It takes a lot of God-given wisdom to wrap our minds, hearts, and souls around these riddles.

Job says that wisdom is worth more than gold and precious stones. Why does he say that? Because Job has learned what true wisdom is. It's the answer to the riddles of life. And life is *riddled* with riddles, isn't it? Job's life has certainly been a baffling search for answers to questions such as *Why does God allow the innocent to suffer? Why is God silent when I need Him most? What is God's purpose for my pain and loss?*

Job doesn't know the answers to these riddles, but he believes that God has the answers he seeks. Job doesn't know what we know, that Satan has challenged God and God is answering this challenge through the life of Job. He doesn't know that God has a plan for strengthening Job's faith and, yes, for deepening Job's wisdom. Because Job doesn't have all of the information regarding his sufferings, he has many unanswered questions.

So Job seeks wisdom as other men seek gold and precious stones, because he knows that wisdom is the knowledge of the nature of things, the reasons behind all that happens in our lives. Wisdom is the ability to make good decisions in life so that everything works out right in the end. The world is full of strife, war, crime, abuse, hatred, racism, addiction, poverty, and neglect because there is so little wisdom in the world. Human beings may have the knowledge of how to build a hydrogen bomb, but they lack the wisdom needed to build a society of peace.

I once shared a speaking platform with Dr. Henry Brandt, the noted Christian psychologist. He told me that on one occasion, a couple came to see him about problems in their marriage. The husband was a professional negotiator who made his living mediating disputes and working out peaceful and mutually agreeable solutions. You might think that this man would have the negotiating skills to settle any dispute between himself and his wife.

But the day this couple came to see Dr. Brandt, they arrived in separate cars; they couldn't stand to be in the same vehicle with each other. On their arrival, they sat as far apart as they could, moving to opposite sides of the room. They spoke only to Dr. Brandt, and they either wouldn't or couldn't communicate directly with each other. The source of their dispute? They couldn't agree on what to do with their cat. These two intelligent, successful people had a desperate need for some wisdom.

Job says that human beings do not know the way to wisdom. This rare commodity called wisdom cannot be found in the land of the living. It cannot be bought at any price. If wisdom could be exchanged for gold or rubies, then the rich would be the happiest people on earth; yet the rich are frequently the most miserable.

Where, then, does wisdom come from? How can we find answers to life's riddles? Job says:

> God understands the way to it
>   and he alone knows where it dwells,
> for he views the ends of the earth
>   and sees everything under the heavens.
> When he established the force of the wind
>   and measured out the waters,
> when he made a decree for the rain
>   and a path for the thunderstorm,
> then he looked at wisdom and appraised it;
>   he confirmed it and tested it (Job 28:23–27).

There is great scientific wisdom running through the analogies Job uses. Previously, in Job 26:7, he said that God "suspends the earth over nothing," a scientifically accurate statement. Here he talks about God establishing the force of the winds, measuring out the waters, and directing the rain and thunderstorms. Today, scientists understand that winds do have mass, velocity, and energy that can be measured, that water has volume that can be measured, the storms have courses that can be charted and even predicted with a surprising degree of accuracy.

These facts were unknown to the nascent science of Job's day, yet they were somehow revealed to Job. God must have given Job an extra measure of wisdom during his time of trial and loss. He began to understand the wisdom that created the universe and ordered the workings of nature. Why did God give such wisdom to Job? What did Job do that made him receptive to the wisdom God wanted to give him? The answer is found in the next verse, where Job says: "And he [God] said to man, 'The fear of the Lord—that is wisdom, and to shun evil is understanding'" (Job 28:28).

The fear of the Lord is wisdom. This means that when a person stands before God in respectful, awed reverence for Him, trusting that He knows what He is doing—*that is the beginning of wisdom.*

We will never possess the answers to life's riddles until we possess what the Bible calls the fear of the Lord. This reverent fear of God is lived out through our obedience to Him. There is only one way we can begin to unravel the riddles of life, and that is through the wisdom God gives as a reward for our obedient fear and love for Him. That is what Job learned in his trials.

You'll recall that Job is the first of five Old Testament books called the Wisdom Books. The other four are Psalms, Proverbs, Ecclesiastes, and the Song of Solomon. Of the five Wisdom Books, the one we most think of as a source of wisdom is Proverbs, because that book condenses the wisdom of God into a series of concise, memorable sayings. It is interesting to note that the book of Proverbs opens with the same observation on wisdom that Job makes in Job 28:28. In Proverbs 1, King Solomon says that these proverbs are "for attaining wisdom and discipline; for understanding words of insight" (v. 2). Then he says, just as Job has said, "The fear of the LORD is the beginning of knowledge, but fools despise wisdom and discipline" (v. 7).

If you want to understand the riddles of life, then this is where you must begin—with the wisdom that comes from the fear of the Lord.

THE "GOOD OLD DAYS"

In the next three chapters, Job takes stock of his life. In Job 29, he begins by looking back at the "good old days"—what Cleopatra in Shakespeare's *Antony and Cleopatra* called "My salad days, when I was green in judgment." First, Job tells us of the blessings he enjoyed in his "salad days":

> How I long for the months gone by,
>   for the days when God watched over me,
> when his lamp shone upon my head
>   and by his light I walked through darkness!
> Oh, for the days when I was in my prime,
>   when God's intimate friendship blessed my house,
> when the Almighty was still with me
>   and my children were around me,

when my path was drenched with cream
 and the rock poured out for me streams of olive oil (29:2–6).

Job uses beautiful poetic language to describe those halcyon days when God smiled upon him. The lamp and the light speak of God's guidance. The cream and streams of olive oil speak of the richness of life—the pleasures and possessions Job once enjoyed. And, of course, Job speaks lovingly and long-ingly of his children, now mourned. He goes on to speak of the honor he received as a leader in his community:

When I went to the gate of the city
 and took my seat in the public square,
the young men saw me and stepped aside
 and the old men rose to their feet;
the chief men refrained from speaking
 and covered their mouths with their hands;
the voices of the nobles were hushed,
 and their tongues stuck to the roof of their mouths.
Whoever heard me spoke well of me,
 and those who saw me commended me,
because I rescued the poor who cried for help,
 and the fatherless who had none to assist him (Job 29:7–12).

Job goes on to describe all the good deeds he was able to do in those days, using his wealth to help the poor and downtrodden:

The man who was dying blessed me;
 I made the widow's heart sing.
I put on righteousness as my clothing;
 justice was my robe and my turban.
I was eyes to the blind
 and feet to the lame.
I was a father to the needy;
 I took up the case of the stranger.
I broke the fangs of the wicked
 and snatched the victims from their teeth (Job 29:13–17).

In those days, he had his life all planned out. He thought he would live out his life as he always had, multiplying his days and enjoying his life until, one day, he would die at peace in his own bed:

I thought, "I will die in my own house,
     my days as numerous as the grains of sand.
My roots will reach to the water,
     and the dew will lie all night on my branches.
My glory will remain fresh in me,
     the bow ever new in my hand" (Job 29:18–20).

Why shouldn't his life continue on as it always had? Here was Job, a godly man who was blessed by God and who used his riches to bless others. Why shouldn't God reward such a man with a long and peaceful life?

I have met many Christians who look at their lives just as Job once did. Their theology is limited, just as his once was. They think, "If I obey God and serve God and do what is right, then God will bless me and take care of me, and I will never be exposed to tragedy or catastrophe." That was Job's view, until his own experience exploded that idea to bits.

Job concludes this reflective section by describing his influence on others in his community:

Men listened to me expectantly,
     waiting in silence for my counsel.
After I had spoken, they spoke no more;
     my words fell gently on their ears.
They waited for me as for showers
     and drank in my words as the spring rain.
When I smiled at them, they scarcely believed it;
     the light of my face was precious to them.
I chose the way for them and sat as their chief;
     I dwelt as a king among his troops;
     I was like one who comforts mourners (Job 29:21–25).

In all of this wistful reflection and recollection of the past, we hear Job longing for the "good old days" to return.

THE HEAVIEST BURDEN OF ALL

In Job chapter 30, Job abruptly shifts to the other side of the ledger of his life. He moves from the halcyon past to the harsh and hurtful present. Whereas Job was once revered as a leader, a counselor, a chief, and even a king, he is now treated with abuse and disdain:

But now they mock me,
>   men younger than I,
whose fathers I would have disdained
>   to put with my sheep dogs.
Of what use was the strength of their hands to me,
>   since their vigor had gone from them?
Haggard from want and hunger,
>   they roamed the parched land
>   in desolate wastelands at night.
In the brush they gathered salt herbs,
>   and their food was the root of the broom tree.
They were banished from their fellow men,
>   shouted at as if they were thieves.
They were forced to live in the dry stream beds,
>   among the rocks and in holes in the ground.
They brayed among the bushes
>   and huddled in the undergrowth.
A base and nameless brood,
>   they were driven out of the land.
And now their sons mock me in song;
>   I have become a byword among them.
They detest me and keep their distance;
>   they do not hesitate to spit in my face (vv. 1–10).

Job goes on to say that God, who was once his defender, has left him defenseless before his enemies and vulnerable to their attacks:

Now that God has unstrung my bow and afflicted me,
>   they throw off restraint in my presence.
On my right the tribe attacks;
>   they lay snares for my feet,
>   they build their siege ramps against me.
They break up my road;
>   they succeed in destroying me—
>   without anyone's helping them.
They advance as through a gaping breach;
>   amid the ruins they come rolling in.
Terrors overwhelm me;
>   my dignity is driven away as by the wind,
>   my safety vanishes like a cloud (Job 30:11–15).

Next, Job describes the physical, emotional, and spiritual anguish of his suffering and loss:

And now my life cbbs away;
    days of suffering grip me.
Night pierces my bones;
    my gnawing pains never rest.
In his great power God becomes like clothing to me;
    he binds me like the neck of my garment.
He throws me into the mud,
    and I am reduced to dust and ashes (Job 30:16–19).

Finally, he describes the heaviest burden of all in this time of suffering: the silence of God.

I cry out to you, O God, but you do not answer;
    I stand up, but you merely look at me.
You turn on me ruthlessly;
    with the might of your hand you attack me.
You snatch me up and drive me before the wind;
    you toss me about in the storm.
I know you will bring me down to death,
    to the place appointed for all the living.
Surely no one lays a hand on a broken man
    when he cries for help in his distress.
Have I not wept for those in trouble?
    Has not my soul grieved for the poor?
Yet when I hoped for good, evil came;
    when I looked for light, then came darkness (Job 30:20–26).

Job feels persecuted by God. He loves and trusts in God, but he feels God has deliberately wounded him, and he can't understand why. So Job cries out as an earthquake victim would call out for help from beneath a heap of rubble. But God doesn't seem to hear his cries.

This is a problem most of us face in times of pressure and pain—the problem of unanswered prayer. This, Job says, is what hurts him the most: He cries out to the heavens, and the heavens are silent.

Job concludes this chapter with a lament on the misery of living:

The churning inside me never stops;
    days of suffering confront me.

I go about blackened, but not by the sun;
> I stand up in the assembly and cry for help.
I have become a brother of jackals,
> a companion of owls.
My skin grows black and peels;
> my body burns with fever.
My harp is tuned to mourning,
> and my flute to the sound of wailing (Job 30:27–31).

These are the words of a man who knows the depths of suffering and loss. He knows the sense of isolation and alienation a sufferer feels. He knows the gradual wasting of body and soul that takes place as he descends into the valley of the shadow of death.

JOB'S FINAL DEFENSE

In Job 31, Job makes a last attempt to understand the reasons for his suffering. He's still searching for wisdom. His theology has deepened and broadened through his time of suffering, but part of his thinking is still stuck in the mire of his old, limited theology. In reviewing his life, he continues to look for some sin that might account for his pain. He begins this review by considering the issue of lust and sexual sin:

I made a covenant with my eyes
> not to look lustfully at a girl.
For what is man's lot from God above,
> his heritage from the Almighty on high?
Is it not ruin for the wicked,
> disaster for those who do wrong?
Does he not see my ways
> and count my every step? (vv. 1–4).

Job knows that in order to keep himself pure before God, he must be careful about what he sees. So Job has made a covenant with his eyes. In order to properly control and channel his sexual urges, he has to watch his thought life. Those who allow lust to rule their lives are courting disaster, because God knows a man's ways and counts every step a man takes.

He goes on to challenge God or other people to inspect his life and see if his claims are true:

If I have walked in falsehood
    or my foot has hurried after deceit—
let God weigh me in honest scales
    and he will know that I am blameless—
if my steps have turned from the path,
    if my heart has been led by my eyes,
    or if my hands have been defiled,
then may others eat what I have sown,
    and may my crops be uprooted (Job 31:5–8).

Job claims to be innocent of the sin of fornication. If he speaks dishonestly, if his eyes have led his heart astray, then may he be judged and punished accordingly. Job is confident that God, who weighs a man's life with honest scales, will find him to be exactly as he claims—sexually pure and morally blameless. Just as he is innocent of fornication, he is also innocent of the sin of adultery:

If my heart has been enticed by a woman,
    or if I have lurked at my neighbor's door,
then may my wife grind another man's grain,
    and may other men sleep with her.
For that would have been shameful,
    a sin to be judged.
It is a fire that burns to Destruction;
    it would have uprooted my harvest (Job 31:9–12).

So Job claims to have been morally blameless. Moreover, he also claims to have been fair and compassionate toward his servants:

If I have denied justice to my menservants and maidservants
    when they had a grievance against me,
what will I do when God confronts me?
    What will I answer when called to account?
Did not he who made me in the womb make them?
    Did not the same one form us both within our mothers?
    (Job 31:13–15).

Notice that while Job has had many employees (servants) working for him, he does not see himself as superior to them. He believes that God made all people equal. He also knows that God will demand an accounting for the way he has treated the people in his employ.

He also says that he has been compassionate and generous toward the poor; he has defended the defenseless:

> If I have denied the desires of the poor
>   or let the eyes of the widow grow weary,
> if I have kept my bread to myself,
>   not sharing it with the fatherless—
> but from my youth I reared him as would a father,
>   and from my birth I guided the widow—
> if I have seen anyone perishing for lack of clothing,
>   or a needy man without a garment,
> and his heart did not bless me
>   for warming him with the fleece from my sheep,
> if I have raised my hand against the fatherless,
>   knowing that I had influence in court,
> then let my arm fall from the shoulder,
>   let it be broken off at the joint.
> For I dreaded destruction from God,
>   and for fear of his splendor I could not do such things (Job 31:16–23).

Though rich, Job has always put his trust in God, not in his riches and certainly not in idols:

> If I have put my trust in gold
>   or said to pure gold, "You are my security,"
> if I have rejoiced over my great wealth,
>   the fortune my hands had gained,
> if I have regarded the sun in its radiance
>   or the moon moving in splendor,
> so that my heart was secretly enticed
>   and my hand offered them a kiss of homage,
> then these also would be sins to be judged,
>   for I would have been unfaithful to God on high (Job 31:24–28).

Job refuses to put anything before God in his life, because to do so would be an act of unfaithfulness, an act of spiritual adultery.

He goes on to show a remarkably Christian attitude toward his enemies. Remember, this is the attitude of a man who lived centuries before Christ said, "Love your enemies" (Luke 6:27). Job says,

If I have rejoiced at my enemy's misfortune
    or gloated over the trouble that came to him—
I have not allowed my mouth to sin
    by invoking a curse against his life— (Job 31:29–30).

This is the spirit expressed by U.S. naval commander John Woodward Philip during the Spanish-American War of 1898. His battleship, the *Texas*, fired upon and destroyed a Spanish cruiser, the *Vizcaya*, in the bay of Santiago de Cuba. As the enemy ship burned and sank, the American sailors broke into cheers of victory. But Commander Philip rebuked and silenced his crew. "Don't cheer, boys," he said. "Those poor fellows are dying."

Job understood that it is a sin to gloat over the misfortune of others— even the misfortune of one's enemies.

He has also been generous with his hospitality:

If the men of my household have never said,
    "Who has not had his fill of Job's meat?"—
but no stranger had to spend the night in the street,
    for my door was always open to the traveler— (Job 31:31–32).

And he has never been a hypocrite, hiding secret sins:

If I have concealed my sin as men do,
    by hiding my guilt in my heart
because I so feared the crowd
    and so dreaded the contempt of the clans
    that I kept silent and would not go outside
(Oh, that I had someone to hear me!
    I sign now my defense—let the Almighty answer me;
let my accuser put his indictment in writing.
Surely I would wear it on my shoulder,
    I would put it on like a crown.
I would give him an account of my every step;
    like a prince I would approach him.)— (Job 31:33–37).

Finally, Job says that he has not abused his land. He has never polluted the environment:

If my land cries out against me
    and all its furrows are wet with tears,

> if I have devoured its yield without payment
>> or broken the spirit of its tenants,
> then let briers come up instead of wheat
>> and weeds instead of barley (Job 31:38–40).

Job didn't need the Environmental Protection Agency or the Sierra Club to force him to be a good environmentalist. He practiced conservation out of respect for God's creation. Being a good steward of the land was simply part of being a good servant of God, who made the land.

And with that, the words of Job are ended; he has nothing more to say. Baffled, wounded, tormented, defensive, yet unwilling to forsake God, Job at last falls silent.

THE GREATEST LESSON OF THE BOOK OF JOB

In his sufferings, Job has learned that God is greater than his theology. This is a truth we all need to learn. We tend to think we know how God will act in every situation. And the moment we have God neatly confined in our little theological box, *He does something surprising!*

God can't be contained by our theology. Though He is never inconsistent with His own nature and His own truth, He often seems to act apart from our ideas about Him. God is loving and good; He's never malicious. But His love sometimes takes forms we cannot understand.

Up to this point, Job has had faith in the benevolent rule of God. No matter how intense his pain and loss, Job has tremblingly held on to his faith in a God who wisely rules the universe. But even though Job has maintained his faith, he has asked deep, tough questions of God. If we are honest, we must confess that Job's questions are our questions.

It's no sin to question God. He welcomes our questions and is patient with our limitations. He understands our pain, and He never blames us or judges us when we cry out to Him. But there is one major flaw in the long monologue of Job that we have just studied: Job insists on defending himself.

If we are honest, we have to admit that we do the same. When we are afflicted, our first response is to justify ourselves: *Why should this happen to me? I haven't done anything to deserve this pain and suffering. I've been faithful to God. It's unfair that I should suffer this way!*

Looking at Job, we truly see ourselves. We realize that Job is not looking at his sufferings from God's point of view, and neither do we.

We have such a woefully inadequate understanding of the depths of our depravity, of how truly lost we are in our sins. As the prophet Jeremiah put it, "The heart is deceitful above all things and beyond cure. Who can understand it?" (Jeremiah 17:9). If there is one lesson that God often teaches us through times of trial, it is this: There are depths of sin within us that we are never fully aware of. Even when we think we are innocent, we are still sinners by birth and by our actions. As the apostle Paul has said: "I care very little if I am judged by you or by any human court; indeed, I do not even judge myself. My conscience is clear, but that does not make me innocent. It is the Lord who judges me" (1 Corinthians 4:3–4).

God knows us better than we know ourselves, and we continually need to gain *His* perspective on our sins.

And there is yet another truth that emerges from the story of Job, a subtle truth that God weaves into the pattern of this narrative. Though this truth is not underscored or highlighted, it is one of the most profound lessons of the story of Job. It is the answer to one of the deep riddles of life: Why is God often silent when we need Him most?

What does Job do from chapters 27 through 31? He defends himself. He vindicates himself. He protests his own innocence.

And that is why God is silent.

Why doesn't God answer Job's questions? Because Job isn't ready to listen. As long as Job defends himself, God cannot defend him.

And as long as Job stands on the ground of his own righteousness, God remains silent. In fact, God does not utter a single word to Job until several chapters after we read that Job's words are ended in Job 31:40.

What is true of Job's life is true of ours as well. As long as you insist on justifying yourself, God will not justify you. That is why Jesus begins the Sermon on the Mount by saying, "Blessed are the poor in spirit, for theirs is the kingdom of heaven" (Matthew 5:3). In other words, blessed are those who are bankrupt in themselves, who have come to the end of themselves, who have stopped defending themselves. When they let go of the need to vindicate themselves, God will rise to take up their cause.

That is what we will soon see in the book of Job: God will begin to speak on Job's behalf. In the New Testament epistle of 1 John we read, "If anybody does sin, we have one who speaks to the Father in our defense—Jesus Christ,

the Righteous One" (1 John 2:1). The Lord is our lawyer, our defense counselor. He will vindicate us if we will let Him speak.

But as long as we insist on justifying ourselves and explaining ourselves
and proclaiming our own innocence, He has nothing to say. This is probably
the greatest lesson we can glean from the book of Job—and the hardest for us
to learn. When the words of Job are ended, when the words of Ray Stedman
are ended, when your own words are ended, then our Defender can rise before
the court of heaven and present an airtight case, resulting in our acquittal on
all charges.

The silence of God ends when our silence begins.

YOUTH ANSWERS AGE

Job 32–33

John Wesley was an eighteenth-century English preacher who, along with his brother Charles, co-founded the Methodist movement. In his later years John Wesley observed, "When I was young I was sure of everything. Now, having been mistaken a thousand times, I'm not half so sure of most things as I was before. At present, I am hardly sure of anything but what God has revealed to me."

That is an appropriate statement to bear in mind as we come to Job 32 and 33. At the end of Job 31, we come to a break in the narrative. Job has just finished a long and impassioned defense of himself, and then the text tells us, "The words of Job are ended" (31:40). At this point, the book of Job takes an unexpected turn. Beginning with chapter 32, a new voice intrudes into the narrative—the voice of a young man named Elihu:

> So these three men stopped answering Job, because he was righteous in his own eyes. But Elihu son of Barakel the Buzite, of the family of Ram, became very angry with Job for justifying himself rather than God. He was also angry with the three friends, because they had found no way to refute Job, and yet had condemned him. Now Elihu had waited before speaking to Job because they were older than he. But when he saw that the three men had nothing more to say, his anger was aroused (vv. 1–5).

In these first five verses, we learn a number of details that haven't previously been revealed. Up to this point, you might have pictured this long debate as involving only four participants: Job and his three "comforters." There has been no mention of other people being present. It is only here, at the beginning of Job 32, that we learn that there was at least one other person on hand—Elihu. Though we aren't told how many others were present, it is possible that there was a crowd of onlookers listening to this exchange between Job and his three friends. Elihu may have been one young man in a crowd of dozens or even hundreds of spectators to this drama. The text doesn't tell us.

Who is this young man, Elihu? Why does he speak at this moment?

ELIHU—A MISUNDERSTOOD YOUNG MAN

The name *Elihu* means "My God Is He." Elihu is the son of Barakel (a name that means "God blesses"). Barakel was a Buzite—a citizen of the land of Buz. At the beginning of the book of Job, we saw that Job lived in the land of Uz. The lands of Uz and Buz were named for two brothers who lived in the time of Abraham (see Genesis 22:21).

We know that Elihu was young; he had kept his peace throughout the prior discussion because Job and the other three men "were older than he." Also, Elihu later says, "I am young in years." We also know that Elihu was angry. He was not only angry with Job for defending himself, but he was angry with Eliphaz, Bildad, and Zophar because they had condemned Job without evidence.

Some people have taken Elihu's anger as proof that the young man was rash, impulsive, and quick-tempered, but the text doesn't support such a con- clusion. After all, Elihu has listened quietly and patiently throughout this long debate, which has taken place over a period of hours or even days. Elihu waits for a lull in the conversation before speaking. Only after Job and his three "comforters" fall silent does Elihu stand and speak. Despite the anger he feels, the words of Elihu are courteous and considerate:

> I am young in years,
>   and you are old;
> that is why I was fearful,
>   not daring to tell you what I know.
> I thought, "Age should speak;
>   advanced years should teach wisdom."
> But it is the spirit in a man,
>   the breath of the Almighty, that gives him understanding.
> It is not only the old who are wise,
>   not only the aged who understand what is right.
> Therefore I say: Listen to me;
>   I too will tell you what I know (Job 32:6–10).

Bible commentators differ on how to view Elihu. Some regard him as a brash young man, full of the arrogance of youth. Some think that Elihu adds nothing to the conversation but merely repeats the arguments of Job's three "comforters." Still others dismiss Elihu's words as a meaningless interruption, noting that God, when He enters the discussion at the end of the book, seems to take no notice of Elihu and his argument at all.

I believe all of these views are mistaken. I don't see Elihu as arrogant or impulsive. His message is distinctly different from that of the three "comforters" in several important respects. And I am convinced that Elihu's argument expresses the very core theme of the book of Job. Let me share with you four important facts about Elihu that students of this book often miss. These four facts tell us much about this young man and the importance of his message:

(1) *God does not rebuke Elihu.* At the end of the book of Job, God rebukes Job's three friends for their folly in all the things they said to Job:

> After the LORD had said these things to Job, he said to Eliphaz the Temanite, "I am angry with you and your two friends, because you have not spoken of me what is right, as my servant Job has. So now take seven bulls and seven rams and go to my servant Job and sacrifice a burnt offering for yourselves. My servant Job will pray for you, and I will accept his prayer and not deal with you according to your folly. You have not spoken of me what is right, as my servant Job has." So Eliphaz the Temanite, Bildad the Shuhite and Zophar the Naamathite did what the LORD told them; and the LORD accepted Job's prayer (42:7–9).

God tells Job's three friends that He is angry with them for speaking falsely of Him. He tells them to offer a sacrifice and have Job pray for them. But God never addresses such a command to Elihu. Why not? Because Elihu is not guilty of speaking falsely of God, as Job's three "comforters" are. God is not angry with Elihu because Elihu spoke rightly.

(2) *Elihu's message occupies a prominent place in the drama.* He speaks for five chapters. Clearly, this is one of the major discourses in the book. If Elihu had spoken falsely at such length, God would have surely included him in the command to offer sacrifices and ask Job to pray for him. The fact that God does not condemn Elihu's message seems to be a tacit endorsement. I believe God approves of what Elihu says, and He approves of the courteous and compassionate spirit in which Elihu speaks.

(3) *Unlike Job's three "comforters," Elihu is sensitive to Job's suffering.* Though Elihu has strong feelings and though he is described as being angry, he controls his emotions and speaks with courtesy and sensitivity to Job. The three friends were caustic and sarcastic and seemed to have no empathy at all for the suffering Job was going through.

(4) *Unlike Job's three "comforters," Elihu claims to speak from revelation, not from age and experience.* This, I believe, is the most important distinctive that separates Elihu from the other three men. I'm reminded of those words of

John Wesley that I cited at the beginning of this chapter: "At present, I am hardly sure of anything but what God has revealed to me." That is Elihu's position. He says:

> But it is the spirit in a man,
> > the breath of the Almighty, that gives him understanding.
> It is not only the old who are wise,
> > not only the aged who understand what is right (Job 32:8–9).

We often assume that age automatically produces wisdom, but this is not necessarily the case. True, experience has a tendency to make us wise. But at the same time, we know young people who are wise beyond their years, and we know old people who are unbelievably foolish. Age is not necessarily a guarantee of wisdom. We who have been "young" for many decades like to think that it is our years and our gray hair that have made us wise, but the truly wise know this isn't so.

In fact, one of the most profound truths to emerge from our study of Job is the fact that *wisdom is something only God can give*. And God can give wisdom to the young as well as to the old.

We can start at any age to show God the reverence, love, and obedience He is due, which the Bible calls "the fear of God." The Bible further tells us that the fear of God is the beginning of wisdom. So if we have true reverence for God and we speak from the wisdom God has given us, then we can be truly wise, regardless of our calendar age.

AN OLD TESTAMENT VERSION OF JOHN THE BAPTIST

I'm reminded of a schoolteacher who was turned down for a promotion. She was upset that a younger teacher, with only three years' experience, was being promoted instead. So she protested to the principal, "I've had twenty-five years' experience, and she's had only three! Why was I passed over in favor of a less experienced teacher?"

"I have to disagree with you," the principal said. "Every year, the other teacher's work improved. Your work hasn't improved in all the time I've been observing you. So I don't agree that you've had twenty-five years' experience. You've had one year's experience twenty-five times."

That principal is right. It's quite possible to go through life, repeating the same way of thinking over and over again, never growing or changing or learning wisdom. That is the point Elihu makes. It's not being old that makes us wise. It is the Spirit of the Almighty who teaches us wisdom.

I believe Elihu plays a vitally important role in this story. God uses Elihu to answer Job's cry for an explanation of his suffering. Throughout Job's trial of pain and loss, God has been silent. Job has cried out for help, and no answer has been given. But God often chooses a surprising and unexpected way to answer our prayers. I believe Elihu delivers God's reply to Job, and he does so in a way that Job does not expect.

You may recall how earlier in the book Job cries out for a mediator between himself and God. He said, "If only there were someone to arbitrate between us, to lay his hand upon us both, someone to remove God's rod from me, so that his terror would frighten me no more" (9:33–34). For a while, it seems that God does not answer Job's cry.

But then Elihu stands and speaks. I'm not saying that Elihu is the mediator Job prays for. Rather, I believe Elihu is a witness who points to the coming Mediator—an Old Testament version of John the Baptist. He's a voice in the wilderness, bearing witness to the Mediator who will bridge the gap between God and humanity.

Read the words of Elihu with care. At first glance, you may think that Elihu sounds very much like Job's three "comforters." You may think he is speaking to Job in an accusing manner, just as the other three men did. But if you read very attentively, you will see that by the end of Elihu's discourse, his words sound very similar to the words spoken a short time later by the voice of God. I believe Elihu is truly speaking words given him by the Spirit of God. Job wanted to hear the message of God, and now at last he hears it from the lips of this wise and godly young man, Elihu.

COMPELLED BY THE SPIRIT

Having introduced himself and asking to be heard, Elihu proceeds to tell Job and the other three men why he has risen to speak:

> I waited while you spoke,
> I listened to your reasoning;
> while you were searching for words,
> I gave you my full attention.
> But not one of you has proved Job wrong;
> none of you has answered his arguments.

Do not say, "We have found wisdom;
　　　let God refute him, not man."
But Job has not marshaled his words against me,
　　　and I will not answer him with your arguments (Job 32:11–14).

Then, speaking of Job's three friends, Elihu says,

They are dismayed and have no more to say;
　　　words have failed them.
Must I wait, now that they are silent,
　　　now that they stand there with no reply? (Job 32:15–16).

Elihu's words are candid, but his tone is courteous as he explains why he feels compelled to speak:

I too will have my say;
　　　I too will tell what I know.
For I am full of words,
　　　and the spirit within me compels me;
inside I am like bottled-up wine,
　　　like new wineskins ready to burst (Job 32:17–19).

Elihu says he feels compelled to speak by "the spirit within me." I believe he uses the word *spirit* in the same way he used it earlier, in verse 8, referring to "the breath of the Almighty," the Spirit of God. He is saying that he speaks according to the urging of God Himself.

Elihu continues:

I will show partiality to no one,
　　　nor will I flatter any man;
for if I were skilled in flattery,
　　　my Maker would soon take me away (Job 32:21–22).

Elihu wanted his hearers to know that he had no intention of showing any favor or disfavor, nor was he seeking anyone's favor. He wanted only to speak according to the will of God, his Maker.

A REFRESHING DIFFERENCE IN TONE

In Job 33, Elihu invites Job to participate in a dialogue with him:

But now, Job, listen to my words;
　　　pay attention to everything I say.

I am about to open my mouth;
> my words are on the tip of my tongue.
My words come from an upright heart;
> my lips sincerely speak what I know (vv. 1–3).

Here, Elihu promises to speak only sincere, honest words. He is not speaking to flatter or condemn. He is not speaking out of mere human experience. He is speaking the words that God has given him, words that come from a humble and upright heart.

The Spirit of God has made me;
> the breath of the Almighty gives me life.
Answer me then, if you can;
> prepare yourself and confront me.
I am just like you before God;
> I too have been taken from clay.
No fear of me should alarm you,
> nor should my hand be heavy upon you (Job 33:4–7).

What a refreshing difference in tone from the approach of the other three men! This young man Elihu says, in effect, "I will speak my peace, and you may answer me and even confront me. I'm just a man like you, made by the same Maker as you. What I say has come from what God has taught me. But you don't have to fear that I will be harsh with you, as those other three men have been. I'm not going to accuse you of sin. I'm not going to browbeat you or harangue you. I'm just going to speak as the Spirit of God leads me to speak, no more, no less."

Next, Elihu analyzes Job's view of God:

But you have said in my hearing—
> I heard the very words—
"I am pure and without sin;
> I am clean and free from guilt.
Yet God has found fault with me;
> he considers me his enemy.
He fastens my feet in shackles;
> he keeps close watch on all my paths" (Job 33:8–11).

Though Job is a godly man, his view of God has been in error throughout this book. Like his three friends, Job has demonstrated a narrow, limited theology that does not leave room for the fact that God's ways are not our ways.

God's thoughts transcend the normal thinking of humanity. Instead of trying to see life from God's perspective, our natural tendency is to view God—and even judge God—according to our own human standards, our own limited perspective.

According to Elihu, Job sees God as capricious. Job has come to suspect that God acts without good reason and even according to changeable moods, just as human beings do. We are quick to project our own fallen self-image onto God and think, "God acts the way we do. He gets cranky and unreasonable, just as we do."

So Elihu summarizes all that Job has been saying, how God has wounded Job without reason and treated him as an enemy. To Job's flawed attitude, Elihu offers this rebuke: "But I tell you, in this you are not right, for God is greater than man" (Job 33:12).

That is what we must always remember about God: His understanding is infinitely greater than ours. His plans and purposes are far deeper than our own. It is never right to lay a charge of capriciousness against God. Behind every act of God is a loving heart, and He always acts in accordance with His loving nature. When we fail to acknowledge His wisdom and His love, it is we who are in error, not God.

This is the argument of the Bible from beginning to end. For example, in his letters to the Romans, Paul writes, "But who are you, O man, to talk back to God?" (Romans 9:20). We are fallen creatures with limited understanding. We don't know the facts as God knows them. How, then, can we challenge the Creator who made us? With these few words—"God is greater than man"—Elihu lays this all to rest.

Then he addresses Job's problem with the silence of God:

Why do you complain to him
     that he answers none of man's words?
For God does speak—now one way, now another—
     though man may not perceive it (Job 33:13–14).

Often we say God hasn't answered our prayers because we prayed ten minutes ago or ten hours ago or ten days ago, and the answer we expected hasn't arrived. At other times, we say God hasn't answered our prayers because the answer that came was not the one we hoped for. God answered, but not according to *our* wishes and *our* timetable.

For some reason, we think God owes us an immediate answer, and He owes us an answer on our terms. But Elihu shows us a different perspective on prayer. He tells us that God always speaks, but sometimes we are deaf to His voice. We do not understand what He is truly saying to us.

GOD SPEAKS THROUGH OUR DREAMS AND OUR PAIN

Elihu then suggests two ways that God speaks to us. First, He speaks in dreams:

> In a dream, in a vision of the night,
>> when deep sleep falls on men
>> as they slumber in their beds,
> he may speak in their ears
>> and terrify them with warnings,
> to turn man from wrongdoing
>> and keep him from pride,
> to preserve his soul from the pit,
>> his life from perishing by the sword (Job 33:15–18).

Here is a profound statement of how God cares for human beings. Though people seem bent upon their own destruction, God is constantly trying to get through to us, to warn us, to keep our souls from the pit, to keep us from perishing by the sword. Even though His efforts to warn us may cause distress or pain, His goal is always to spare us from even greater pain, such as the loss of our eternal souls.

One of the ways God reaches out to us is by speaking to us in dreams. You may say, "You're not suggesting that I should analyze all of my dreams as if they are messages from God!" No, I'm not. Some of our dreams may well represent God speaking to us, but others are simply the result of eating cold pizza before bedtime!

Psychologists tell us that dreams are a way by which suppressed and denied truth percolates up into our consciousness. We all tend to deceive ourselves. We tend to push unpleasant truths out of sight and out of mind. But these unpleasant truths aren't really gone, they're just "swept under the rug" of our minds. These truths sometimes reappear before us in our dreams.

Sometimes these unpleasant realities take the form of warnings in which we see ourselves doing things that horrify us or make us ashamed. These are usually warnings that the potential for sin lurks within us. I believe God may use these dreams to speak to us by showing us truths that we suppress and hide from ourselves.

At other times God may speak to us more directly through our dreams. We see examples of such dreams in both the Old and New Testaments. Men like Joseph, Daniel, and Ezekiel were able to understand much of what God was saying to them through their dreams.

Second, Elihu says God speaks to us through our pain:

> Or a man may be chastened on a bed of pain
>   with constant distress in his bones,
> so that his very being finds food repulsive
>   and his soul loathes the choicest meal.
> His flesh wastes away to nothing,
>   and his bones, once hidden, now stick out.
> His soul draws near to the pit,
>   and his life to the messengers of death (Job 33:19–22).

Notice how Elihu's argument in these verses describes all that Job has gone through. The young man is saying, "God is speaking to you, Job. You think He has been silent, but He has been speaking volumes to you. True, the pain and loss you suffered was not (as your three friends claimed) a punishment for hidden sin. You're right about that. But you're wrong in thinking that God is silent. He's speaking to you through your pain."

Pain has a way of getting our attention when nothing else will. An experience of suffering or loss can produce a profound change in our values, our priorities, and our outlook on life. C. S. Lewis put it this way in his book, *The Problem of Pain*:

> We can rest contentedly in our sins and in our stupidities, and anyone who has watched gluttons shoveling down the most exquisite foods as if they did not know what they were eating, will admit that we can ignore even pleasure. But pain insists upon being attended to. God whispers to us in our pleasures, speaks in our consciences, but shouts in our pains. It is his megaphone to rouse a deaf world.

Has God ever shouted at you through your pain? A man once said to me, "For most of my adult life, I thought my career was the most important thing in life. Then I had a heart attack. Believe me, God got my attention!" Sometimes God, out of the great love He has for us, must allow pain to enter our lives in order to rouse us out of our deafness. If there is no other way to get our attention, He is sometimes forced to shout to us in our pain.

THE GOSPEL ACCORDING TO ELIHU

Next, Elihu makes an astonishing prophetic statement:

> Yet if there is an angel [or messenger] on his side
>> as a mediator, one out of a thousand,
>> to tell a man what is right for him,
> to be gracious to him and say,
>> "Spare him from going down to the pit;
>> I have found a ransom for him"—
> then his flesh is renewed like a child's;
>> it is restored as in the days of his youth (Job 33:23–25).

According to the Amplified Bible, that word translated *angel* could also be translated *messenger*. In that day, long before people became accustomed to thinking in terms of millions of people or billions of tax dollars, the largest numbers imaginable were thousands. In Elihu's thinking, "one out of a thousand" was the equivalent of saying, "a unique individual, one who stands out as unique among an infinite number." The only mediator in history who stands out as totally unique, of course, is Jesus Christ, the Son of God.

So Elihu's message could be paraphrased this way: "Let's say a man is suffering and sorrowing. Suppose a special, unique, one-of-a-kind messenger comes alongside him. Suppose this messenger tells this suffering man how to live an upright life. What's more, suppose this messenger acts as a mediator between the suffering man and God. And suppose this messenger brings good news to this suffering man and says to God, 'Spare this man from eternal punishment; I have found a ransom for his soul.' What would be the result in that man's life? He would feel young, strengthened, and renewed like a child, like a youth. It would be as if he had been *born again!*"

Isn't that amazing? Elihu is describing exactly what happened when Jesus came into the world. Jesus is the unique messenger of the good news of the kingdom of heaven. He came to us and told us what is right for us and how to live an upright life. He acted as a mediator between a lost humanity and a righteous God. He stepped into our place and said, "Spare them from eternal punishment; I have found a ransom for them, and the ransom is my own blood." And the result? We are born again.

This passage is an amazing Old Testament foretaste of the New Testament gospel of the grace of God. It reminds us of Paul's triumphant statement when he reminds the suffering and persecuted Christians in Rome "we also rejoice in our sufferings, because we know that suffering produces perseverance; perseverance, character; and character, hope. And hope does not disappoint us, because God has poured out his love into our hearts by the Holy Spirit, whom he has given us" (Romans 5:3–5).

For those who are apart from God, suffering only produces bitterness, resentment, despair, and hopelessness. But for those whose lives have been touched by the Mediator whom God provides, suffering produces perseverance, character, and hope; in short, suffering can actually produce blessing in our lives. Why? Because we can see God's loving purpose in our times of suffering as He uses our pain and stress to train us, teach us, and prepare us for an eternity in glory with Him.

Throughout his trial of suffering, Job has experienced the emergence of a slow and certain light within his heart. Suffering has produced a depth of understanding in Job's life that he never had when his bank account was full, his body was healthy, and his life was easy and free from sorrow. Just look at the progressive growth in his understanding of God's ways:

In Job 9, he cried out for a mediator between himself and God. "If only there were someone to arbitrate between us," he said (v. 33). Later, in Job 16, he experienced this glimmer of insight: "Even now my witness is in heaven; my advocate is on high" (v. 19). Job was beginning to understand that the mediator he cried out for was already interceding on his behalf before God.

Then, in Job 19, Job came out clearly and said, "I know that my Redeemer lives, and that in the end he will stand upon the earth. And after my skin has been destroyed, yet in my flesh I will see God" (vv. 25–26). Job's understanding had deepened to the point where he understood that this Mediator and Redeemer would not only intercede with God in heaven but also would stand upon the earth and enable Job to experience a resurrection and eternal life.

Finally, in Job 23, we see that Job has gained a sense that God may actually have a purpose for his suffering. Job didn't know yet what that purpose might be, but he began to see that God was testing and refining Job's character. So he said of God, "But he knows the way that I take; when he has tested me, I will come forth as gold" (v. 10).

Through his sufferings, Job has gradually been learning the truth of the gospel. Though he lived centuries before the birth of Jesus Christ, Job was learning the truth of Jesus Christ: that He is our Mediator, our Advocate and Intercessor on high; that He is our Redeemer and the Door that leads to eternal life. Job was learning that through his sufferings his character was being refined like gold. Elihu now adds to Job's understanding, telling him that this Mediator brings good news of redemption, of freedom from eternal punishment, so that this old man Job can be renewed like a child, can be "born again."

That is the Gospel According to Elihu.

THE SILENCE OF JOB

Elihu goes on to tell Job that if he will pray to God, then he will find favor with God and be restored:

> He [the suffering man] prays to God and finds favor with him,
>> he sees God's face and shouts for joy;
>> he is restored by God to his righteous state.
> Then he comes to men and says,
>> "I sinned, and perverted what was right,
>> but I did not get what I deserved.
> He redeemed my soul from going down to the pit,
>> and I will live to enjoy the light."
> God does all these things to a man—
>> twice, even three times—
> to turn back his soul from the pit,
>> that the light of life may shine on him (Job 33:26–30).

How patient God is! He waits for us and allows us to struggle in our relationship with Him. He will bring us back to him again and again, as long as it takes for us to learn and understand His ways.

Next, Elihu appeals directly to Job:

> Pay attention, Job, and listen to me;
>> be silent, and I will speak.
> If you have anything to say, answer me;
>> speak up, for I want you to be cleared.
> But if not, then listen to me;
>> be silent, and I will teach you wisdom" (Job 33:31–33).

What is Job's answer to Elihu's appeal? Silence.

Job's silence indicates that he is finally ready to listen. He is willing to be taught wisdom by this young but Spirit-led man, Elihu. By his silence, Job shows he wants to learn what God seeks to teach him about the meaning of his sufferings.

Elihu's message continues.

YOUR GOD IS TOO SMALL

D r. Francis Schaeffer once said that the first argument of the gospel is not, as we often think, *Jesus died for your sins*. Nor is it, as we are sometimes told, *God loves you and has a wonderful plan for your life*. Dr. Schaeffer said that the first argument of the gospel is *God is there*. The Scriptures begin by informing us that there is a God, that He is wise and all-powerful, and He is in control of life.

This is one of the great lessons of the book of Job. The omnipotent God of the universe is also the Lord of our suffering. When we hurt, we may not sense His presence. We may not feel that He is listening or answering our prayers, but He is present even in our pain.

Elihu begins the next section of his monologue with an invitation to all who are listening: Listen to me, test my words, and judge whether I speak rightly or not.

> Hear my words, you wise men;
> > listen to me, you men of learning.
> For the ear tests words
> > as the tongue tastes food.
> Let us discern for ourselves what is right;
> > let us learn together what is good (Job 34:1–4).

Again and again, God invites us to examine and test His Word in a logical, reasonable way. Isaiah wrote:

> "Come now, let us reason together,"
> > says the LORD.
> "Though your sins are like scarlet,
> > they shall be as white as snow;
> > though they are red as crimson,
> > they shall be like wool" (Isaiah 1:18).

And the apostle Paul, writing to the Christians in Corinth, said of the message God had given him: "I speak to sensible people; judge for yourselves what I say" (1 Corinthians 10:15).

In the same way, Elihu invites everyone within the sound of his voice to judge the truth of what he was about to say regarding the power and wisdom of God.

ELIHU CONFRONTS JOB'S FLAWED VIEW OF GOD

Elihu begins by examining Job's problem with God:

> Job says, "I am innocent,
>   but God denies me justice.
> Although I am right,
>   I am considered a liar;
> although I am guiltless,
>   his arrow inflicts an incurable wound" (Job 34:5–6).

That is Job's first complaint against God in a nutshell. Job says, "I haven't done anything wrong. I'm innocent." Job implies, therefore, that God should bless him. But instead of blessing Job, God allows him to be afflicted. In other words, God denies Job justice by denying him the blessing he feels he has earned. That was Job's theology.

Many people have the notion that if they live a good life, God is *obligated* to reward them. So when life doesn't go the way they expect, they accuse God of being unjust. That was Job's complaint against God: "I am innocent, but God denies me justice."

Job protested the fact that this seeming injustice of God was compounded by the false accusations of three people he had thought of as friends: "Although I am right, I am considered a liar."

So Elihu says, "This is the key to your problem, Job. You think that when bad things happen to good people, it's because God is unjust and unfair." Then Elihu goes on to say:

> What man is like Job,
>   who drinks scorn like water?
> He keeps company with evildoers;
>   he associates with wicked men.
> For he says, "It profits a man nothing
>   when he tries to please God" (Job 34:7–9).

These are tough words for Elihu to level at Job. Remember that at the very beginning of his trial, after he had lost everything, Job responded with words of trust and faith: "Naked I came from my mother's womb, and naked I will depart. The LORD gave and the LORD has taken away; may the name of the LORD be praised" (Job 1:21).

Now Elihu says that Job's response to God is one of scorn, just like the attitude of the ungodly. Elihu sums up Job's thinking this way: "It profits a man nothing when he tries to please God." In other words, "What good does it do to behave myself? I might as well indulge in sin, because God doesn't reward you when you try to please Him."

Have you ever thought that way? Sometimes when we face trials and we see ungodly people prospering and enjoying life, we are tempted to make such complaints about God.

Remember, at the beginning of the book of Job, Satan declares that he is going to get Job to curse God to His face. There are two things Satan must do in order to make Job curse God. First, Satan must make Job distrust God and feel that God has mistreated him. Second, Satan must increase Job's resentment to the point where Job curses and rejects God. That is what Satan is after.

As we have followed this story, we have seen that Satan has, at times, succeeded in his first objective. He has gotten Job to feel that God is not fair and can't be trusted to act justly. But Satan has not succeeded in getting Job to reject God. At times, it seems that Job has come dangerously close to this point, but he has never crossed that fateful line.

In verses 7 through 9, Elihu warns Job of the dangerous place Job's doubts are leading him. Once a person begins to distrust God and view Him as unfair, that person is keeping company with the ungodly. Elihu doesn't want Job to cross that fatal boundary line. Job has not yet cursed God, and Elihu is warning Job to pull back from that perilous brink.

WHY GOD CANNOT BE UNFAIR

Next, Elihu takes up the truth of who God is and what He is truly like. He begins by saying that God cannot be unjust or unfair:

> So listen to me, you men of understanding.
> > Far be it from God to do evil,
> > from the Almighty to do wrong.

He repays a man for what he has done;
 he brings upon him what his conduct deserves.
It is unthinkable that God would do wrong,
 that the Almighty would pervert justice (Job 34:10–12).

Elihu says that God will judge the wicked and bless the righteous, no matter how long it takes. God may not balance the scales of justice immediately, He may not do so in a timeframe that suits you and me, but He will achieve justice in His own time and His own way. God is the author of all justice, so He cannot be unjust.

Earlier in the book of Job, the three friends argued that God is so mighty that no matter what He says, man simply has to take it. But Elihu is not saying that. He is saying that God always acts in accordance with His nature, a principle that is taught throughout the Old and New Testaments. For example, the apostle James tells us, "Every good and perfect gift is from above, coming down from the Father of the heavenly lights, who does not change like shifting shadows" (James 1:17–18).

There is no changeability in God. He is always true to His character. Our circumstances may be painful and trying at the moment, but if we cling to the truth that God's character and love are unchangeable, our faith will rescue us from the temptation Job faces here.

Next, Elihu argues that God, being infinite and all-wise, is not accountable to finite and limited human beings:

Who appointed him over the earth?
 Who put him in charge of the whole world?
If it were his intention
 and he withdrew his spirit and breath,
all mankind would perish together
 and man would return to the dust (Job 34:13–15).

Elihu asks, "What human authority appointed God to be in charge of everything?" In other words, to whom is God accountable for His decisions? No one! God was not appointed to rule the universe. He is sovereign because He *made* the universe. He is accountable to no one.

The godless say, "Leave me alone, God! I don't need You! I don't want You in my life!" But what if God answered the rebellious prayer of godless people? Their lives would collapse, and they would fall to dust. Every breath they take comes from God.

Next, Elihu points out that we derive our sense of justice from God Himself. He is the Author of justice; He teaches us what fairness is:

> If you have understanding, hear this;
>> listen to what I say.
> Can he who hates justice govern?
>> Will you condemn the just and mighty One?
> Is he not the One who says to kings, "You are worthless,"
>> and to nobles, "You are wicked,"
> who shows no partiality to princes
>> and does not favor the rich over the poor,
>> for they are all the work of his hands?
> They die in an instant, in the middle of the night;
>> the people are shaken and they pass away;
>> the mighty are removed without human hand (Job 34:16–20).

We human beings complain loudly about injustice, yet we tend to show partiality and flattery toward those who are in authority over us or those who can do favors for us. In other words, we behave unjustly, favoring the rich and powerful over the poor and powerless. God does not do that. As Elihu says here, God governs without partiality. He treats princes and paupers alike. How can human beings be more fair than God?

RIGHTEOUSNESS LIKE FILTHY RAGS

Elihu then makes the point that God does not need to conduct an inquiry or convene a jury trial in order to know a human heart. God sees everything we do and knows everything we think. Even the darkness cannot hide our sins from Him:

> His eyes are on the ways of men;
>> he sees their every step.
> There is no dark place, no deep shadow,
>> where evildoers can hide.
> God has no need to examine men further,
>> that they should come before him for judgment.
> Without inquiry he shatters the mighty
>> and sets up others in their place (Job 34:21–24).

Since God knows us completely, He judges us fairly. He is not account-able to us for the judgments He makes. We are accountable to Him for our deeds and thoughts. As the psalmist expressed it,

> O LORD, you have searched me
>> and you know me.
> You know when I sit and when I rise;
>> you perceive my thoughts from afar.
> You discern my going out and my lying down;
>> you are familiar with all my ways.
> Before a word is on my tongue
>> you know it completely, O LORD (Psalm 139:1–4).

God sees the depths of the heart; He understands the thoughts of the mind. We cannot say that God is unjust when He judges us, because He knows us more completely than we know ourselves. Elihu continues:

> Because he takes note of their deeds,
>> he overthrows them in the night and they are crushed.
> He punishes them for their wickedness
>> where everyone can see them,
> because they turned from following him
>> and had no regard for any of his ways.
> They caused the cry of the poor to come before him,
>> so that he heard the cry of the needy (Job 34:25–28).

Here we see the standard of performance that God righteously expects of human beings. God holds the world in His grasp, and people are accountable to Him for their actions, including how they treat other people. The wicked and unjust should not expect mercy from God. If they do not love God, respect God, and trust in God during this life, then they have rejected Him for all eternity, and God will judge them accordingly.

Elihu then asks how any mere human being can demand that God account for His actions and decisions:

> But if he remains silent, who can condemn him?
>> If he hides his face, who can see him?
> Yet he is over man and nation alike,
> to keep a godless man from ruling,
>> from laying snares for the people.

Suppose a man says to God,
> "I am guilty but will offend no more.
Teach me what I cannot see;
> if I have done wrong, I will not do so again."
Should God then reward you on your terms,
> when you refuse to repent?
You must decide, not I;
> so tell me what you know (Job 34:29–33).

God's decisions cannot be questioned because He is an absolute sovereign over individuals and nations, and He accepts no substitute for righteousness. People sometimes want to come to God on their own terms and invent their own salvation. They say, "I promise to be a better person. I promise to reform." But reform is not what God wants from us.

Our Lord is not in the business of reforming people. He's in the business of renewing people. He doesn't want to make us better; He wants to make us new. God desires our repentance and relationship, not reform. It's not enough to say to God, "I'm guilty, but I will try not to do that again." What God demands of us is unconditional surrender, completely giving up the right to run our own lives. That is what God seeks from us, and He will accept no other basis for a relationship with Him.

Elihu closes chapter 34 by addressing God's problem with Job:

Men of understanding declare,
> wise men who hear me say to me,
"Job speaks without knowledge;
> his words lack insight."
Oh, that Job might be tested to the utmost
> for answering like a wicked man!
To his sin he adds rebellion;
> scornfully he claps his hands among us
> and multiplies his words against God" (vv. 34–37).

Elihu is saying that Job speaks out of ignorance of the true nature and character of God. As a result, Job needs further testing. "Oh, that Job might be tested to the utmost," this young man says. Do you find those words appallingly insensitive? You might say, "After all Job has been through, how could Elihu say such a thing? How could he wish further testing on a man who has already suffered to the limits of human endurance?"

I don't believe Elihu is being cruel. He doesn't want to increase Job's agony. He only wants Job to be brought to the truth. So he says, in effect, "If suffering brings knowledge of God to a man, then let Job be tested until he no longer accuses God of injustice. Let Job be tested until he lets go of his own meager righteousness and clings only to the righteousness of God."

At the beginning of the book of Job, we see that Job is a godly and upright man who wants to serve God. The problem that emerges is that Job thinks he can achieve righteousness by his own efforts. The toughest lesson Job has to learn (and which we all have to learn) is that we can't even begin to recognize how much evil lurks in what we see as our own righteousness. As one Old Testament prophet said,

> All of us have become like one who is unclean,
>   and all our righteous acts are like filthy rags;
> we all shrivel up like a leaf,
>   and like the wind our sins sweep us away (Isaiah 64:6).

We think our own efforts are sufficient to make us acceptable to God. We think that if we obey the truth as we understand it, it is only fair that God reward us. We tend to think that God will grade us on a curve. "Sure, I know I'm a sinner," we say, "but on the whole, I'm a pretty good person."

One of the hardest lessons we have to learn in life is that in God's sight our righteousness truly is nothing more than filthy rags. When we read this in God's Word, it is not mere metaphor, not an overstated hyperbole—it is the literal truth. What we call righteousness or good deeds or innocence is foul and wretched in God's sight.

That is the wisdom Job is finally learning, as taught to him by this young wise man, Elihu. That is the wisdom expressed by the apostle Paul when he cried out, "What a wretched man I am! Who will rescue me from this body of death?" (Romans 7:24).

Our own good works can never save us because they are not truly good. They are the best we can do, but they are still wretched. We can never be declared righteous by God as a result of our own efforts. We can only become righteous by accepting the free gift of God's own righteousness by faith in Jesus Christ.

Remember how in Job 1 God initiated this contest involving Job? The testing of Job wasn't Satan's idea, but God's. It almost seems as if God were maneuvering Satan into achieving His own ends:

Then the LORD said to Satan, "Have you considered my servant Job? There is no one on earth like him; he is blameless and upright, a man who fears God and shuns evil."

"Does Job fear God for nothing?" Satan replied. "Have you not put a hedge around him and his household and everything he has? You have blessed the work of his hands, so that his flocks and herds are spread throughout the land. But stretch out your hand and strike everything he has, and he will surely curse you to your face."

The LORD said to Satan, "Very well, then, everything he has is in your hands, but on the man himself do not lay a finger."

Then Satan went out from the presence of the LORD (vv. 8–12).

Satan thinks he is going to prove God wrong by afflicting Job. The reality is that God has something to teach Job, and He is using Satan as an instrument to achieve something good in Job's life. Satan seeks to hurt Job, but God is using Satan to bring Job to a place of deeper maturity, understanding, and personal knowledge of God.

WHY GOD IS SOMETIMES SILENT

Next, Elihu answers Job's complaint against God in greater detail:

Do you think this is just?
  You say, "I will be cleared by God."
Yet you ask him, "What profit is it to me,
  and what do I gain by not sinning?"
I would like to reply to you
  and to your friends with you.
Look up at the heavens and see;
  gaze at the clouds so high above you.
If you sin, how does that affect him?
  If your sins are many, what does that do to him?
If you are righteous, what do you give to him,
  or what does he receive from your hand?
Your wickedness affects only a man like yourself,
  and your righteousness only the sons of men (Job 35:2–8).

Job has been saying, "I'm innocent, yet God lets me suffer. I might as well have lived like a sinner since God doesn't reward good behavior."

Elihu puts this complaint into proper perspective. He says, in effect, "Job, you seem to think you're doing God an enormous favor by living a good and upright life. But God isn't affected by your good deeds. You have nothing to offer God. He is as high above you as the clouds are above the earth. Whether you do good deeds or evil deeds, the only ones who are affected are other human beings, not God Himself. So don't think that when you suffer, God is acting out of spite toward you. He will never treat you unjustly. That is not His nature."

Elihu then explains why God sometimes appears indifferent toward us:

> Men cry out under a load of oppression;
>> they plead for relief from the arm of the powerful.
> But no one says, "Where is God my Maker,
>> who gives songs in the night,
> who teaches more to us than to the beasts of the earth
>> and makes us wiser than the birds of the air?"
> He does not answer when men cry out
>> because of the arrogance of the wicked (Job 35:9–12).

Why is God silent? People cry out to Him for help, but God knows that they are crying for relief, not necessarily the help they need. They want to be taken out of the pain of their circumstances, especially the painful consequences of their selfishness and sin. The moment the pain is removed, they will go right back to the selfishness and sin that caused their pain in the first place. So they cry out to God.

And God's answer is silence.

I believe this is why our prayers so often go unanswered. Our selfishness has produced agony in our lives, and we want to escape the penalty we have incurred. We are not concerned about God's will for our lives or righteousness and God's glory. We are only thinking, "It hurts! Make it stop!"

Next, Elihu points out another reason for God's silence toward Job:

> Indeed, God does not listen to their empty plea;
>> the Almighty pays no attention to it.
> How much less, then, will he listen
>> when you say that you do not see him,
> that your case is before him
>> and you must wait for him (Job 35:13–14).

Here, Elihu refers to Job's words about wanting to have a trial before God, how he would be his own defense attorney and prove he is in the right.

Elihu says, in effect, "How can you say that to God? Do you think God is really waiting for you to prove him wrong?" Elihu continues:

> And further, that his anger never punishes
>> and he does not take the least notice of wickedness.
> So Job opens his mouth with empty talk;
>> without knowledge he multiplies words" (Job 35:15–16).

This wise young man, Elihu, puts it as gently as he can to Job. He is "speaking the truth in love," as Paul says in Ephesians 4:15. Elihu says, "Job, the problem is that you want to prove God is wrong and you are right. How can God respond to that? He doesn't punish you for it. He's patient with you. But even though He is patient with you, the fact remains: You are speaking out of ignorance, not knowledge of the true nature of God."

THE GLORY OF GOD REVEALED

In Job 36 and 37, Elihu makes a powerful presentation about the glory of God. As he begins this section of his discourse, Elihu claims to speak with divine authority:

> Bear with me a little longer and I will show you
>> that there is more to be said in God's behalf.
> I get my knowledge from afar *[that is, from God]*;
>> I will ascribe justice to my Maker.
> Be assured that my words are not false;
>> one perfect in knowledge is with you (Job 36:2–4).

Elihu shows us that the place to start is with the mind of God. The Lord is right. His knowledge is infallible; therefore, anything that deviates from what He says is false. We should never start with our thoughts, our opinions, or our feelings. That is how we get into trouble. Our starting point must always be, "Let all men be liars; God's Word is true." It is not important that God agree with us, but that we agree with God.

Elihu makes a strong (some would say arrogant) statement when he says, "Be assured that my words are not false; one perfect in knowledge is with you" (Job 36:4). Some commentators think that Elihu brashly refers to himself as "one perfect in knowledge." That's a misinterpretation of Elihu's words. Who does Elihu mean? If you look ahead a few verses, to Job 37:16, you see that Elihu says, "Do you know how the clouds hang poised, those wonders of him who is perfect in knowledge?" Elihu is clearly speaking of God, not himself! So Elihu's claim here is that he is speaking with the authority and inspired knowledge of God.

Next, Elihu declares that God is both merciful and just:

> God is mighty, but does not despise men;
>   he is mighty, and firm in his purpose.
> He does not keep the wicked alive
>   but gives the afflicted their rights.
> He does not take his eyes off the righteous;
>   he enthrones them with kings
>   and exalts them forever.
> But if men are bound in chains,
>   held fast by cords of affliction,
> he tells them what they have done—
>   that they have sinned arrogantly.
> He makes them listen to correction
>   and commands them to repent of their evil.
> If they obey and serve him,
>   they will spend the rest of their days in prosperity
>   and their years in contentment.
> But if they do not listen,
>   they will perish by the sword
>   and die without knowledge.
> The godless in heart harbor resentment;
>   even when he fetters them, they do not cry for help.
> They die in their youth,
>   among male prostitutes of the shrines (Job 36:5–14).

God is merciful and just. Though He is mighty and omnipotent, He does not despise human beings for their weakness. God exalts the powerless and abases tyrants and oppressors. He instructs the human race in righteousness and urges people to repent of their sin. He warns evildoers and comforts the poor in heart. God takes no pleasure in the suffering of human beings, even when they bring suffering on themselves through sin, idolatry, and depraved practices.

Then Elihu makes a statement that has great bearing on the sufferings of Job and on your suffering and mine: "But those who suffer he delivers in their suffering; he speaks to them in their affliction" (Job 36:15).

I like the way the New American Standard Bible renders this verse because it is more literal and preserves the imagery of the original Hebrew: "He delivers the afflicted in their affliction, and opens their ear in time of oppression."

Notice that phrase: "He . . . opens their ear in time of oppression." God doesn't merely *speak* to us when we are afflicted. He actually uses our trials of suffering to *open our ears* so that we can hear what He is saying to us. Remember C. S. Lewis's words in *The Problem of Pain*: "God whispers to us in our pleasures, speaks in our consciences, but shouts in our pains. It is his megaphone to rouse a deaf world." If you are going through pain or trying circumstances right now, it may be that God is trying to open your ear and get your attention. He wants you to listen to what He is saying to you.

Next, Elihu warns Job against dangers that threaten his soul:

He [God] is wooing you from the jaws of distress
    to a spacious place free from restriction,
    to the comfort of your table laden with choice food.
But now you are laden with the judgment due the wicked;
    judgment and justice have taken hold of you.
Be careful that no one entices you by riches;
    do not let a large bribe turn you aside.
Would your wealth
    or even all your mighty efforts
    sustain you so you would not be in distress?
Do not long for the night,
    to drag people away from their homes.
Beware of turning to evil,
    which you seem to prefer to affliction (Job 36:16–21).

Elihu says, "Job, God is calling you out of the affliction you are in and into a place of comfort and refreshment. But in order to go where God is leading, you must give up this complaint you make against God that He is unjust. In your anguish, do not reject God by turning to sin. Don't lust for riches or bribes, because riches mean nothing in times of affliction. Don't commit sins or oppress people under the cover of darkness, because there is no sin that is hidden from God. You've said, with some bitterness, that living a good life hasn't helped you to win God's favor and blessing. That's a dangerous attitude because it could lead you into evil. Remain faithful to God, and you will find the place of refreshment He has prepared for you."

ELIHU'S GLORIOUS CONCLUSION

Elihu's magnificent conclusion is a hymn to the glory of God. It runs from Job 36:22 through the end of chapter 37. Here is the beginning of that passage:

> God is exalted in his power.
>   Who is a teacher like him?
> Who has prescribed his ways for him,
>   or said to him, "You have done wrong"?
> Remember to extol his work,
>   which men have praised in song.
> All mankind has seen it;
>   men gaze on it from afar.
> How great is God—beyond our understanding!
>   The number of his years is past finding out.
> He draws up the drops of water,
>   which distill as rain to the streams;
> the clouds pour down their moisture
>   and abundant showers fall on mankind.
> Who can understand how he spreads out the clouds,
>   how he thunders from his pavilion?
> See how he scatters his lightning about him,
>   bathing the depths of the sea.
> This is the way he governs the nations
>   and provides food in abundance.
> He fills his hands with lightning
>   and commands it to strike its mark.
> His thunder announces the coming storm;
>   even the cattle make known its approach (36:22–33).

The theme of this section is that God is great and His ways are beyond our understanding. He is omnipotent, eternal, and all wise. We human beings divide knowledge into categories and theories, but God, who spreads the clouds out like a blanket and holds lightning bolts in His hands, shatters our categories and confounds our theories.

Beginning with Job 37, Elihu presents a powerful description of a great electric storm. Some Bible commentators feel that this description is so eloquent and vivid that an actual storm may have broken as Elihu was speaking. Here is what Elihu says:

At this my heart pounds
> and leaps from its place.
Listen! Listen to the roar of his voice,
> to the rumbling that comes from his mouth.
He unleashes his lightning beneath the whole heaven
> and sends it to the ends of the earth.
After that comes the sound of his roar;
> he thunders with his majestic voice.
When his voice resounds,
> he holds nothing back.
God's voice thunders in marvelous ways;
> he does great things beyond our understanding.
He says to the snow, "Fall on the earth,"
> and to the rain shower, "Be a mighty downpour."
So that all men he has made may know his work,
> he stops every man from his labor.
The animals take cover;
> they remain in their dens.
The tempest comes out from its chamber,
> the cold from the driving winds.
The breath of God produces ice,
> and the broad waters become frozen.
He loads the clouds with moisture;
> he scatters his lightning through them.
At his direction they swirl around
> over the face of the whole earth
> to do whatever he commands them.
He brings the clouds to punish men,
> or to water his earth and show his love (vv. 1–13).

The power of the storm is Elihu's context for describing the power of God exhibited in nature. It is fascinating once again to notice how the book of Job—probably the most ancient book in the Bible—seems to anticipate today's scientific knowledge. Elihu speaks of how the clouds swirl over the face of the whole earth.

The next time you look at a satellite weather photo on TV, notice how the clouds form spiral-shaped swirls over the face of the earth. Those swirl patterns are not discernable from the ground, and Elihu never saw a satellite photo. So how did he know about the swirl patterns they form as seen from space? This detail, easily missed by the casual reader, suggests once again that the Spirit of God inspires Elihu's message.

Elihu continues:

> Listen to this, Job;
>   stop and consider God's wonders.
> Do you know how God controls the clouds
>   and makes his lightning flash?
> Do you know how the clouds hang poised,
>   those wonders of him who is perfect in knowledge?
> You who swelter in your clothes
>   when the land lies hushed under the south wind,
> can you join him in spreading out the skies,
>   hard as a mirror of cast bronze?
> Tell us what we should say to him;
>   we cannot draw up our case because of our darkness.
> Should he be told that I want to speak?
>   Would any man ask to be swallowed up?
> Now no one can look at the sun,
>   bright as it is in the skies
>   after the wind has swept them clean.
> Out of the north he comes in golden splendor;
>   God comes in awesome majesty.
> The Almighty is beyond our reach and exalted in power;
>   in his justice and great righteousness,
>   he does not oppress.
> Therefore, men revere him,
>   for does he not have regard for all the wise in heart? (vv. 14–24).

Here is a picture of the majesty of God. No human being can control the weather, the storm, or the lightning, but God does. No human can spread out the sky or hang the clouds in place, but God does. No human being can look directly at the sun without being blinded, yet God comes to us in golden splendor that surpasses the brilliance of the sun.

The Lord is exalted and glorious, and not merely because of His omnipotent power. He is exalted also by His absolute justice and righteousness. Though He could rule us as a tyrant, He chooses to rule us with love. Though we have nothing to offer Him, He has a tender and loving regard for those who fear Him.

Throughout the Bible we see that the only people who receive anything from God are those with a humble and contrite heart. If you think you have something to offer God, if you think He needs your achievements or your worthless-as-rags righteousness, then your God is too small. You haven't learned to recognize His majesty and glory. If you come to God in your own self-sufficiency, proud of the "good life" you have lived, then you have cut yourself off from true knowledge of God.

But if you come to Him empty-handed, humble, broken, teachable, and sorrowful for your sins, then God will lift you by His power and grace and restore you to service for Him. That is what Job will soon discover.

THE GOD OF NATURE

In 1950, an MGM motion picture was released called *The Next Voice You Hear*. In that movie, an American factory worker named Joe Smith and his pregnant wife are caught up in a global drama when the human race hears the voice of God broadcasting a series of messages over the radio. It's the story of how individual lives—and human society—are transformed when God speaks to humanity in an audible voice.

We have reached a similar point in the book of Job. Elihu's discourse has ended. As we turn to Job 38, we hear a new voice—a voice of power and authority. The next voice you hear will be the voice of God Himself, speaking directly to Job.

"WHERE WERE YOU, JOB?"

As we open Job 38, a strong storm whips up, and the voice of God sounds forth from the whirlwind:

> Then the LORD answered Job out of the storm. He said:
> "Who is this that darkens my counsel
>   with words without knowledge?
> Brace yourself like a man;
>   I will question you,
>   and you shall answer me (vv. 1–3).

Some Bible commentators have suggested that these words are addressed to Elihu. Even though the opening sentence states that "the Lord answered Job out of the storm," these commentators think that God may be saying to Job, "Who is this young man who has been speaking to you, Job, and darkening counsel by uttering ignorant words?" Later, however, Job clearly applies these words to himself, not Elihu, when he says to God:

You asked, "Who is this that obscures my counsel
    without knowledge?"
Surely I spoke of things I did not understand,
    things too wonderful for me to know (Job 42:3).

Clearly the Lord Jehovah was speaking about Job, not Elihu, when He demanded to know who had obscured the truth with ignorant words. God comes to Job and says that Job has uttered words that darkened the light of God's truth. I wonder how many times we have done the same thing. God tries to speak to us, but we darken the light of His message to us with ignorant words of complaint and rebellion against His will.

In the Lord's great discourse (chapters 38 through 41), we see God subjecting Job to a series of penetrating questions in the following three areas.

1. God's wisdom as displayed in the created universe (38:4–38)
2. God's care for the animal kingdom (38:39–39:30)
3. God's restraint of the forces of evil in the world (40:1–41:34)

As God's discourse begins, He challenges Job, saying, in other words, "Job, you claim you want a trial before Me. Well, let's examine your competence to stand trial. Let's see if you can answer some simple questions first." Then the Lord begins with the subject of the created universe, the earth and the heavens:

Where were you when I laid the earth's foundation?
    Tell me, if you understand.
Who marked off its dimensions? Surely you know!
    Who stretched a measuring line across it?
On what were its footings set,
    or who laid its cornerstone—
while the morning stars sang together
    and all the angels shouted for joy? (Job 38:4–7).

As God's great discourse to Job begins, we see Him subjecting this man to a series of penetrating questions. He asks Job about his knowledge of the earth and the heavens. The poetry in this section of the book of Job is magnificent. Here God poetically describes the earth as a structure built on a foundation with a cornerstone, its dimensions carefully marked off by a Master Architect. As the earth was being constructed, the stars sang as a choir and the angels rejoiced.

God speaks of setting limits for the sea, marking off the horizon where the sun will rise, and determining a place where the gates of death will stand. Then He challenges Job to explain these wonders. Notice how simply God puts these questions to Job. They are practically kindergarten-level questions, dealing with who, what, when, where, and why.

First, God asks questions about the origin of the earth. The origin of the universe has been a subject of scientific inquiry and philosophical debate for thousands of years, and the debate still rages to this day. Why? Because no human being was there to observe and record the event. Human beings may catch a glimpse of what the creation event was like, but we can only imagine it. We did not witness creation with our own eyes.

Job has some understanding of the nature of the universe. In Job 26:7, he made a startlingly accurate statement about the earth's place in space, saying that God "spreads out the northern skies over empty space; he suspends the earth over nothing." But how did God achieve such a feat? Job doesn't know. He has no answer when God asks him about the creation of the earth's foundations in Job 38:6–7.

According to the primitive science of Job's day, the earth was a flat disk that rested on pillars or on the backs of giant elephants or turtles. As we have seen, however, God enabled Job to catch a glimpse of physical reality so that he understood that the earth hangs upon nothing. Yet Job could not begin to understand *how* God could lay the cornerstone of the earth upon nothing at all—not even thin air.

If you ask a physicist or astronomer how God hung the earth upon nothing, you will get an answer about the principles of celestial mechanics, the mass and motion of celestial objects, and the force of gravity. If you ask what gravity is, the learned scientist will say, "Well, it's the force of attraction between massive particles. According to Einstein, mass causes space-time to be curved, and that produces a phenomenon we call gravity."

Scientists can describe how gravity works and can even compute the force of gravity with mathematical precision, but they can't tell us what gravity *is*. The word *gravity* is merely a label for a natural phenomenon. As believers, we know that this mysterious thing called gravity was conceived by the mind of God and that it was somehow linked to that tremendous event at the dawn of creation when the morning stars sang together and all of the angels shouted for joy.

MYSTERIES OF THE EARTH AND SEA

Next, God reminds Job of the most prominent feature on the earth, covering three-quarters of the earth's surface: the sea. God employs beautifully symbolic language, describing the oceans as a newborn baby:

> Who shut up the sea behind doors
>   when it burst forth from the womb,
> when I made the clouds its garment
>   and wrapped it in thick darkness,
> when I fixed limits for it
>   and set its doors and bars in place,
> when I said, "This far you may come and no farther;
>   here is where your proud waves halt"? (Job 38:8–11).

Water is made up of two elements, hydrogen and oxygen, which exist as invisible gases in our atmosphere. When these two elements combine, they form an abundant and life-sustaining liquid, water. What a dramatic moment it was when God caused these elements to merge in such quantities that an ocean was born, filling the seabeds of our world.

What did Job know of the birth of the oceans? Nothing.

God adds that He set boundaries on the waters. Because it is a liquid, water is one of the unstable and uncontrollable substances we know of, yet God commands the ocean to stay in its bed, and the beaches of sand hold it within its borders.

What did Job know of the boundaries that the oceans obey? Nothing.

Next, God examines Job regarding some of the secret processes of the earth and sky, of day and night:

> Have you ever given orders to the morning,
>   or shown the dawn its place,
> that it might take the earth by the edges
>   and shake the wicked out of it?
> The earth takes shape like clay under a seal;
>   its features stand out like those of a garment.
> The wicked are denied their light,
>   and their upraised arm is broken (Job 38:12–15).

Though the sun always rises in the east and sets in the west, it rises in a slightly different place every morning, changing according to the seasons. God is the one who causes the dawn to know its place.

What does Job know about the ordering of the cosmos or the placement of the dawn? Can Job control the sun so that it marks the seasons of the year? Of course not.

Notice the subtle imagery God uses when He says that the dawn takes the earth by the edges and shakes the wicked out of it. This metaphor reflects the idea that evildoers like to do their deeds in the dark of night. But when the dawn comes, the solar rays appear in the morning sky like the fingers of a hand, reaching out to grasp the earth by the edges and shake it. When the dawn arrives, the wicked—those who break into houses in the dead of night—are shaken out of the city by the light. They scurry to their dens to await the arrival of another night.

As the day progresses, the sun moves in its course across the heavens, altering the colors of the world. Shadows move and shift with the changing position of the sun, reshaping the scenery from hour to hour.

God asks Job, "Can you do this? Can you govern how light affects the world? Can you control the time of darkness, when the wicked come out in force? Can you summon forth the sun to expose the wicked and stop their evil deeds?" Of course not. Job has no such knowledge or power.

Then God speaks of the deep things of the earth and sea: "Have you journeyed to the springs of the sea or walked in the recesses of the deep?" (Job 38:16).

Today some daring adventurers have descended by bathysphere into the depths of the Marianas Trench, nearly seven miles below the surface of the South Pacific, east of the Philippines. Over in the North Atlantic, explorers have descended to the wreckage of the RMS *Titanic*, which sank in 1912 after colliding with an iceberg on her maiden voyage. But no human being can walk in the recesses of the deep, where the water exerts a bone-crushing pressure of up to fifteen thousand pounds per square inch. Most of the secrets of the deep are still hidden from us. We know almost as little about "liquid space" as we know of outer space.

Then God speaks of the great mystery of our mortality: "Have the gates of death been shown to you? Have you seen the gates of the shadow of death?" (Job 38:17).

What happens to us when we die? What lies beyond the gates of death? Science is unable to help us understand this mystery. Today we can learn a great deal about heaven and hell by reading the Bible, but there was no Bible in Job's day. Death is a mystery to Job.

When God asks Job what he knows of the deep things of the earth and sea or the deep mysteries of life and death, Job can only answer, "Nothing, Lord. Nothing at all."

If there is one question out of this entire list that we can answer today, it is the next one: "Have you comprehended the vast expanses of the earth? Tell me, if you know all this" (Job 38:18).

Job would have to answer no, but we can answer yes. We know that the earth has a surface area of roughly 196,940,400 square miles and that the diameter of the earth is roughly 7,913 miles. We have globes and maps of the earth with which we can locate every city, country, continent, island, lake, sea, and mountain on the planet. Today we can board a jet plane in London, have lunch in New York, then dinner in San Francisco while, of course, our baggage is winging its way to Buenos Aires.

But from Job's day to our own, how long has it taken to acquire this knowledge? Roughly four thousand years!

MYSTERIES OF LIGHT AND LIFE

Next, God turns Job's attention to mysteries of some of the commonplace phenomena we observe around us:

> What is the way to the abode of light?
>   And where does darkness reside?
> Can you take them to their places?
>   Do you know the paths to their dwellings?
> Surely you know, for you were already born!
>   You have lived so many years! (Job 38:19–21).

God heaps irony on Job. He asks, in effect, "Do you understand how light is produced?" Though modern physics can tell us much about the nature of light, there is still much to be learned. Again, Job must answer God's question, "No, I don't understand the origin of light."

Then God asks what Job knows about the weather:

> Have you entered the storehouses of the snow
>   or seen the storehouses of the hail,
> which I reserve for times of trouble,
>   for days of war and battle?
> What is the way to the place where the lightning is dispersed,

or the place where the east winds are scattered
> over the earth?
Who cuts a channel for the torrents of rain,
> and a path for the thunderstorm,
to water a land where no man lives,
> a desert with no one in it,
to satisfy a desolate wasteland
> and make it sprout with grass?
Does the rain have a father?
> Who fathers the drops of dew?
From whose womb comes the ice?
> Who gives birth to the frost from the heavens
when the waters become hard as stone,
> when the surface of the deep is frozen? (Job 38:22–30).

Notice that God tells Job that there are "storehouses" of snow and hail that He reserves for times of war. This is an intriguing verse. God may be suggesting that there is some secret hidden in ice and snow that might release tremendous power as a weapon of war. Or He may be saying that in the last days, when the entire world is engaged in battle and war, He will unleash storehouses of ice and snow that will strike at the armies under Satan's control.

There is some profound meaning in this verse that is unclear today, but which, I believe, may become a stark reality in the future. I have asked a number of scientists about the verse, and they shake their heads and say, "I can't tell you what that means. I just don't know."

Notice that God says He has reserved these storehouses of ice and snow "for times of trouble." In the Scriptures, that is almost always a reference to the last days, the terrible time of Jacob's trouble, also known as the great tribulation. God says, "I have hidden a terrible secret of war in the snow and hail, which will be revealed in the end times."

God goes on to examine other phenomena associated with storms: lightning, winds, torrents of rain, and thunder. He speaks about the way He takes care of the deserts. We think of the desert as a desolate wasteland, yet God causes the desert to grow flowers and grasses that human beings never see. God sees, and He finds it all good to behold. Human beings go about their busy lives, thinking only of their worries and busy schedules. But God cares for the deserts of the earth.

God then asks Job, "Does the rain have a father? Who fathers the drops of dew?" (Job 38:28). Science now tells us that rain is "fathered" in an amazing way. Before rain can form into droplets, there must be dust in the air. The raindrops form around these little specks of dust. That is why we can "seed" the clouds with certain substances to increase rainfall. We have learned the truth first revealed by God: The rain has a father.

Then God asks Job about the ice and frost. "From whose womb comes the ice? Who gives birth to the frost from the heavens when the waters become hard as stone, when the surface of the deep is frozen?" (Job 38:29–30). It's significant that God confronts Job with a question about ice and frost. When ice freezes, it does something that hardly any other substance does: It expands. Why does frozen water expand in volume when virtually every other substance contracts (becomes smaller in volume) when it freezes?

The answer has to do with the fact that water freezes in a crystalline structure because the hydrogen atoms in ice bond together in a lattice-like formation. The crystal lattice has an open shape that causes ice to expand; it also causes ice to be less dense than liquid water, which is why ice floats. If ice did not expand and float, fish and other living creatures could not live in frozen ponds. When ice forms on top of a pond, that layer of expanded (less dense) ice helps insulate the water below and keeps it from freezing solid. This property enables fish to live in frozen ponds.

The expansion of ice also helps make the soil more fertile. Rain and dew soak into the soil. When this moisture freezes, it forms ice crystals. These crystals expand, and in the process they break down hardened earth into a fine-grained soil that allows seeds to more easily sprout.

So when God asks what Job knows about ice, He is asking Job about one of the basic processes of life. Even so, Job is unable to answer the question.

MYSTERIES OF THE NIGHT SKY

Next, God points Job's attention heavenward:

> Can you bind the beautiful Pleiades?
>   Can you loose the cords of Orion?
> Can you bring forth the constellations in their seasons
>   or lead out the Bear with its cubs?
> Do you know the laws of the heavens?
>   Can you set up God's dominion over the earth? (Job 38:31–33).

From the beginning of time, human beings have believed that the stars have a mysterious effect on the earth. A strange pseudo-science called astrology is based on that belief—a belief that the stars rule the destinies of human beings. To this day, millions of people believe in astrology and consult their horoscopes (astrological forecasts) to see what the stars have planned for their lives that day.

When God speaks to Job of the stars and constellations, He is not talking about astrology, but astronomy, the truly scientific and evidence-based study of the stars and planets. God says, in effect, "Job, what do you know about the influence the stars seem to have upon the seasons? You've seen the Pleiades, that little circle of stars high in the heavens. How do those distant stars appear right on time every year, ushering in the spring? And what of Orion, the mighty hunter? You see him every December, striding across the winter skies. Can you cause the constellations to appear in their seasons?"

The answer, of course, is no. Job does not have the power to order the movements of the stars and constellations.

Then God asks, "Can you lead out the Bear with its cubs?" The Bear is what we call the Big Dipper. It points unerringly to the north. In Scripture, the north always symbolizes the dwelling place of God. Just as the stars appear to revolve around the north, so the whole universe seems to revolve around the throne of God. God asks Job if he understands the motion of the stars around the heavens. Job, of course, does not.

To this day the universe appears more strange and complex than ever, featuring an endless variety of objects that astronomers are just beginning to understand: neutron stars, pulsars, white dwarfs, brown dwarfs, red giants, protostars, collapsars, eclipsing binaries, magnetars, X-ray bursters, nebulae, globular clusters, spiral galaxies, ring galaxies, Seyfert galaxies, quasars, circumstellar matter, dark matter, and more. No wonder some astronomers refer to the universe as a "cosmic zoo." Job was amazed by the night sky he knew; imagine what he would think of a light-swallowing black hole or an exploding supernova.

Next, God asks Job what he knows about the atmospheric phenomena of the earth:

> Can you raise your voice to the clouds
>   and cover yourself with a flood of water?
> Do you send the lightning bolts on their way?
>   Do they report to you, "Here we are"?

Who endowed the heart with wisdom
　　or gave understanding to the mind?
Who has the wisdom to count the clouds?
　　Who can tip over the water jars of the heavens
when the dust becomes hard
　　and the clods of earth stick together? (Job 38:34–38).

Here God speaks of the inadequacy of human efforts to solve some of the
most fundamental problems of life. Even with all of our advanced science,
our satellite technology, and our understanding of climatology and weather
patterns, we cannot control the weather. We can't cause rain to fall when and
where we need it.

Job, in all honesty and humility, must confess before Almighty God that
he has no power to affect the weather. He does not even have sufficient knowledge to understand what causes changes in the weather.

GOD BLESSES THE BEASTS OF THE WILD

In the last three verses of Job 38 and all of Job 39, God speaks to Job of His
providential care for the animal world. He begins by saying that He supplies
food for the beasts of the wild:

Do you hunt the prey for the lioness
　　and satisfy the hunger of the lions
when they crouch in their dens
　　or lie in wait in a thicket?
Who provides food for the raven
　　when its young cry out to God
　　and wander about for lack of food? (Job 38:39–41).

What if God made humanity completely responsible for taking care of
the animal world? Our track record as care providers is not very good. Today,
a sixth of the world's population subsists on less than a dollar a day in wages.
Nearly two hundred million of the world's children under the age of five are
underweight and undernourished; twelve million of them die every year, usually of hunger-related causes.

We can't even feed and care for the human race, so how could we hope to
meet the needs of the animal world? In fact, the animal world is endangered

by human civilization. God preserves the species; it is humanity who wipes them out.

So God says to Job, "Would you be capable of caring for the animal kingdom?" The obvious answer is no. Job wouldn't know where to begin. No human being is capable of providing for the vast variety of species on this planet, yet God has done so for thousands of years.

God continues:

> Do you know when the mountain goats give birth?
>> Do you watch when the doe bears her fawn?
> Do you count the months till they bear?
>> Do you know the time they give birth?
> They crouch down and bring forth their young;
>> their labor pains are ended.
> Their young thrive and grow strong in the wilds;
>> they leave and do not return (Job 39:1–4).

The animals do not have hospitals, obstetricians, midwives, pharmaceuticals, painkillers, Lamaze techniques, or health insurance, yet God has made it possible for animals to give birth and nurture their young. God asks Job, "Do you watch over the animals as they multiply and replenish their species? Do you enable them to give birth in safety?" Of course Job can only shake his head in humility.

God continues:

> Who let the wild donkey go free?
>> Who untied his ropes?
> I gave him the wasteland as his home,
>> the salt flats as his habitat.
> He laughs at the commotion in the town;
>> he does not hear a driver's shout.
> He ranges the hills for his pasture
>> and searches for any green thing.
> Will the wild ox consent to serve you?
>> Will he stay by your manger at night?
> Can you hold him to the furrow with a harness?
>> Will he till the valleys behind you?
> Will you rely on him for his great strength?
>> Will you leave your heavy work to him?

Can you trust him to bring in your grain
    and gather it to your threshing floor? (Job 39:5–12).

Wild animals are driven by powerful instincts, and they will invariably do what they were made to do. Some animals are untamable and cannot be made to serve humanity, yet they manage to survive in the wild because of their natural instincts. Who gave them those instincts? Certainly Job did not. Only a wise and loving God could do that.

Next comes a humorous passage of Scripture. God says,

The wings of the ostrich flap joyfully,
but they cannot compare with the pinions
    and feathers of the stork.
She lays her eggs on the ground
    and lets them warm in the sand,
unmindful that a foot may crush them,
    that some wild animal may trample them.
She treats her young harshly, as if they were not hers;
    she cares not that her labor was in vain,
for God did not endow her with wisdom
    or give her a share of good sense.
Yet when she spreads her feathers to run,
    she laughs at horse and rider (Job 39:13–18).

I love the comical imagery of this passage! God speaks of the stupidity of the ostrich, and then He takes responsibility for the bird's stupidity. He says that He "did not endow her with wisdom or give her a share of good sense." An ostrich can outrun a horse and rider, yet she is so foolish that she walks off and leaves her eggs right out in the open. She does not take care of her young.

But God says, "I made her that way." The ostrich is one of many animals that show God's rich sense of humor.

Once while I was visiting Australia, I saw a duck-billed platypus, an animal that appears to be assembled from spare parts left over from creation. God makes some animals beautiful for their coloration, their stripes, their spots, their plumage, or their sculpted bodies. He makes other animals that are awe-inspiring in their fierce majesty. And He makes still others that are ridiculous and comical. Why? I believe God created a variety of animals to mirror back to us certain aspects of our humanity: our human beauty, our human nobility, our human frailty, and our human folly.

"I AM UNWORTHY!"

Next, God speaks poetically of the courage of one of the noblest of creatures, the horse:

> Do you give the horse his strength
> > or clothe his neck with a flowing mane?
> Do you make him leap like a locust,
> > striking terror with his proud snorting?
> He paws fiercely, rejoicing in his strength,
> > and charges into the fray.
> He laughs at fear, afraid of nothing;
> > he does not shy away from the sword.
> The quiver rattles against his side,
> > along with the flashing spear and lance.
> In frenzied excitement he eats up the ground;
> > he cannot stand still when the trumpet sounds.
> At the blast of the trumpet he snorts, "Aha!"
> > He catches the scent of battle from afar,
> > the shout of commanders and the battle cry (Job 39:19–25).

From ancient times, the horse has courageously served humanity in battle. Why? Because God endowed horses with a unique character; they love conflict and competition.

When I was a boy in high school, I had a horse named Shorty. He was a maverick—not very tall, not very powerful, but he had an unconquerable spirit. He would never let another horse get ahead of him. It was all I could do to keep him under control when some other horse tried to pass him. He would put on a burst of speed to stay in front because he had a competitive spirit. He loved to race, and he was determined to win.

That's the nature of a horse. Who made horses that way? That is the question God asks Job. And Job knows the answer: Only God has the wisdom and power to create such a wonderful creature as the horse.

God continues:

> Does the hawk take flight by your wisdom
> > and spread his wings toward the south?
> Does the eagle soar at your command
> > and build his nest on high?
> He dwells on a cliff and stays there at night;

> a rocky crag is his stronghold.
> From there he seeks out his food;
>> his eyes detect it from afar.
> His young ones feast on blood,
>> and where the slain are, there is he (Job 39:26–30).

Finally, God points Job to the birds of prey, the hawk and the eagle. He speaks of the strange and fierce ways of these creatures, of their amazingly keen eyesight, of the fact that they live on the rocky crags of high cliffs, and they can detect their prey from a great distance. God gave these birds their instincts and abilities.

Again, Job stands confounded by the wisdom and power of Jehovah God, maker of heaven and earth, Lord of all kingdoms, including the animal kingdom.

At the beginning of Job 40, God confronts Job with a convicting question: "Will the one who contends with the Almighty correct him? Let him who accuses God answer him!" (vv. 1–2).

How has Job fared in this examination by almighty God? Does Job still feel he has the right to accuse God of being unfair? Job responds:

> I am unworthy—how can I reply to you?
>> I put my hand over my mouth.
> I spoke once, but I have no answer—
>> twice, but I will say no more (Job 40:3–5).

Job is silenced by God's display of His creative wisdom and is forced to conclude, in effect, "I am not in the same league as You, Lord. My puny wisdom is no match for the wisdom that created the universe."

Earlier, Job had said that if he could just confront God face to face, "I would give him an account of my every step; like a prince I would approach him" (Job 31:37). But now Job can only say, "I feel like two cents waiting for change. I'm small potatoes. I'm not in God's league at all."

But Job has not gone deep enough with God—not yet. He is silenced, but he is not convinced. He still does not yet understand his basic problem. He has not learned what God had in mind when He invited Satan to test Job in the first place.

Sometimes our troubles bring us to a place where we are silent before God. We stop complaining, but that is not all that God wants to accomplish in our lives. He doesn't want our silence; He wants our trust and our love.

God wants us to place our lives in His hands and believe that He does all things well. So in the next section of the book of Job, He will take Job even deeper into an understanding of His purposes and His loving heart.

The God of nature has just instructed Job. Now Job is about to venture deeper into the nature of God.

THE NATURE OF GOD

For years the iron-mining town of Wabush, Canada, in Labrador province was accessible only by railroad or airplane; there was no road leading to the town. Wabush was built in the early 1960s as a residential community for workers at the mines. But it wasn't until the late 1980s that a road was built, making Wabush accessible by car. That road is still the only road into Wabush. If you want to leave Wabush, you must turn around and take that same road, moving in the opposite direction.

My point is simply this: Life is like the town of Wabush. In our lives, we eventually reach the end of the road. We can go no further. If we want to get out of the place we're in, we have to turn around and go in the opposite direction. That's what it means to repent: to turn completely around and go back the opposite way. When we come to the end of ourselves, there is no other road but the road of repentance.

Job has come to his own Wabush. He has been going the wrong way with God. Now it's time for him to stop, turn completely around, and take the road of repentance.

Throughout this book Job has been crying out in his pain, his bewilderment, and his tortured heart, pleading for a chance to make his case before almighty God. Now God has answered Job out of the whirlwind—a voice out of the storm—and Job has been silenced.

But God is not through with Job. This man who has suffered so much is about to be taught by God Himself about the deep realities of life. Job is about to learn that he has been wrong about God, wrong about life, and wrong about himself. This will be a tough lesson for him. There is no more bitter pill to swallow than the pill of finding you are wrong when you thought you were right.

Life has a way of changing our perspective as we grow older. Sometimes when people reach a certain stage of life, they look back on the convictions of their youth—the values they have stood for, the attitudes they have held—

and they realize that they have been wrong in their approach to life. Carl Jung, the Austrian psychologist, put it this way:

> In the second half of life the necessity is imposed of recognizing no longer the validity of our former ideals but of their contraries; of perceiving the error in what was previously our conviction; of sensing the untruth in what was our truth, and of weighing the degree of opposition, and even of hostility, in what we took to be love.

If you have reached "the second half of life," then you probably identify with those words. Looking back on your life, you may realize that what you thought was selfless love was actually self-centered pride and desire. What you thought was idealism was actually arrogance and egotism. What you thought was truth was an illusion. That's what God is teaching Job in the closing chapters of this book. He is helping Job to realize that what he saw as righteousness and innocence were only external matters. Internally, there was a deep and serious problem.

This is a tough lesson for Job to learn. In truth, it's a difficult lesson for us all to learn.

IT'S NOT EASY TO RUN THE WORLD

In Job 38 through 40:5, God took Job on an extended tour of the universe, the earth, and the animal kingdom. He showed that in accusing the maker of heaven and earth of injustice, Job was challenging a source of wisdom and power that was infinitely superior to his own. As God subjected Job to an exam on various subjects regarding the created order, Job was not able to answer a single question—not one! So Job ended the exam utterly silenced but not yet convinced.

Now Jehovah speaks again from the whirlwind of a storm:

> Brace yourself like a man;
> > I will question you,
> > and you shall answer me.
> Would you discredit my justice?
> > Would you condemn me to justify yourself? (Job 40:6–8).

Here God brings before Job another issue, saying, in effect, "Are you capable of managing the moral government of earth? What about the moral realm, Job? You say I'm being unfair and flawed in My judgment. Are you able to prove Me wrong in the realm of morality, justice, and fairness?"

Then God invites Job to ascend to His throne and deal with the issues that He deals with:

> Do you have an arm like God's,
>   and can your voice thunder like his?
> Then adorn yourself with glory and splendor,
>   and clothe yourself in honor and majesty.
> Unleash the fury of your wrath,
>   look at every proud man and bring him low,
> look at every proud man and humble him,
>   crush the wicked where they stand.
> Bury them all in the dust together;
>   shroud their faces in the grave.
> Then I myself will admit to you
>   that your own right hand can save you (Job 40:9–14).

This, in other words, is God's challenge to Job: "Can you clothe yourself with majesty so that the proud will be humbled and the wicked will fear you? Can you deal authoritatively with sinful, arrogant people?" It is not easy to run the world or bring justice to humankind.

God speaks of the need to humble the proud. This, in fact, is the problem God is dealing with in Job's heart, though Job doesn't yet know it. Job is not an evil man; he is honest and upright. He loves the Lord. But he does have a pride problem.

Pride is a sneaky thing. We Christians have figured out some ingenious ways to disguise our pride and even make it look like humility. It is said that a church once gave their pastor a medal for humility, but they had to take it away because he wore it. Everyone is susceptible to pride, including that faithful and sincere believer, Job.

So God says to Job, "One problem I continually have to deal with is the problem of the proud. I continually have to bring them low and humble them in the hope that they will turn to me and find grace. If they will not, then I have to crush the wicked, bury them in the dust, and consign them to eternal punishment. Can you do that, Job? Are you capable of dealing with pride in others when pride is still an issue in your own life?"

BEHEMOTH AND LEVIATHAN

Next God summons two strange and amazing animals. One is called behemoth, a land animal; the other is called leviathan, a sea creature. First, God speaks of behemoth:

Look at the behemoth,
    which I made along with you
    and which feeds on grass like an ox.
What strength he has in his loins,
    what power in the muscles of his belly!
His tail sways like a cedar;
    the sinews of his thighs are close-knit.
His bones are tubes of bronze,
    his limbs like rods of iron.
He ranks first among the works of God,
    yet his Maker can approach him with his sword.
The hills bring him their produce,
    and all the wild animals play nearby.
Under the lotus plants he lies,
    hidden among the reeds in the marsh.
The lotuses conceal him in their shadow;
    the poplars by the stream surround him.
When the river rages, he is not alarmed;
    he is secure, though the Jordan should surge
    against his mouth.
Can anyone capture him by the eyes,
    or trap him and pierce his nose? (Job 40:15–24).

Bible commentators are unsure what this animal might be. Some think behemoth is the hippopotamus, the elephant, or the rhinoceros, but the language God uses goes far beyond the realm of known zoology. Previously, when God took Job on a tour of the created universe, all the animals were recognizable and identifiable. But when God speaks of behemoth, He describes a creature that transcends the natural world.

The name *behemoth* is significant. It's the Hebrew word for beasts, and it's a plural word, suggesting not just one beast but all beasts joined into one.

God goes on to speak of the legendary sea creature, leviathan:

Can you pull in the leviathan with a fishhook
    or tie down his tongue with a rope?

Can you put a cord through his nose
    or pierce his jaw with a hook?
Will he keep begging you for mercy?
    Will he speak to you with gentle words?
Will he make an agreement with you
    for you to take him as your slave for life?
Can you make a pet of him like a bird
    or put him on a leash for your girls?
Will traders barter for him?
    Will they divide him up among the merchants?
Can you fill his hide with harpoons
    or his head with fishing spears?
If you lay a hand on him,
    you will remember the struggle and never do it again!
Any hope of subduing him is false;
    the mere sight of him is overpowering (Job 41:1–9).

The name of leviathan is also significant. In Hebrew, it means "the folded one." You can see in this single word the image of a dragon with its elongated body snaking through the sea, with loop after folded loop jutting up out of the waves.

Some Bible commentators believe leviathan is the crocodile, though others think leviathan could be the whale. But I think that if we admit that God is using mythical language, then it becomes clear that He is speaking symbolically of real but supernatural beings. These beasts, behemoth and leviathan, are symbolic creatures God uses to represent beings that are real, but invisible and supernatural.

Scripture uses such symbols in other places. In the books of Isaiah, Daniel, Zechariah, and Revelation, beasts that rise up out of the sea and come up out of the earth symbolize forces on the earth. Such creatures symbolize movements, institutions, individuals, leaders, and even supernatural powers. The prophet Isaiah describes leviathan as a twisting, coiled, folded serpent that is also called "the monster of the sea" (or, as in the New American Standard Bible, "the dragon who lives in the sea"):

In that day,
    the LORD will punish with his sword,
    his fierce, great and powerful sword,
    Leviathan the gliding serpent,

> Leviathan the coiling serpent;
> he will slay the monster of the sea (Isaiah 27:1).

So God speaks to Job of two beasts of legend and myth. There is behemoth—a single creature called "the beasts"—a creature with a tail like a cedar tree, with bones like tubes of bronze, with limbs like rods of iron, ranking first among the works of God. And there is leviathan, the coiled and folded dragon of the sea, a creature of overwhelming power and intimidating size, a sea monster so awesome and destructive that no one can stand against him.

Where have we heard of two such creatures before? If you open the New Testament book of Revelation to chapter 13, you read:

> And I saw a beast coming out of the sea. He had ten horns and seven heads, with ten crowns on his horns, and on each head a blasphemous name. The beast I saw resembled a leopard, but had feet like those of a bear and a mouth like that of a lion. The dragon gave the beast his power and his throne and great authority. One of the heads of the beast seemed to have had a fatal wound, but the fatal wound had been healed. The whole world was astonished and followed the beast. Men worshiped the dragon because he had given authority to the beast, and they also worshiped the beast and asked, "Who is like the beast? Who can make war against him?" . . .
>
> Then I saw another beast, coming out of the earth. He had two horns like a lamb, but he spoke like a dragon. He exercised all the authority of the first beast on his behalf, and made the earth and its inhabitants worship the first beast, whose fatal wound had been healed . . . He also forced everyone, small and great, rich and poor, free and slave, to receive a mark on his right hand or on his forehead, so that no one could buy or sell unless he had the mark, which is the name of the beast or the number of his name (Revelation 13:1–4, 11–12, 16–17).

This prophetic passage speaks of two frightening creatures that will dominate the world scene in the last days. One is a beast that comes up out of the sea. The other is a beast that comes up out of the earth. Behind both of these beasts is a third creature called "the great dragon." This great dragon is identified as Satan:

Then another sign appeared in heaven: an enormous red dragon with seven heads and ten horns and seven crowns on his heads. His tail swept a third of the stars out of the sky and flung them to the earth . . .

And there was war in heaven. Michael and his angels fought against the dragon, and the dragon and his angels fought back. But he was not strong enough, and they lost their place in heaven. The great dragon was hurled down—that ancient serpent called the devil, or Satan, who leads the whole world astray. He was hurled to the earth, and his angels with him (Revelation 12:3–4, 7–9).

This dragon, Satan, gives power and authority to the two beasts. In other words, these two beasts—the beast from the sea and the beast from the earth—represent Satan's power as it is manifested on earth in the last days.

I believe God, in His interrogation of Job, is speaking symbolically of the same forces that will be present on the earth in the last days. The first of these beasts, behemoth, represents the satanic warping of human nature that the Bible calls "the flesh." It's the fallen nature within us, with its continual desire to assert the self and live to gratify the self.

The second beast, leviathan, represents the world in all its influence upon our souls, pressuring us to conform and adopt the values and attitudes of the dying and fallen world around us. Leviathan seeks to dominate our thinking in every way.

Behind behemoth and leviathan is the great dragon, Satan himself, the malevolent and cunning devil who rebels against the authority of God and who manipulates human events for his own ends.

THE WORLD, THE FLESH, AND THE DEVIL

God sets a crucial question before Job and before you and me. His question is, "Are you strong enough to stand up to these two great beasts, the enemy without and the enemy within? And are you strong enough to stand up against that malicious and dreadful force that is behind them both, the devil? Can you stand firm against the world, the flesh, and the devil?" One biblical commentator, Bishop Christopher Wordsworth, put it this way:

It seems probable that Behemoth represents the evil one acting in the animal and carnal elements of man's own constitution, and that Leviathan symbolizes the evil one energizing as his external enemy.

Behemoth is the enemy within us; Leviathan is the enemy without us—the world, the flesh, and the devil.

The world, the flesh, and the devil: We could call these three forces Satan's unholy trinity. The devil always imitates; he never comes up with anything original, for he cannot. In a twisted and distorted way, Satan is continually imitating God and trying to sell us a cheap and shabby imitation of the real thing. He imitates the Holy Trinity (the Father, Son, and Holy Spirit) by substituting a false trinity (the world, the flesh, and the devil).

It is important to understand that these three forces—the world, the flesh, and the devil—are not three co-equal enemies. The first two—the world and the flesh—are mere channels used by our true enemy, the devil. There is only one enemy, Satan, and he uses the world and the flesh as channels with which he ensnares our hearts, minds, and souls.

Paul writes of the world, the flesh, and the devil in his letter to the church at Ephesus:

> And you were dead in your trespasses and sins, in which you formerly walked according to the course of *this world* [the first channel, the world], according to *the prince of the power of the air* [a description of the devil], of the spirit that is now working in the sons of disobedience. Among them we too all formerly lived in *the lusts of our flesh* [the second channel, the flesh], indulging the desires of the flesh and of the mind, and were by nature children of wrath, even as the rest. (Ephesians 2:1–3 NASB, emphasis added).

In the entire span of human history, no one has ever been able to reform the world and make it serve humanity. The story of human history is the story of the individual against the world system. Every government in every nation struggles with this problem.

Often the younger generation senses a need to rebel against something called "the system." What many people today call "the system" is what the Bible calls "the world." We all feel the heavy hand of control that the system places on us—a pressure to conform to the world's values and its illusory standards of what's important in life. We cannot control the system, for it continually demands that we obey and serve it.

Leviathan is the symbol God uses for this world system. With this symbolism in mind, it becomes much easier to understand what God means when He tells Job:

Can you fill [leviathan's] hide with harpoons
 or his head with fishing spears?
If you lay a hand on him,
 you will remember the struggle and never do it again!
Any hope of subduing him is false;
 the mere sight of him is overpowering (Job 41:7–9).

The world system is a brutal force that cannot be killed or defeated by human means. Attack the world system, and you will find that you have awakened a vicious and deadly sea dragon that shows no mercy.

God goes on to say:

No one is fierce enough to rouse him.
 Who then is able to stand against me?
Who has a claim against me that I must pay?
 Everything under heaven belongs to me (Job 41:10–11).

He is telling Job, in effect, "If no human being can hope to stand against the power of this sea beast, Leviathan, which symbolically represents the world system, then how can any human being hope to stand against Me? How can you claim that I, the maker of heaven and earth, owe you a debt? The entire universe is mine. It's irrational to suppose that the one who owns everything could possibly owe anything to anyone."

Though human beings can't hope to slay the sea beast that is the world system, God is in control of His universe. He is infinitely greater than leviathan. The world system is His problem, and He can handle it. With this realistic perspective in mind, Job should realize the utter futility and absurdity of challenging God and trying to hold Him accountable.

A STRUGGLE AGAINST SATANIC FORCES

God then returns to the subject of leviathan and further describes this symbolic sea monster, focusing on its ability to defend itself:

I will not fail to speak of his limbs,
 his strength and his graceful form.
Who can strip off his outer coat?
 Who would approach him with a bridle?
Who dares open the doors of his mouth,
 ringed about with his fearsome teeth?

His back has rows of shields
    tightly sealed together;
each is so close to the next
    that no air can pass between.
They are joined fast to one another;
    they cling together and cannot be parted.
His snorting throws out flashes of light;
    his eyes are like the rays of dawn.
Firebrands stream from his mouth;
    sparks of fire shoot out.
Smoke pours from his nostrils
    as from a boiling pot over a fire of reeds.
His breath sets coals ablaze,
    and flames dart from his mouth.
Strength resides in his neck;
    dismay goes before him.
The folds of his flesh are tightly joined;
    they are firm and immovable.
His chest is hard as rock,
    hard as a lower millstone.
When he rises up, the mighty are terrified;
    they retreat before his thrashing (Job 41:12–25).

Here is a picture of a powerful sea dragon, armored with scales like shields, snorting fire and brimstone, spreading dismay and terror among the mighty, sending humanity in retreat with the thrashing of his massive tail. Again, this is a symbolic picture of a deeply entrenched, well-defended world system that cannot be overthrown. The world system intimidates and terrorizes humanity with its seemingly invincible power. God continues:

The sword that reaches him has no effect,
    nor does the spear or the dart or the javelin.
Iron he treats like straw
    and bronze like rotten wood.
Arrows do not make him flee;
    slingstones are like chaff to him.
A club seems to him but a piece of straw;
    he laughs at the rattling of the lance.

His undersides are jagged potsherds,
>   leaving a trail in the mud like a threshing sledge.
He makes the depths churn like a boiling caldron
>   and stirs up the sea like a pot of ointment.
Behind him he leaves a glistening wake;
>   one would think the deep had white hair.
Nothing on earth is his equal—
>   a creature without fear.
He looks down on all that are haughty;
>   he is king over all that are proud" (Job 41:26–34).

Here again we see a picture of utter invincibility. And in the very last verse of this chapter, we see a revealing insight: This sea dragon, leviathan, is the lord and master of a certain segment of humanity: the haughty and the proud. Wherever you see pride, arrogance, egotism, narcissism, insolence, vanity, selfishness, and scorn, you see the spirit of leviathan.

Leviathan is the lord of the proud, the ruler of all who live to glorify the almighty self. This sea beast fills human hearts with ambition, envy, and a lust for power, status, fame, possessions, and wealth. Where do we find such arrogance and selfishness? Certainly we can find it in the corridors of the government, the studios of the entertainment industry, and the corner offices of the financial towers. But we can also find it in our churches, in the pulpit, on the church board, or in the church pew. We can find it in our own homes and in our own hearts.

This beast perverts things that are good and pure. It twists the desire to serve God and minister to others into a prideful lust to be lauded by the congregation and recognized as a "church boss" and a power broker. Leviathan stirs up factions in the church, sets laypeople against pastors, and pits one ministry against another, shattering entire churches and causing some people to leave the faith in disillusionment.

Leviathan is the world system. Along with the flesh and the devil, it is one of the three forces that is continually at war with our souls. The world system is the reality behind the symbolic beast God describes to Job. God says, in effect, "Job, are you up to doing battle against such a monster?" He wants to bring Job to an awareness that there are powers in the world and in Job's own heart and life over which he has no control.

God does not come right out and tell Job about the discussion He had with Satan at the beginning of the book. But God makes it clear to Job that behind his pain, loss, and sorrow, there is an intense struggle against satanic forces. At last Job is given a strong hint that the reason he has suffered such agony is not because of his own failure or sin. The source of his suffering is a problem that is embedded so deeply in human nature and the nature of this fallen world that it is hard for any human being to recognize it.

We are at war with Satan. He seeks to destroy us and torture us and kill our faith. That is what God has been dealing with even in the depths of Job's suffering and loss.

JOB FINDS HIMSELF

We turn to the opening verses of Job 42, and there we hear Job's response to all that God has told him: "I know that you can do all things; no plan of yours can be thwarted" (vv. 1–2).

Job begins by expressing a new and transformed view of God. Notice the distinction Job makes here: "I know that You can do all things." God is omnipotent. Though Job believed in an omnipotent God at the beginning of this story, He now understands God's majesty and might in a totally new and expanded way. He sees that God is all wise and all knowing; therefore, His judgments must be true and just, even if they are mysterious to human beings. He sees that God is all powerful and that no plan of His could ever be thwarted. Neither leviathan nor Satan nor the will of man could ever frustrate God's purposes.

Isn't that amazing? Job has now learned that God is a sovereign being. All that God does is right. His works are consistent with His character, His justice, and His love. When Job is able to see God more clearly, he can see himself more clearly as well.

What's true in Job's life is true in your life and mine. When we lose sight of God, we lose sight of ourselves. When we discover the reality of God, we find the reality of ourselves.

Job has a new view of himself, so he says:

> You asked, "Who is this that obscures my counsel
>   without knowledge?"
>   Surely I spoke of things I did not understand,
>   things too wonderful for me to know.
> You said, "Listen now, and I will speak;
>   I will question you,
>   and you shall answer me."

My ears had heard of you
> but now my eyes have seen you.
Therefore I despise myself
> and repent in dust and ashes (Job 42:3–6).

Notice the changed perspective Job describes. Before, he had only heard of God. Now, it's as if he has seen God with his own eyes—the eyes of his soul. Before, Job believed in God like he would believe a story he heard with his ear. Now Job believed because he had personally witnessed the reality of God's power and wisdom. That's quite a difference!

And the result in Job's own life? He says, "Therefore I despise myself and repent in dust and ashes." Now that is repentance!

Job is doing nothing more than agreeing with what God has said about him. He quotes God, saying, "Lord, You asked me, 'Who is this that obscures my counsel without knowledge?' You were right, Lord. It was me. That's what I've been doing. I'm an ignorant man, so ignorant that I dared to challenge the wisdom and justice of the Almighty."

Then he quotes God a second time, saying, "Lord, You said, 'Listen now, and I will speak; I will question you, and you shall answer me.' Lord, You were right about that, too. I not only thought I could answer any questions You put to me, but I even thought I could ask questions You could not answer. I've been arrogant and self-righteous. I've been wrong all along. Lord, when I see what a fool I've been, I despise myself."

Job has never been in this place before. At last, he is learning one of life's hardest lessons: The source of our problems is not God. It's not other people. We are the source of our problems. And the problem within us is one that only God can cure. We're incapable of handling these problems; we must place them in the loving, gracious, and strong hands of God.

These humble words of Job are often misunderstood: "Therefore I despise myself and repent in dust and ashes." Some people think that God has cruelly humiliated this man, crushed his spirit, and caused him to hate himself. That's not an accurate understanding of Job's words, and those who view God this way are falling into the same trap of misjudging and accusing God that Job had fallen into. God's dealings with Job have been loving, not cruel.

When Job finally gives up trying to defend and justify himself, God begins to heal him. Now God can bless Job as never before. Job discovers that truth Jesus spoke of in the Sermon on the Mount:

Blessed are the poor in spirit,
> for theirs is the kingdom of heaven.

Blessed are those who mourn,
    for they will be comforted.
Blessed are the meek,
    for they will inherit the earth.
Blessed are those who hunger and thirst for righteousness,
    for they will be filled (Matthew 5:3–6).

Job has come to the town of Wabush—the end of the line, the end of himself. He realizes he has been going the wrong way with God. He has turned around and is on the road of repentance. He has confessed his sin and discovered God's gift of forgiveness. Though Job doesn't know it, there's unimaginable blessing awaiting him just around the corner.

A NEW BEGINNING

Niccolò Paganini is considered one of the most brilliant violinists in the history of music. He played concerts in the great symphony halls of Europe, drawing standing-room-only crowds. A master showman as well as a musical virtuoso, Paganini perfected a unique ability to perform entire sonatas on a single violin string. In fact, audiences clamored for a piece he composed called "Variations for the Fourth String." In that piece, he reached notes three octaves higher than a G string was normally capable of producing, having perfected a harmonic technique that few other violinists could imitate.

Paganini also devised a dramatic way of demonstrating his skill with a single string. He would secretly tie a penknife to his right wrist, and then begin playing a sonata on all four strings. At a dramatic moment in the piece, he would draw the blade across the E string, causing it to snap. The crowd would gasp as Paganini continued playing on three strings. Later, the A string would break. Then the D string. Paganini would continue playing effortlessly and beautifully on one string. Amazingly, the piece had all the richness and intricacy of a sonata played on all four strings.

When does a master violinist display his greatest skill? When he has only one string to play upon. A virtuoso is always the most impressive when he has the least to work with.

The same is true of God. He is the Great Virtuoso who wants to transform your life into a masterpiece of His power and grace. His brilliance is displayed most dramatically when he has the least to work with—when the strings of our lives have been broken and there is nothing left for Him to play on but a single string.

That's the truth Job is about to learn. Job's life has been reduced to a single strand, but that strand has been stretched taut and finely tuned by the Master. Beautiful music is about to burst forth from Job's life.

A DISTORTED IMAGE OF GOD

The last time we saw Job, he was flat on his face before God, having experienced a breathtaking vision of the power and wisdom of God. He cried out to God, "My ears had heard of you but now my eyes have seen you. Therefore I despise myself and repent in dust and ashes" (Job 42:5–6).

Now we come to the epilogue of the book of Job. Here we see that God gives Job a new beginning in his life, and the Lord begins by rebuking the three friends who tormented Job with their arguing and accusations:

> After the LORD had said these things to Job, he said to Eliphaz the Temanite, "I am angry with you and your two friends, because you have not spoken of me what is right, as my servant Job has. So now take seven bulls and seven rams and go to my servant Job and sacrifice a burnt offering for yourselves. My servant Job will pray for you, and I will accept his prayer and not deal with you according to your folly. You have not spoken of me what is right, as my servant Job has" (Job 42:7–8).

Job has already been humbled before God. He has seen his own sin, and he has repented in dust and ashes. Now it his friends' turn. God now summons the three men, beginning with Eliphaz. They have dropped out of sight for a while, but now God calls them and says, "I'm angry with all three of you because you spoke falsely about Me. You haven't spoken what is right, as My servant Job has."

What a shock it must have been for Eliphaz and his two companions to hear this indictment from the Lord. Throughout their dialogues with Job, they were utterly convinced they were defending the righteousness and truth of God. They prided themselves on their zeal for the Lord and their denunciation of sin and wickedness. Now, to their startled amazement, they hear God Himself accusing them of defaming Him!

To make matters worse, God says, "You have not spoken of Me what is right, as My servant Job has." God says Job is right and they're wrong. What a blow to their pride *that* must have been!

What did these three men say that God found so offensive? They had made God out to be nothing but a cosmic judge who punished wrongdoers and rewarded the righteous. The image of God they presented was a distortion. It completely left out God's qualities of compassion, love, and mercy. It omitted His patience in giving sinners the opportunity to repent.

Many Christians are like these three men. They present a picture of a God who is concerned only with defending truth and punishing evildoers. They imagine that God is a stern and harsh being who leans out over the battlements of heaven shouting, "Cut that out!" the moment anyone steps out of line. No wonder the world has such a distorted view of God!

There is no biblical support for the idea that God withholds blessing or inflicts instant punishment on evildoers. The Bible says that God sends the rain upon the just and the unjust alike (see Matthew 5:45). God gives good things to all people, even those who rebel against Him. He gives them the blessings of food, shelter, family life, peace, and prosperity. The apostle Paul wrote that God is good to all because His kindness is intended to show human beings where blessings come from so that they will turn to Him: "Or do you show contempt for the riches of his kindness, tolerance and patience, not realizing that God's kindness leads you toward repentance?" (Romans 2:4).

It is God who tilts the wineskins in heaven and pours out His blessing upon us. This is a truth that Job's three comforters failed to acknowledge. In everything they said they presented a distorted and false image of our gracious and merciful God.

A FALSE ACCUSATION AGAINST JOB

God was also angry with these three men because they presented a false accusation against Job. They accused this suffering man of hypocrisy and outright wickedness, and they had no basis for the accusation. They hounded this man relentlessly about his supposed sins, yet he was morally upright in all of his conduct. They insisted that Job's misfortune was the result of some terrible sin that he hid and denied. They claimed to speak for God, yet they were doing the devil's work, and that was offensive to God.

Satan is the accuser of the brethren (see Revelation 12:10); he is the accuser in heaven and the destroyer on earth. So these three men—Eliphaz the Temanite, Bildad the Shuhite, and Zophar the Naamathite—became Satan's instruments to ratchet Job's torment even higher. God now calls them to account because of the way they have falsely accused Job and allowed themselves to be used for the devil's purposes.

It is fascinating to notice that twice in this account God says, "You have not spoken of me what is right, as my servant Job has." God has just spent four chapters—Job 38 through 41—telling Job how wrong he has been. But here He commends Job for having spoken rightly! Isn't this a contradiction?

No. Job did have a problem with pride, and he was wrong when he thought he had a right to hold God accountable. But Job also said a number of things that were true and that pleased God. That's why God commended Job. Let me suggest four truthful, accurate statements that Job made about God.

First, when God pointed out Job's folly, Job admitted it without hesitation, argument, or self-defense. True, Job had charged God with unfairness, but the moment God showed Job how foolish this charge was, Job instantly repented.

Second, Job always adhered to the facts as he saw them. He didn't always see reality very clearly, especially in the depths of his pain, but he was always honest. He never tried to distort or twist the facts to fit an inadequate theology.

Third, Job took his problem straight to God. That's an admirable trait. Throughout this account, no matter how deep his anguish and torment, Job continually sought God in prayer. We never saw Job's three friends praying for him; they never asked God to relieve Job's suffering or to give them wisdom and understanding. Job, unlike his three "miserable comforters," was a man of prayer and faith.

Fourth and finally, when Job repented, he declared without reservation that God is holy, wise, and good. This is the highest expression of faith. Job didn't trust his own limited human observations about God; instead, he trusted God's own words about Himself, and he pronounced God to be just and holy in all of His deeds.

To their credit, Job's three friends also obey God and instantly do as He commands: "So Eliphaz the Temanite, Bildad the Shuhite and Zophar the Naamathite did what the LORD told them; and the LORD accepted Job's prayer" (Job 42:9).

They do not argue, resist, or protest their innocence. They do not defend themselves, even though they now must humble themselves, go hat in hand to Job, and ask him to pray for them. How humiliated they must feel! These three men must go to the man they've accused and scorned, and they must say, "Job, old friend, we're sorry for all we said. I know we've hurt you, but please pray for us."

So these men bring the offering of seven bulls and seven rams because seven is the number of perfection in Scripture. The bull is always the picture of service that is rendered unto death. The ram is a picture of life and energy offered up in sacrifice to God. In this burnt offering, the seven bulls and seven rams symbolize the true basis for humanity's acceptance before God, the sacrificial service and the sacrificed life of Jesus Himself.

All the offerings and sacrifices of the Old Testament picture Christ. The Old Testament saints looked forward to the work of Christ just as we look back to the cross. These offerings of bulls and rams pictured the sacrificial death of the sinless Son of God upon the cross of Calvary. The Old Testament saints' understanding of this symbolism was dim at best, but they acted in obedience to God. In offering these sacrifices, they indicated that they recognized that their own pride was laid low and that their best efforts at righteousness were utterly foolish and futile.

God showed the people of the Old Testament that they could do nothing to save themselves; their salvation depended on a substitute. The righteousness of Christ had to be substituted for our sin so that God could accept us. The New Testament tells us "no flesh should glory in his presence" (see 1 Corinthians 1:29 KJV). We must rest on the sacrifice God has made on our behalf, the righteousness of Christ Himself.

THE POWER OF INTERCESSORY PRAYER

Notice, too, the emphasis God places on intercessory prayer. He tells Job's friends, "My servant Job will pray for you, and I will accept his prayer and not deal with you according to your folly" (Job 42:8). In other words, "There will be no pardon for you without Job's petition on your behalf. If you want to be received and forgiven, you must not only bring the sacrifices; you must also have my servant Job pray for you."

This is an instructive lesson on prayer. Many of us grow up with the idea that prayer is a way of manipulating God into doing our bidding, a kind of heavenly Aladdin's lamp. But that's not the purpose of prayer. God has not given us access through prayer so that we can bend His will to serve our own. Prayer is the way in which God enlists us in His plans and purposes.

As James tells us in the New Testament, "You do not have, because you do not ask God" (4:2). How impoverished our lives are—and the lives of our friends and loved ones—simply because we do not bother to pray for one another. God underscores the fact that Job's friends will not be accepted and forgiven unless Job prays for them. When this humble and upright man prayed for his friends, they were forgiven and pardoned.

Here is a beautiful picture of forgiveness. I love to picture this scene in my imagination. How easy it would have been for Job to have said, "I told you I was innocent, but did you listen to me? No! You falsely accused me! And now you come crawling, wanting me to pray for you, do you?" That's what you or I might have said, but not Job.

I wish we could have heard Job's prayer. Perhaps it went something like this: "O Lord, here are these three friends of mine. They've been stubborn, foolish, and ignorant, just as I was. Lord, You forgave me, and now I ask You to forgive them as well. I called them 'miserable comforters,' and that's what they were! I said they were prideful and that wisdom would die with them. But Lord, I was just as proud and ignorant myself. You forgave me, and so, Lord, I ask You to forgive them as well."

We don't know exactly what Job prayed, but I believe his prayer must have been much like that. The Scriptures tell us that the Lord heard Job's prayer and accepted it, and Job's three friends were forgiven. I'm reminded of Paul's words to the Ephesians: "Be kind and compassionate to one another, forgiving each other, just as in Christ God forgave you" (Ephesians 4:32).

What a beautiful thing it is to see Job praying for his friends without a hint of resentment or a desire to get even. He simply lifts them up in prayer, and God honors Job's prayer.

RESTORATION AND RENEWAL

Next we see the restoration and renewal that God brings into the life of His servant Job: "After Job had prayed for his friends, the LORD made him prosperous again and gave him twice as much as he had before" (Job 42:10).

Some people look at this stage in Job's life and say, "Well, finally! After all the cruelty God inflicted on Job, He decided to be merciful and compassionate in the end." That's a distorted view. God didn't suddenly decide to show mercy to Job. He has been compassionate and merciful all along! God's character is unchanging. His compassion never fails, and His love endures forever.

When we go through times of trial, it's not because God is angry or cruel. If we will patiently endure, God will bring us to a place of blessing, just as He did in Job's life. As the prophet Jeremiah wrote:

> For men are not cast off
> 　　by the Lord forever.
> Though he brings grief, he will show compassion,
> 　　so great is his unfailing love.

For he does not willingly bring affliction
 or grief to the children of men (Lamentations 3:31–33).

Isn't that encouraging? God does not willingly afflict or grieve the children of men. If it is necessary for our growth and spiritual well being, He will allow grief to come into our lives, but He also shows us His unfailing love. When we hurt, He hurts with us. When we cry, He mingles His tears with our own. As a loving heavenly parent, He knows the heartache of hurting for a child, even when He must afflict that child to bring about repentance. At those times when God must cause grief in our lives, He also has compassion for us according to His abundant love.

A FAMILY GATHERING

God then moves Job's relatives and friends to bring him gifts and surround him with fellowship and consolation:

All his brothers and sisters and everyone who had known him before came and ate with him in his house. They comforted and consoled him over all the trouble the LORD had brought upon him, and each one gave him a piece of silver and a gold ring (Job 42:11).

The first thing we notice about this occasion is that it is a family gathering. Job's brothers and sisters (we do not know how many) and all of his friends are gathered together. The uncles and aunts are there, plus cousins, nephews, nieces, and grandchildren. At this time, Job is probably seventy years of age or more. He has been through an ordeal that has lasted months, and perhaps as long as a year. Though his own children have perished, he must have had grandchildren and great grandchildren by now. With all the neighbors and friends and their families, it was a huge and joyous family gathering.

The second thing we notice is that it was a feast. They all gathered and ate with Job in his house. I don't know what they served at this feast, but in Bible times it was common to roast a well-fattened calf. However, in view of God's description of how stupid the ostrich is (see Job 39:13–18), they may have served a roasted ostrich with stuffing and cranberry sauce! Whatever they served, you can be sure there was plenty for everyone.

The third thing we notice is that Job's friends and family come together for a time of fellowship. The passage tells us that they showed Job sympathy, and they comforted him for all the pain and sorrow he had endured. Whether in Job's day or our own time, fellowship is a beautiful thing. We were all made to enjoy fellowship with others; no one was ever meant to go through life alone. Job needed his family and friends, and we Christians need one another in the body of Christ.

In the late 1700s, a young pastor named John Fawcett served a poor church in the village of Wainsgate, England. Fawcett became widely known as a gifted writer and preacher and was soon called to serve in a large and influential church in London. He accepted the call, and John and his wife, Mary, prepared to move to London.

On the day the Fawcetts were loading the wagons with their furnishings for the move, all the people from the little village church came to bid them an emotional farewell. There were hugs and tears all around.

Finally, Mary Fawcett turned to John and, with tears in her eyes, said, "John, I can't bear to leave our friends!"

"Neither can I," John said. "I've changed my mind. We'll remain here with the people we love."

And John Fawcett spent the rest of his ministry—all fifty-four years—in the village of Wainsgate. As a result of that experience, he wrote a hymn called "Blest Be the Tie That Binds"—a song that expresses the true depths of genuine fellowship:

> Blest be the tie that binds
> Our hearts in Christian love;
> The fellowship of kindred minds
> Is like to that above.

Job must have experienced the emotions expressed in that hymn. He must have been grateful for the tie of fellowship that binds many hearts together as one. His family and friends offered their comfort and shared his woes. He was surrounded with prayer, comfort, sympathy, and hope.

USING OUR "BAPTIZED IMAGINATIONS"

But there is a strange note to this scene. Notice that the text reads, "They comforted and consoled him over all the trouble the Lord had brought upon him." That's a strange way to put it, isn't it? It sounds as if Job's family and friends are blaming God for Job's troubles.

What did Job say in response? The Scriptures do not tell us. But using my "baptized imagination" (a phrase coined by C. S. Lewis), I want to express my own opinion of what Job must have said. Bear in mind, I am reading into the text some dialogue that is not there. But I simply can't believe that this dear old patriarch—after all he has suffered and after all of his discussions with Eliphaz, Bildad, Zophar, Elihu, and God Himself—would allow his neighbors, friends, and family members to accuse God of bringing evil into his life.

I believe that on hearing this charge against God, old Job must have raised his hand and said, "Wait! You've got it all wrong! Once I thought as you do. I assumed that that God inflicted these events on me to hurt me. I lost seven fine sons and three beautiful daughters, killed by a whirlwind that destroyed the house where they had gathered. That same day, I lost all my livestock and my wealth. Impoverished and heartbroken, I said, 'The Lord gave and the Lord has taken away; may the name of the Lord be praised.'

"I believed my calamity would not last and that God would rescue me from my pain and make up for my losses. Instead, my life got worse! I developed awful boils over my entire body. All over my body, I have scars from these terrible boils that tormented me day and night. I sat in the garbage heap, scraping my sores with pieces of broken pottery. I prayed for relief, but none came. I began to doubt. I began to wonder whether Jehovah was indeed the God of love and justice He claimed to be.

"Then I began to complain. You all heard me. I charged God with doing harm to me without cause. I said that God had no right to treat me this way. I accused Him of unfairness.

"My suffering was made worse by three well-intentioned but misguided men. They falsely accused me of unconfessed sin. In my pain, I spoke just as bluntly to them.

"But through that experience, I discovered that God was not doing evil to me at all. He was teaching me two mighty truths. Though I wouldn't want to go through such an experience again, I'm glad I learned these two lessons, and I can honestly say I'm thankful for the suffering I've endured. Let me share these two truths with you:

"First, God showed me that I have a mediator, a redeemer. There is one who acts as an intercessor between God and me. In my pain, I felt isolated from God. I saw Him as great and powerful and myself as weak and wounded. I asked myself, 'How could God, the all-powerful maker of the universe, know how I feel?' But the Spirit of God invaded my heart and taught me something amazing. I saw this truth so clearly that I cried out, 'I know that my Redeemer lives and that in the end he will stand upon the earth. And after my skin has been destroyed, yet in my flesh I will see God!'

"I don't know when my Redeemer will come and stand upon the earth. It may be soon. It may be two thousand years from now. But I know He lives, and He is coming. And when He comes, I don't believe He will arrive in a pretentious display of glory. God doesn't work that way. I've come to learn that God loves humility. Knowing Him as I now do, I suspect He'll probably arrive in some obscure little place. He may even come as a tiny baby, the most helpless creature in the universe. It would be like God to send the Redeemer that way.

"Second, God showed me that my problem is not God. I am my problem. The reason I need a Redeemer is that I have a sin problem. The worst evil I face is not in the things that happen to me. It's in the dark and ugly sin that lurks within me. My sin is so deceptive that I don't even see it. I think I'm innocent, yet God knows how desperately wicked my heart is. He saw the pride of my self-centered flesh, and He held up a mirror to my soul so that I could finally see it for the first time.

"Friends, I had to humble myself and see that God's diagnosis was accurate. My problem was me and the sin that lurked inside me. Once God had brought me to a place where I could see myself as I really am, I repented in dust and ashes. I cast myself upon His grace. When I did that, my Redeemer, my Mediator, brought God and me together. My sins were forgiven, and an incredible peace flooded my heart.

"You know, I don't care whether I'm poor or rich. I don't care whether I'm sick or well. I don't care whether I'm alone or surrounded by friends and family. The joy I've found with God is so wonderful that it's worth everything I've suffered and more besides! No, God didn't send evil into my life. Don't comfort me for that! God sent good into my life, and I thank Him every day for that experience."

There is one more interesting detail in the account of this gathering of Job's family and friends. The text tells us that his brothers, sisters, and friends came and ate with him in his house—"and each one gave him a piece of silver and a gold ring." Job's friends gave him gifts of silver and gold, two metals that symbolize redemption in the Bible. Silver is the sign of redemption; gold is the picture of deity, of God redeeming lost humanity.

Job's friends were probably moved by God to give him these gifts of silver and gold in order to provide a foundation for the restored wealth that God was bringing into Job's life. At the same time, I think God had an even deeper symbolism in mind for these gifts, a symbolism that the gift-givers themselves probably never imagined. These gifts were God's sign that His redemption was at work in Job's life. Job wasn't being redeemed merely in the realm of his finances or his family or his health; God was redeeming him spiritually by pointing Job to the Redeemer who was to come, who would save His people from their sins.

DOUBLED BLESSINGS

Next we see how God dramatically restored Job back to health and wealth and the love of his family: "The LORD blessed the latter part of Job's life more than the first. He had fourteen thousand sheep, six thousand camels, a thousand yoke of oxen and a thousand donkeys. And he also had seven sons and three daughters" (Job 42:12–13).

Notice that Job ended up with double of everything he had before. He started out with seven thousand sheep; he ended up with fourteen thousand. His three thousand camels were doubled to six thousand. His five hundred yoke of oxen became a thousand. His five hundred donkeys also became a thousand.

But what about Job's children? You might think that since Job's seven sons and three daughters were killed, he would receive double the number of children—fourteen sons and six daughters. But no, when God restored Job, He gave him seven sons and three daughters, the same number of children Job had at the beginning. Why?

Because Job *still* had seven sons and three daughters in heaven!

Job hadn't truly *lost* his first ten children—not in the same sense that he had lost his wealth and possessions. He was separated from his children by death, but he would be together with them again. Job's first ten children were safe in the arms of the Lord. And now he had seven *more* sons and three *more* daughters. So God *did* double the number of Job's children!

God doubled every blessing that Job had to start with. He does not willingly afflict or grieve the children of men. Instead, He longs to bless our lives, richly and abundantly. That is the mercy of God.

PEACE, FRAGRANCE, AND BEAUTY

We encounter another surprise when we read about the young daughters of Job: "The first daughter he named Jemimah, the second Keziah and the third

Keren-Happuch. Nowhere in all the land were there found women as beautiful as Job's daughters, and their father granted them an inheritance along with their brothers" (Job 42:14–15).

The text places a special emphasis on Job's daughters. Here, the last chapter of Job contrasts sharply with the first. In Job 1, the sons of Job were at the forefront of the story. They had a birthday party every year and invited their sisters to come and share with them. Here in Job 42, the daughters of Job take center stage.

One detail worth noting is that Job gives his daughters an inheritance along with their brothers. This was unheard of in the culture of Job's day. I believe that this detail, which many pass over without noticing, gives us a profound insight into what God has been doing and is still doing in Job's life. Through His Spirit, God is revealing truth to Job that he could never learn any other way.

Job began this book as an upright and righteous man who wanted to serve God, at least to the limited degree that he understood God's will. But as faithful and sincere as Job was, he still had much to learn about his own sinfulness and fallibility and about God's greatness. By the end of the book, God had instructed Job in many amazing truths, including the truth that a great Mediator-Redeemer was coming who would bring eternal life to Job and to every human being who would believe in Him.

Here this old patriarch shows that God has taught him yet another principle of life that he could not have learned from his culture. This truth could only be taught him directly by the Spirit of God, a truth we find in the New Testament: "There is neither Jew nor Greek, slave nor free, male nor female, for you are all one in Christ Jesus" (Galatians 3:28).

In the culture of Job's day, women were second-class citizens. But God was teaching Job that in His kingdom, there are no second-class citizens. Before God, there are no distinctions between men and women. All are equal—all are one—in the Lord.

Each of the names of these three daughters has a special significance. *Jemimah* means "dove." Throughout the Scriptures, and even today, the dove is a symbol of peace.

Keziah is another spelling of "cassia," a spice with a sweet cinnamon-like fragrance. This spice is mentioned in Psalm 45, which is a symbolic wedding hymn for the Messiah-King, a prophetic psalm of Jesus. In that psalm, the Messiah-King comes for His bride and is greeted with this song: "All your robes are fragrant with myrrh and aloes and cassia; from palaces adorned with ivory the music of the strings makes you glad" (v. 8).

The Messiah-King has prepared Himself for the wedding by making himself fragrant with the scent of myrrh, aloes, and cassia. These spices are significant because they are *burial spices*. After Jesus was crucified and placed in the tomb, women came with these burial spices to apply them to His body in order to preserve it. The Messiah-King of Psalm 45 was fragrant with burial spices at His wedding because His marriage to the bride (which is the church, the body of believers) is made possible by His death, which occurred, of course, upon the cross.

So Job named his daughter Keziah after cassia, a rare and costly burial spice that has great symbolic significance. Cassia points to the fact that Job's longed-for Mediator-Redeemer, the Messiah-King, must die in order to accomplish His mission on earth.

Finally, we come to Job's youngest daughter, Keren-Happuch. This name literally means "the horn of adornment," and it refers to the container that holds the cosmetics that make a young woman beautiful. This girl's name speaks of the outward beauty that comes from inner loveliness. The horn symbolizes the comely spirit from which her true beauty flows.

So Job's three daughters were given names that mean peace, fragrance, and beauty. The passage tells us, "Nowhere in all the land were there found women as beautiful as Job's daughters." These young women possessed rare beauty—an inner beauty as well as physical loveliness.

Peace, fragrance, and beauty are the fruit of Job's trials. This is the result that suffering brings in the lives of all who learn to receive trials as evidence of God's love. As Paul tells us:

> Not only so, but we also rejoice in our sufferings, because we know that
> suffering produces perseverance; perseverance, character; and character,
> hope. And hope does not disappoint us, because God has poured out his
> love into our hearts by the Holy Spirit, whom he has given us (Romans
> 5:3–5).

When we learn to maintain an attitude of faith, trust, and joy in our sufferings, then we experience peace, fragrance, and beauty at the end of our trials.

The book of Job closes on a note of contentment and peace: "After this, Job lived a hundred and forty years; he saw his children and their children to the fourth generation. And so he died, old and full of years (Job 42:16–17).

Job was probably at least seventy years old at the beginning of the story. His death comes a hundred and forty years after going through his time of pain and testing. By the time Job died, he had undoubtedly lived to be more than two hundred years old.

At the close of the story, we see Job as a contented man—a man at peace with God, at peace with himself, and at peace with everyone around him. He has gone through a stormy time in his life, but God has sustained him and richly blessed him.

We all go through stormy times in life. We all suffer pain and loss. But if we learn the lessons of our pain, if we learn to trust the wisdom and love of God, then we will come through it with our souls intact, with our lives blessed with peace, fragrance, and beauty. That is the lesson of the suffering, restoration, and peaceful passing of Job into life everlasting.

Job has gone to meet his Redeemer face to face. He has left this world and entered a world beyond his imagining. Like Paul, Job has finished his course; he has kept the faith. Like a violin with only one string remaining, stretched taut but tuned and played by the Master, Job has seen a beautiful song pour forth from his life.

But we are not quite finished. Turn the page with me, and let's take a final look at Job and the deep meaning of his story.

SOME FINAL THOUGHTS

Epilogue

If you've seen *The Sound of Music*, then you know just a little of the real-life story of the Trapp Family Singers. The patriarch of this Austrian singing family was Georg Ritter von Trapp (1880–1947), a decorated submarine captain during World War I. When von Trapp lost his wife Agathe to a scarlet fever epidemic in 1922, he became the sole parent of seven children. After one of his daughters came down with the fever, he hired Maria Kutscher, a convent novitiate, as the child's nurse. Maria stayed on as the children's governess and eventually married Ritter von Trapp.

The Trapps' home was always filled with music, and the children learned to sing and harmonize. The Trapp Family performed in concert halls and festivals, becoming famous all over Europe.

During the 1930s, Ritter von Trapp watched the rise of Naziism with alarm. When the Trapps were invited to sing for Adolf Hitler's birthday celebration, von Trapp refused. In 1938, the Nazi government pressured him to accept a new commission as a submarine commander, and Ritter von Trapp decided it was time to escape.

He had his family dress for a short walk in the woods. Then, accompanied by the family priest, they hiked across the Austrian Alps to a tiny Italian village. From there, they took a train down the Italian coast and booked passage to New York. They arrived in America with nothing but the clothes on their backs and $3.50 in cash. They performed their music around the country and soon rebuilt their fortunes.

In 1942, the Trapp Family bought a six-hundred-acre farm near Stowe, Vermont, and remodeled the farmhouse as an Austrian chalet. The Trapps continued to tour even after Georg Ritter von Trapp passed away in 1947. Later, Maria and the Trapp children turned their chalet into the world-famous Trapp Family Lodge. Guests could ski and hike in the daytime, then be treated to a Trapp Family concert in the evening.

On December 20, 1980, the lodge burned to the ground. Maria and the children were devastated. They had endured so much adversity, and now the lodge was gone. In their discouragement, they questioned whether they should rebuild.

The day after the fire, a package arrived for the Trapp Family. A friend had sent it several days before. When the Trapps unwrapped the package, they found it was a gift for the lodge, a large rug bearing a Latin inscription: *Nec Aspera Terrent* (Do not be terrified by adversity).

Encouraged by the gift, the Trapps immediately began rebuilding. Today, a new and more beautiful Trapp Family Lodge stands on the site of the old lodge. When you enter the lobby, the first thing you notice is a large rug with a Latin inscription, reminding you not to be terrified by adversity.

That is one of the great lessons of the book of Job, but it's not the only lesson. Having reached the end of the book, I would like to look back and recall some of the great truths that God has set before us through the life of this suffering servant, Job.

TRADING OUR ILLUSIONS FOR GOD'S TRUTH

As we have already noted, the book of Job is probably the first book of the Bible ever written. It takes us back to the most primitive days of human culture and reveals to us that God was working out His plan for human redemption even then.

Job was probably a contemporary of Abraham. He lived before the Jewish people existed and before the Bible was written, making his home in a place called Uz. Yet his faith reflects a heritage of revelation, the revealed truth about the one true God. This revealed truth was preserved by oral traditions dating back to Adam and Eve. The truth was handed down, generation by generation, to a faithful descendent named Noah. It was Noah who preserved this revealed faith when the world was destroyed by a global catastrophe, the great flood. After the flood, the descendents of Noah scattered throughout the world (see Genesis 10) and carried this faith wherever they went.

One of those who inherited this tradition of revealed truth was Job. He had no Scriptures on which to base his beliefs. Moses, David, and the prophets would not be born until centuries after the time of Job. This man received the revealed truth of God purely through the oral traditions that had been handed down from father to son through the generations.

So the faith of Job was, you might say, a primitive faith. Yet as we have seen in our study, everything the book of Job reveals about God is consistent with the larger revelation of the Old and New Testaments. None of the teaching in the book of Job conflicts with any other part of God's revealed Word.

The book of Job accomplishes the same goal that every other book of the Bible does: It strips away the illusions of life and permits us to see reality. That is why this book is so valuable to us. If you have lived long at all, you have probably discovered that life isn't what you thought it was when you were young. There are many things we hold to be true that turn out to be illusions. Through a careful study of the book of Job, we learn to trade our illusions for God's truth.

The world around us seeks to squeeze us into a mold of false and delusional thinking about reality, God, and ourselves. The entire Bible, including the book of Job, challenges and corrects our false thinking. Through His Word, God shakes us out of our illusions and brings us back to our senses so that we can see His truth. That's why it's important for us to come together and allow the Spirit of God to speak to our hearts through the Word of God, so that we can correct our thinking and (as the apostle Paul has said) renew our minds: "Do not conform any longer to the pattern of this world, but be transformed by the renewing of your mind. Then you will be able to test and approve what God's will is—his good, pleasing and perfect will" (Romans 12:2).

We have been looking at the book of Job in detail, verse by verse, incident by incident. Now it's time to pull back and take an aerial view of the book of Job and Job's life. Before we take our leave, let's make sure we haven't overlooked any of the truths God has for us in this ancient book of wisdom.

THERE IS NO SAFE PLACE IN A WAR

In Job 1, we caught a glimpse behind the scenes of this world and were shown what takes place in the heavenly realm when a believer is tried or tempted here on earth. From time to time we are all tested in much the same way Job was, even if not to the same degree. We all undergo pressure, stress, pain, and loss. We all face the temptation to compromise our faith and integrity.

The book of Job shows us how we should view our times of testing and temptation. When trials come, we rarely recognize them for what they are. We think they are simply the result of adverse circumstances or perverse people. We don't look at the larger picture and see the hand of Satan or the plan of God in our troubles. We cry out to God and plead with Him to remove our problems.

Job reminds us that when we are in the midst of trials, we don't know the whole story. We can't see behind the scenes of reality. We are often unaware that there is a profound reason for the pain and loss we suffer. The reason we suffer is that *we live in a universe at war*.

You and I are in the middle of a cosmic struggle that has been going on since before the creation of Adam and Eve. C. S. Lewis put it this way in *Mere Christianity*: "Enemy-occupied territory—that is what this world is. Christianity is the story of how the rightful king has landed, you might say landed in disguise, and is calling us all to take part in a great campaign of sabotage." The apostle Paul describes the nature of this war: "For our struggle is not against flesh and blood, but against the rulers, against the authorities, against the powers of this dark world and against the spiritual forces of evil in the heavenly realms" (Ephesians 6:12).

We tend to think that we are noncombatants living in peacetime. That's not how Satan views us. To him, we are military targets. If we don't wish to become casualties, we had better wake up to the reality of this war and prepare to fight back.

One of the reasons Job was so bewildered by the suffering he experienced is that he didn't understand that his life was a battlefield in this great cosmic war. He didn't realize that Satan had him in the crosshairs. All the things Satan did to torture Job and destroy his spirit were part of the satanic strategy.

In the midst of the troubles, temptations, and pressures of our lives, we dare not become complacent. Life is not a Sunday school picnic, even though we wish it could be. We wish we could relax, enjoy life, and never have to suffer pain, loss, stress, or temptation. We wish we could be safe and secure from all harm, but that's not realistic. There is no safe place in a war.

That's why Christians should not plan their lives the same way as those I call worldlings, the people of this world. Just as our Lord's kingdom was not of this world, we are not citizens of this world. When we have God's perspective on our lives, we realize that we don't live on the same plane as the worldlings. We don't live for the same plans and goals and purposes as the worldlings. We live to serve God's eternal purpose.

It may sound harsh, but it's true: God didn't put us here to have a good time. Yes, He does give us good times and blessings to enjoy, but each one is a gift of His love and grace. We should never assume that we are entitled to God's blessings or that we deserve them. We are here to fight a battle against the powers of darkness. We are engaged in an unending combat with powerful forces that seek to control human history.

When I was in the U.S. Navy during World War II, there were many things about navy life that I enjoyed, but I knew I wasn't in the navy to have a good time. In fact, I considered my time in the service to be a temporary phase in my life, and I looked forward to the end of my enlistment. I believed that my *real* life would begin when I got out of the navy.

That's how we should view our lives on earth. Yes, there's much to enjoy, but we are here for a deeper and larger purpose than merely having a good time. We are here to win a war. At some point, our time of enlistment in this war will be over, and our real lives in eternity will begin. But for now we must fight this fight and serve our Lord and Commander.

That is one of the key lessons of the book of Job. God wants us to know that there are momentous events taking place behind the scenes of history. He is weaving our lives and even our pain into a great cosmic battle plan. And He is winning! That is the assurance we have in the book of Job.

THE TRUE NATURE OF FAITH

Job thought he was exercising faith when he obeyed God and did what was right. But was it really faith? Before his trials began, Job believed just as his three "comforters" did: God punishes you if you're wicked and blesses you if you're good. So what kind of faith does it take to live a good life if that is your theology? That's not faith; it's simple self-interest.

Many people still think this way today. They live as "good people" and they think God owes them blessings in return. They feel entitled to God's blessings because they have earned the right to be blessed. In reality, they are just living the way they do so they won't get in trouble with God. There's an element of faith in the way they live, but it's a very weak faith.

Remember, this was Satan's accusation before God: "Does Job fear God for nothing? . . . You have blessed the work of his hands, so that his flocks and herds are spread throughout the land. But stretch out your hand and strike everything he has, and he will surely curse you to your face."

In other words, "Job's faith is nothing more than self-interest. Let me at him, and I'll show you just how shallow his faith really is." Satan isn't right about very much, but he is right about this: It's a weak faith that only serves God in times of blessing. The book of Job teaches us that true faith, genuine faith, great faith is revealed only when we serve and trust God in the hard times, the times of suffering, loss, and opposition. That's the kind of faith that makes the world sit up and take notice.

When Jesus wrestled in prayer in the garden of Gethsemane, just hours before He went to the cross, He was deeply afraid. He told His disciples that His heart was filled with sorrow and anguish, even to the point of death. He asked them to pray for Him, and then He went a short distance away and fell to the ground. "My Father," He cried out, "if it is possible, may this cup be taken from me. Yet not as I will, but as you will" (Matthew 26:39).

That is great faith! In the midst of His fear and horror of the cross, Jesus expressed the faith of an obedient servant: "Not as I will, but as You will!"

That is Job's attitude. He trembles, he falters, he questions, he pleads with God—but he never lets go of God. He never stops loving God. He continues to be the man God calls "My servant Job." That is why Job ultimately becomes an example of faith. The greatest faith is that which is demonstrated when we feel the least faithful, when we feel so weak we can't do anything but cling by our fingernails. That is what the book of Job teaches us about genuine faith.

THE TRUE NATURE OF FALLEN HUMANITY

The book of Job also confronts us with an accurate view—God's view—of our fallen condition. We tend to think we are pretty good people. We compare ourselves with the evildoers in the world, and we seem almost perfect by comparison (at least, that's what we tell ourselves).

Then we read the book of Job. Here we find a man who is truly upright and godly, putting us to shame. In fact, Job may well represent humanity at its absolute best. He is a highly respected and greatly honored man—a man who is sincere, moral, devoted, selfless, and compassionate toward the poor and needy. He has devoted his life to serving God and doing His will. God Himself said, "There is no one on earth like him; he is blameless and upright, a man who fears God and shuns evil." If any man deserved God's blessing, wouldn't that man be Job?

There are many people in the world who are wonderfully kind, moral, unselfish, and sincere. Many of them are not Christians and don't even believe in God, but they believe in living good lives. We look at such people and think, "I know they don't believe in God, but they are such good people that they deserve to go to heaven. God should make an exception in their case."

But the book of Job makes it clear that this is a faulty and misleading way of looking at life. The story of Job strips away outward appearances and forces us to see our fallen humanity as it is. Job thinks he is a good man—an innocent man—and he is, compared to the rest of the fallen human race. But he is still fallen. He is self-deceived. There is sin lurking within Job that he doesn't even see. So it is with all of us, even the best of us: We are fallen. We are sinners. We deserve nothing from God.

Through his sufferings, Job discovered some very unpleasant truths about himself. He learned that he was a lover of status and prestige. When his illness made him repulsive to the community and he took refuge in the rubbish heap, Job longed for the days when he had honor and dignity, when people bowed before him and spoke well of him. Job liked that because there was a sneaky bit of selfish pride lurking in the recesses of his heart.

The book of Job shows us that we human beings long to possess some of the glory that is due to God alone. Our motives are tainted by pride. Yes, we want to serve God if in doing so, we will gain some glory. We want other people to speak well of us and to say, "What a great man of God he is! What a wonderful woman of faith she is!" As good a man as Job was, he was not immune to the sin of pride. God used a trial of pain and loss to burn that sin out of Job's life.

WHY WE SUFFER

If bad things happen to bad people, that makes sense to us; we do not struggle with that. But when bad things happen to good people, we are stunned. Our sense of justice and fairness is offended. We say, "Why, Lord? Why do You allow the wicked to prosper and the righteous to suffer?"

The book of Job teaches us a difficult truth about suffering: Sometimes we suffer because our affliction accomplishes God's purposes. This principle always seems to catch us by surprise, even though it should be obvious to us all. After all, the New Testament makes it abundantly clear that God allows the innocent to suffer in order to achieve His purposes. The most innocent man to ever live was Jesus of Nazareth. He suffered and died on the cross not because He was an evildoer, not because He deserved to suffer, but because He was carrying out God's purpose in the world.

Jesus always did what was pleasing in the sight of the Father, yet His life was filled with suffering from beginning to end. He suffered rejection, false accusation, humiliation, violence, and death by torture. He was, as the prophet Isaiah prophetically described Him, "despised and rejected by men, a man of sorrows, and familiar with suffering" (53:3).

Why did Jesus suffer? Why did Job suffer? Why do you and I suffer? Because suffering, in the life of a godly person, is a way of allowing God to demonstrate that Satan is a liar and a cheat. Satan claims that we human beings serve God only out of self-interest. When people continue to love and serve God even in the depths of their suffering, they prove that Satan is a liar who richly deserves the eternal punishment that awaits him.

Unfortunately we Christians have all too often confirmed the lie of Satan instead of the truth of God. When we have suffered, we have ceased to serve God and have instead accused Him and dishonored Him. We have proved that our own faith is shallow and weak, a matter of self-interest, not unselfish service and love for God.

Job teaches us that suffering is a means by which Satan is silenced and God is vindicated. It's a high and holy privilege to uphold the glory of God against the accusations of the devil. If we will learn to see our sufferings in light of the spiritual war that has been raging since before the creation of the human race, it will transform our lives and our pain. It will awaken us to the high and holy privilege of (as Paul says in Philippians 3:10) sharing in the sufferings of our Lord Jesus Christ.

I once knew a woman who had lost both her husband and her son in an auto accident. When I went to see her, she was weeping and hardly able to speak. I wondered what I could say to her that might bring her any comfort at all. I asked God for wisdom, then said, "You've been given a high and holy honor."

"What do you mean?" she asked.

I sat down beside her and went through the Scriptures with her, pointing her to a number of Scriptures that speak of the privilege of suffering for Christ. "God has given you the privilege of bearing this trial so that you can demonstrate that God's strength, love, and grace are present in all circumstances, even in the worst that life can throw at us."

As we talked together, a new look came over her face. The pain was still there in her eyes, but there was also a new look of peace on her face. She said, "I think I see what you mean." And we prayed together.

Over the weeks and months that followed, her life was a radiant testimony to hundreds of people. Lives were touched and God was glorified because this woman was able to see her sufferings in a new way. She was able to look at her loss as Job did.

Understand that it's not always the best practice to quote Scripture to a person who is in the depths of suffering and loss. We should avoid preaching to people or dispensing platitudes as Job's three "comforters" did. But sometimes, as we seek to be sensitive to the leading of the Holy Spirit, we may feel God leading us to help a suffering friend to find God's perspective on pain and loss.

God wants us to look at our afflictions from His perspective, from the long view of eternity. That is one of the great lessons of the book of Job. That is one of the reasons we need to lay hold of the truths in this book.

THE CHARACTER OF GOD

But there is yet another theme that emerges from our study of the book of Job, and it is probably the most important and life-changing truth in the entire book: Even in the depths of our sufferings, the character of God never changes. He is what He has always been: a God of power, wisdom, and love.

If we do not have an accurate understanding of God's unchanging character, then we run the risk of having our faith destroyed by times of trial and suffering. Even in the best of times, many people see God through a distortion lens. To them God is a cold, impersonal, uncaring Being at best, and cruelly vindictive at worst. Some see God as angry, judgmental, and unfair. Others divide God into two beings: a distant and threatening Old Testament God versus a loving and forgiving New Testament God. Even Job had a distorted image of God, especially when He thought God was being unfair to him.

But God doesn't change, and He is not unfair. There are not two Gods, one for the Old Testament and one for the New; our God, the God of the Bible, is one God. He is loving, just, and unchanging. The God of the Bible, the Lord of our lives and our sufferings, is not ruthless and cold; He is deeply concerned about us and aware of our problems. He maintains sovereign control of the universe, and He limits the power of Satan. God never tests us beyond what we can bear. He is patient, forgiving, and ultimately responsible for everything that happens in our lives.

At the beginning of the book of Job, we see three characters: God, Satan, and Job. By the end of the book, Satan has disappeared from view. There are only two characters left onstage: God and Job. At this point, Job begins to see what God is working out through his sufferings. He realizes that God has purposes and plans that he, as a finite human being, can scarcely imagine, much less understand. Job also knows that in some mysterious way, God is able to use Job's sufferings to fulfill those purposes and plans.

At one point in the book, God speaks to Job of the moment when the earth was created and "the morning stars sang together and all the angels shouted for joy." In the original Hebrew, that word *angels* is literally "the sons of God." Other passages of Scripture speak of a time yet to come when "the sons of God" will be revealed. Paul writes: "The creation waits in eager expectation for the sons of God to be revealed" (Romans 8:19).

An even greater shout of joy will shake the heavens when God reveals the new creation He is building out of the lives of His people. He is using the sufferings, trials, and tribulations of this present life to reveal a future glory. As Paul put it: "I consider that our present sufferings are not worth comparing with the glory that will be revealed in us" (Romans 8:18).

What a thrilling thought! The God who created the universe has chosen us to be the ones to bear His name in the hour of affliction. There is no higher honor than that. This is why Jesus says: "Blessed are you when people insult you, persecute you and falsely say all kinds of evil against you because of me. Rejoice and be glad, because great is your reward in heaven, for in the same way they persecuted the prophets who were before you" (Matthew 5:11–12).

What does it mean to share in the sufferings of Christ? As Jesus Himself says, it means bearing insult, persecution, false accusation, and reproach for His sake. But it means more than that. It also means bearing accidents, injuries, cancer, Alzheimer's disease, multiple sclerosis, arthritis, emphysema, heart attacks, strokes, amputations, physical deformities, grief, financial loss, bankruptcy, the end of a career, invalid parents, rebellious children, a troubled marriage, an unwanted divorce, old age, and more.

All the painful experiences of our lives become ways of sharing the sufferings of Christ—*if* we view those experiences as a privilege and not as a reproach. When we learn to see life from God's perspective, we realize that (as songwriter Randy Stonehill put it) "this life is just a moment in the morning of our day." Suffering is temporary; life with God is forever.

In this brief moment of time, we have a great opportunity to bear the honor of suffering for Christ. It's an opportunity that will never be ours in eternity; it is only ours right here, right now. So my prayer, as we close the book of Job, is that we will learn to stop grieving and complaining about our affliction and learn to count it a great joy and privilege to bear suffering and reproach for the sake of Jesus Christ.

And to share in the eternal glory to come.

Enjoy this book? Help us get the word out!

Share a link to the book or
mention it on social media

Write a review on your blog, on a retailer site,
or on our website (dhp.org)

Pick up another copy to share with someone

Recommend this book for your
church, book club, or small group

Follow Discovery House on
social media and join the discussion

Contact us to share your thoughts:

 @discoveryhouse   @DiscoveryHouse

Discovery House
P.O. Box 3566
Grand Rapids, MI 49501 USA

Phone: 1-800-653-8333
Email: books@dhp.org
Web: dhp.org

NOTE TO THE READER

The publisher invites you to share your response to the message of this book by writing Discovery House, Box 3566, Grand Rapids, MI 49501, USA. For information about other Discovery House books, music, or videos, contact us at the same address or call 1-800-653-8333. Find us on the Internet atdhp.org or send e-mail to books@dhp.org.